Reality by Design

The Rhetoric and Technology
of Authenticity in Education

RHETORIC, KNOWLEDGE, AND SOCIETY
A Series of Monographs Edited by
Charles Bazerman

Winsor • *Writing Like an Engineer: A Rhetorical Education*

Van Nostrand • *Fundable Knowledge: The Marketing of Defense Technology*

Petraglia • *Reality by Design: The Rhetoric and Technology of Authenticity in Education*

Reality
by Design

The Rhetoric and Technology
of Authenticity in Education

JOSEPH PETRAGLIA

Georgia Institute of Technology

LEA

LAWRENCE ERLBAUM ASSOCIATES, PUBLISHERS

1998   Mahwah, New Jersey   London

Lawrence Erlbaum Associates, Inc., Publishers
10 Industrial Avenue
Mahwah, New Jersey 07430

Cover design by Kathryn Houghtaling Lacey

LIBRARY OF CONGRESS CATALOGING-IN-PUBLICATION DATA
Petraglia, Joseph.
    Reality by design : the rhetoric and technology of authenticity in
education / Joseph Petraglia.
        p.   cm.
    Includes bibliographical references and indexes.
    ISBN 0–8058–2041–8 (alk. paper). — ISBN 0–8058–2042–6 (pbk. :
alk. paper)
        1. Constructivism (Education) 2. Authenticity (Philosophy)
3. Reality. 4. Cognitive learning theory. 5. Educational
technology. 6. Education—Philosophy. I. Title.
LB1062.P42 1997
370'.1—dc21   97–28104
                                                            CIP

Books published by Lawrence Erlbaum Associates are printed
on acid-free paper, and their bindings are chosen for strength
and durability.

Printed in the United States of America
10 9 8 7 6 5 4 3 2 1

To my parents,
Charles and Patricia Rossi,
and, of course,
to Deepika

Contents

Editor's Introduction

CHARLES BAZERMAN
University of California, Santa Barbara

As HUMAN MATERIAL and symbolic artifice become ever more clever and pervasive, the real takes on greater and greater importance, yet seems ever more elusive. We live increasingly in an environment built not only of concrete cities, but of symbolic realms, electronic environments, and novel social relations. People living in hunter–gatherer societies tend to know what is real for them, and do not lose their ways trying to find worlds of personal meaning in a confusing and alienating world; perhaps even more fundamentally, children grow up with clear imperatives and motives within an identifiable set of adult practices. They do not need to ask what is real. But as the products of human cleverness proliferate, it becomes increasingly difficult to identify which artfully constructed alternative offers something that seems real to us, and it becomes increasingly difficult for youth to pursue wholeheartedly the wisdom, practices, and arts the previous generations offer them.

The issue of the real is more than a philosophic, moral, or existential question that may occupy the intellectual leisure of those who find themselves at personal sixes and sevens. Because of the peculiarities of human psychology, the real is a matter of motivation, participation, and organization of cognition and behavior. That is, people are more engaged (and thus learn more) the more real and meaningful they find tasks. What people find real and engaging, nonetheless, may be of the greatest human artifice. Some people find crafting sailboats, or acting in costume upon a stage, or documenting literary history, or working on string theory far more real than gathering berries. Modern society's concern for authenticity, honest expression of feelings, following one's heart and conscience, and similar motives attests to the difficulties and importance we attach to locating what we find personally real.

If the sense of the real is so important, especially in a world that seems to offer so much variety, then the learning, attention, and development of children are closely tied to what they find (or can be convinced is) real and engaging, even if at certain moments play is what strikes them as most real. The progressive reforms of twentieth-century education have at their heart, as Joseph Petraglia documents in *Reality by Design*, this recognition of the importance of a sense of reality or authenticity—culminating in the current educational movement called constructivism, in which each student constructs his or her own knowledge of the world. Petraglia places this historical development in education side by side with developments in psychology that have led to the current concern for situated cognition—an approach that again emphasizes the individual's perception of and responsiveness to the immediate ambient world and motivating activities that seem personally real. Petraglia then examines how these lines of thinking come together and are operationalized in the new field of educational technology, which designs learning environments. Educational technologies offer the promise of realistic, motivated learning matched to the needs, desires, and learning styles of individual students—situating them in personalized interactive environments within which they can construct their own knowledge.

However, Petraglia points out, constructivism and situated cognition have a hidden kicker. In pointing toward the importance of the individual's sense of reality, they destabilize the very notion of a consistent and knowable reality—as has been elaborated in the social constructionist movement. If realities are constructed through individual activity and perception, then realities are multiple, and we cannot rely on any reality we offer students to be authentic prior to their engagement with it. How can we determine what realities would engage each student? Even more confusingly, how could what we know as reality be of interest or use to students' constructions of their realities? Alternatively, how might we convince students that the realities we have to offer have any real or authentic value to them?

Petraglia finds the way out of our dilemma in the key term *persuasion*. People find some environments and tasks persuasive, and thus authentic, engaging, and motivated. Other environments and tasks leave them cold and appear to be artifice. In addressing educational situations and in designing electronic educational environments, we need to start thinking rhetorically—not about what is real in an absolute sense, but about what may appear as real and motivating to the students. To help us on this path, Petraglia describes some examples of educational tools he and others have created. But even more, he has created intellectual tools to help us determine how to realize educational realities in a world of increasing artifice, a world where we make our own realities.

Acknowledgments

W RITING ON the subject of constructivism in education does a great deal to concentrate one's attention on the impact of others' thinking on one's own. In working through the many issues surrounding authenticity, I have been fortunate to find ready assistance from many sources. At Lawrence Erlbaum Associates, former editor Hollis Heimbouch was instrumental in helping me formulate the broad outlines of this project and eliciting very useful feedback on the prospectus. Her successor, Linda Bathgate, has been equally supportive as the manuscript moved into the production phase, and it has been a real pleasure working with Barbara Wieghaus and her very accommodating production staff. Special thanks are due Charles Bazerman, the Rhetoric, Knowledge, and Society series editor. Chuck knew me well enough to wield editorial carrots and sticks in a way that produced optimal motivation; his expert criticisms helped clarify my writing and moved the project along relatively quickly. Even greater, perhaps, are the thanks owed Chuck for providing me and the field of rhetoric and writing with a model of *rhetoric scholarship* that bridges saying and doing.

Here at Georgia Tech, the EduTech Institute and the Cognitive Science program have provided a multidisciplinary community in which to explore authenticity in education. Mark Guzdial, Cindy Hmelo, Janet Kolodner, Nancy Nersessian, Wendy Newstetter, and Ashwin Ram have each, in different ways, facilitated my interest in authenticity's centrality to education and educational technology. Far-ranging discussions with Cindy on anchored instruction and situated cognition and team-teaching a course on qualitative research methods with Wendy were especially helpful in understanding the relationship of authenticity to pedagogy and scientific method. I benefited greatly from discussions with many graduate students whose own run-ins with the rhetoric of authenticity have found their way onto many of these pages. I gratefully acknowledge support from the Georgia Tech Foundation that enabled me to meet with educators and technologists at national and international fora.

Within my own School of Literature, Communication, and Culture, colleagues Jay Bolter, Daryl Ogden, Kavita Philip, and Greg VanHoosier-Carey have been gracious, astute, and encouraging readers of some pretty awful prose. Many thanks to them all. More of a colleague than a research assistant, Bryce Glass spent many hours with me, thinking about the relationship of learning theory to technology, and I appreciate the efforts he and Greg have expended to make *Reality Check* real. Thanks too to Kathleen Bergin at Tech's Center for Education Integrating Science, Mathematics, and Computing for lending a teacherly perspective to *Reality Check* and knowledge negotiation that provides a needed hedge against ivory-towerism. Colleagues elsewhere have also contributed greatly. I would like to express my appreciation to Bernie Baars, Allan Collins, Maureen Daly Goggin, David Jonassen, Charlie Hill, David Russell and Rand Spiro for talking through some of the issues authenticity raises and (in the case of Maureen, Charlie, and David Russell) for providing excellent feedback on drafts of various chapters. Closer to home, any words of thanks here can only hint at my profound gratitude to Deepika Petraglia-Bahri for her editing acumen and general encouragement throughout this project.

Finally, I am glad to have an opportunity to acknowledge my debt to my former professors at Carnegie Mellon, and especially to Preston Covey, Rich Enos, Linda Flower, Dick Hayes, and Richard Young. It was at CMU where I learned two valuable lessons: that an academic life without interdisciplinarity is not worth living, and that the study of rhetoric, when done right, has everything to do with everything.

—Joseph Petraglia

Introduction:
Why an Interest in the Authentic?

A PEDAGOGICALLY committed colleague recently delivered a lecture to assembled engineering, computer science, and cognitive science faculty to explain the theoretical underpinnings of his popular course on Decision Making in Engineering. A recurring theme of his talk was the contrast between what he called the Traditional Model and his Emergent Model of education. The last item on a transparency he had put up indicated that the Traditional Model required students to "solve puzzles," whereas the Emergent Model required students to "learn-by-doing with real-world problems." Tapping on an egg-carton-on-wheels contraption that he had brought with him, the professor behind the podium proclaimed ". . . and you don't get any more real world than *this*." The statement caught my attention, for only a few minutes earlier, he had explained that the rolling egg carton was designed by his students to be used by the enslaved inhabitants of the planet Algar for the laudable purpose of launching a sleeping gas canister at the tyrant Rhapton.

During the question and answer period, I asked the speaker whether a machine designed for an extraterrestrial environment and built to sedate a mythical creature was a suitable exemplar of an authentic task. It seemed to me that the task environment went far beyond being merely hypothetical, and I was unclear as to how the real world came into the picture. I wondered aloud whether there might be some conflation of materiality with reality, and whether the fact that the task resulted in the construction of a physical object was being offered as proof of its authenticity. The question seemed to annoy my colleague, for, *of course*, the situation was fictive and mere "things" did not confer authenticity on teaching, but the *problem* was real. The two students who accompanied the professor to offer the learners' perspective on the course quickly agreed. One enthused, "It *was* a real-world problem for us. The fact that it happened as part of a science fiction scenario, if anything, freed us up to be more creative. We could do anything we want, and set our own limits. We weren't constrained by stuff that would happen, say, if we had to do something that had to work on Earth." Looking around the room, I observed that this rather remarkable sequence of statements was widely met with murmured approval and the nodding of sympathetic heads.

The point in relating this story is not to suggest the pedagogical unsoundness of my colleague's task, for I know of few educators who are as committed to student-centered learning, and, by all accounts, the course and task are ones that most students find very valuable. Instead, what I find interesting is that no one in the room seemed to notice or care about the vagueness and contradictions in the discourse on authenticity and reality. The anecdote provides what I think is a characteristic illustration of both the unquestioned value of authenticity in education and the often unreflective ways in which we speak of it. In what might be called an authenticity paradox, we see that the purported real worldliness of a learning environment, technique, or task is so rhetorically potent that we frequently call attention to it in pedagogical conversations to legitimate our undertakings, yet it is so inconsequential to the job at hand, that terms such as *real world* and *authentic* do not require (or even resist) precise delineation. Another colleague at the lecture dismissed my follow-up question with the pronouncement, "This is getting religious around the edges . . . let's move on."

Yet, does the purported existence of this paradox in education merit extensive attention or, put another way, might I be accused of taking talk of the real world too seriously? One could argue that our references to the authenticity of a particular environment, the everyday nature of given tasks, and the real-world orientation of a curriculum are merely turns of phrase. After all, over the course of time, authentic and real-world have become the preferred adjectives applied to everything from the infamous elementary school word problem with real-world referents (e.g., "Two trains leave the station at the same time . . .") to the ornate and cue-filled realm of computer simulations and multi-user dungeons (MUDs). The certain buzzword quality about such terms might signal that they should be left alone or relegated to the world of innocuous clichés. However, the point I wish to argue in this introduction is that claims of authenticity are not inconsequential rhetorical flourishes—twenty years ago, they might have been, but they are no longer considered as such. Unlike earlier, more commonsensical imperatives to motivate students by "making learning real," today's educators are facing a much more weighty challenge for our current interest in pedagogical contextualization and authenticity has grown more culturally significant and intellectually demanding even as it remains imprecise and untheorized. This is a result, in part, of a corresponding move in many areas of education (especially in educational psychology) toward viewing the mind in context—a move that is making discussions of the everyday and the authentic unavoidable. Although the meaning of authenticity in education may be interesting for its own sake, my real argument is that it serves as an especially useful window into our current theories of cognition and learning. I would even go so far as to suggest that an understanding of contemporary education hinges on what we take *authentic learning* to mean and how we believe it is achieved.

CONSTRUCTIVISM IN EDUCATION
OR "THE IMPORTANCE OF BEING AUTHENTIC"

To suggest that formal education has undergone an enormous shift over the course of the last century is safely banal. Education, like so many other academic enterprises, has been caught up in the postmodernity of the century. Contemporary theories of language, learning, social behavior, and knowledge have drawn back from what is generally characterized as a modernist, Enlightenment faith in objectivity and the univocality of knowledge. The abbreviated and unflattering version of the objectivistic model of education, which most of us have rejected, is one that my colleague's transparency identified as the Traditional Model. According to this model, the principal challenges faced by teachers were essentially those of greasing the student's mental machinery and packaging discrete, decontextualized bits of information in such a way that he or she could easily grasp and commit them to memory. This emphasized accuracy and demonstrability: the student learned the "right" information and proved this to his or her evaluator in an unambiguous fashion. Idiosyncratic interpretation was discouraged and the correspondence of the correct information with the external world was, for the most part, unquestioned.

With the coming of industrialism, these educational ideals, responding to social and economic restructuring both in the United States and abroad, came under attack. Allegiance to the belief that formal education served a civilizing mission lost ground in favor of the more democratic and practical values of mass participation and economic efficacy. The educational program known as *progressivism* in the United States harnessed these values and set the stage for a focus on authenticity as the embodiment of Deweyan philosophical and pedagogical ideals. Consequently, in our own times, sociologically and culturally sensitive theories of education have emphasized the social and economic viability of learning with the goal of preparing students for full participation in the world around them, and we now accept that education is an ongoing process that is informed at least as much by what transpires outside the classroom as by what we teach within those confines. Of course, the presumption that education entails a relatively uncomplicated transfer of information from the knowable to the knower and from the expert to the novice has largely disappeared, at least in the annals of educational theory if not in practice.

Yet, the story of authenticity does not lie solely in the realm of educational values; to the degree that it has met with popular success, progressivism in education has been abetted by the corresponding drive to acknowledge the importance of everyday contextualization in the behavioral sciences and especially in cognitive psychology. The cognitivist tradition, which has steadily sought to integrate the role of context in learning since its origins in the first half of this century, has lent the weight of science to our sense of the desirability of authenticity in our pedagogy. From its break with Wundt's experimentalism and early interests in conditioned response and behavioralism, cognitivism has embarked on the quest for a more satisfying model of human information processing and has quickly, though incrementally, exploited the potential latent in *constructivism*—the interdisciplinary view that we construct knowledge based on our cultural assumptions and prior experiences rather than through the efficient and rational calculation of the information at hand. Therefore, constructivism can be understood as a natural and social scientific complement to the progressivism which it developed alongside of.

Constructivist and other sociocognitivist inroads into education are widening with each passing year, following the path initiated by cognitivists in the first half of this century. Modern constructivism, Resnick argues (1991), obliges us to view social behavior not just as an influence on thought, but also, as itself, a manifestation of cognitive processing that leads us to "analyze the ways in which people jointly construct knowledge under particular conditions of social purpose and interaction" (p. 2). In this view, knowing cannot be separated from the activities in which one engages, and learning is intimately connected to its contexts and purposes. In short, constructivism alerts us to a more encompassing notion of context than previously available to psychology, one in which everyday social, cultural, and material constraints cannot be discounted when studying learning or formulating pedagogical approaches. It is only reasonable then, for Dunn (1994) to conclude that, "if we do indeed construct our reality and learn nothing that is not somehow context-specific, then instruction should take place in rich contexts that reflect the real world and are as closely related as possible to contexts in which this knowledge would subsequently be used.... In a word, they need to be authentic" (p. 84). In this way, the desirability of authenticity in learning, a cornerstone of American educational philosophy throughout the twentieth century, has been given psychological teeth, validation within the social sciences that has moved the *desideratum* from the status of a somewhat inchoate cultural value to one that is defensible on the grounds of empirical research.

ENTER TECHNOLOGY

Although it has seesawed with elitist educational ideals for centuries (e.g., the notion that education is a good in and of itself), authenticity has stealthily pervaded educational theory and practice to become the criterion by which we adjudicate pedagogical options and alternatives. As Honebein, Duffy, and Fishman (1993) suggest, "Authentic activity is one of the most cited features of a constructivist learning environment.... Indeed, the common quest today is for 'authentic learning'" (p. 89). In a society (such as our own) that views education as an extension of national economic and social policy, the applicability of learning, to the real world, is a usually tacit, but increasingly formal, objective of the educator, determining, in large part, the tools he or she chooses to deploy in the classroom. Certainly, this seems to be the conclusion of educational technologists who have been working to apply multimedia and hypermedia to the task of contextualizing information.

The process of integrating constructivism into educational practice is clearly mirrored in the field of educational technology which, like education generally, draws on constructivist theories of learning to justify pedagogical innovations that encourage "everyday" thinking within "authentic" tasks in an attempt to situate learning. Indeed, educational technology arguably provides what may be the best illustration of constructivist thinking as it relates to education today, thereby providing a keyhole through which the application of constructivism to the broader enterprise of education can be seen to best advantage.

As has already been suggested, authenticity in learning is not necessarily a high-tech objective. High school social studies instructors, primary school science and math teachers, and practically any conscientious teacher having come of age in post-Dewey America almost intuitively seeks to design classroom assignments and problems whose fulfillment or solution will have implications beyond the classroom. However, advances in educational technology have raised the stakes and moved the contextualization of learning from a loric "knack" to a full-fledged intellectual enterprise with the interest in real-world learning serving as a theme for special issues of professional journals and conferences. Educators and technologists have held out great hopes for the prospect of increased student engagement in activities that use multimedia, hypertext, and other electronic-based learning applications. These hopes have been largely rooted in the belief that new technological advances will enable educators to contextualize, and thus, bring authentic learning materials and environments into the classroom.

Not surprisingly, a general interest in constructivism and the enthusiasm generated by its enactment in educational technology have sparked a lively debate into the differences between thinking and learning in formal environments as opposed to learning within more informal, everyday contexts. Together, these moves are fueling greater attention to nuances of nomenclature meant to better describe and advocate the sort of thinking we want and need to support in our schools. As Vosniadou (1994) puts it, "Technology can help in this process [of rethinking schooling] because it makes it possible to create learning situations that mirror what is happening in the real world in ways that are difficult to realize in a traditional classroom" (p. 12). This possibility is echoed in the literature reviews of research papers and reports in educational technology where terms like *anchored instruction* and *participatory learning* are being explicated along with notions of *apprenticeship* and *student-centeredness*.

Authenticity is not, of course, the only issue confronting educational technologists. The concerns of educators, generally, and educational technologists, in particular, are manifold, and rationales for using technology are similarly varied. Other commonly stated rationales for the use of other media and modalities in learning include learner engagement through sheer novelty value and/ or enthusiasm for technology; improvement of the logistics of teaching (i.e., technologies have traditionally been seen as labor-saving devices with the potential to deliver more personalized instruction than a human teacher has the time to do, and, more recently, distance learning has become an issue of note); and the increased effectiveness of information delivered using new media. Still, authenticity is perhaps the most interesting of these other possible arguments for investment in educational technology both for its apparent imperviousness to empirical investigation and for its rhetorical force. Other rationales for educational technology are, bluntly, less sexy. Technology's potential for motivating students with its novelty and glitz, some may argue, rests on educationally dubious practices of titillation. The puritans among us might argue that there is something unseemly about having students engage in learning just because it might be entertaining, but less prudish educators might justifiably worry about the transience of novelty and the quickness with which students tire of bells and whistles. Improvement of the logistics of teaching is suspect because it seems too mundane on one hand, and too technical on the other. Efficacy of learning is certainly educational technology's strong suit, but it is too dry. Empirical claims about technology's efficacy are testable, but only crudely so, and even worse, such claims are boring.

In contrast, authenticity's charms for educational technology lies in its rhetorical power and constructivist pedigree; it is a dimension of a learning environment that rises above the showbiz aspects of novelty-motivation, our work-a-day, blandly utilitarian interest in serving the greatest number of students most effectively and the often reductive empirical efforts to demonstrate that technology "works" in true or quasi-experimental studies. Of course, as with novelty, authenticity is promoted for its ability to intrinsically motivate learners, but even without playing the motivation card, technology's capacity to bring the real world to the student is an argument that is seen as needing no warrant. Thoroughly interwoven with prior and broader commitments to progressivism and constructivism, authenticity has a cultural significance for educators of every kind that these other rationales do not possess, and its cachet is bound up in its promise of revolutionizing learning in every domain. Technologists and educators generally understand, of course, that in practice, technology is often anything but revolutionary, and that an accommodatingly inexact vocabulary of authenticity may lead us to an understanding of human learning that is driven by the technological tools we develop and use rather than the other way around. Some excesses aside, however, educational technologists have nevertheless advanced compelling arguments that technology really does contextualize learning. They suggest that, using features such as multimediation, interactivity, and collaborative modalities, apprenticeship conditions for learning can be approximated and students can be engaged in the authentic activities of experts.

THE EPISTEMOLOGICAL CRISIS
CONFRONTING EDUCATION

In a preface to his account of the sociocognitive process of navigation, Hutchins (1995) voices his regret at cognitive anthropology's failure to realize its full potential. In his view, this field's continued reliance on traditional "indoor" methods, despite its own disciplinary origins in a concern for context, had made it either unable or unwilling to make a clean break with traditional social science (xii). I sympathize with Hutchins' complaint, but also note that even the study of cognitivism *al fresco* (i.e., research growing out of situated cognition and constructivist theories) poses challenges that we have not been able to engage. Papert (1995), in his recent remarks to a House of Representatives panel on technology and education, identifies the obstacles in radically reforming education as rooted largely within our image of school as we have known it, a representation deeply ingrained in the consciousness of educators whose own experience of schooling resists profound change. I would go a step further to suggest that, as the field of educational technology illustrates, the real obstacle facing the implementation of a full-bodied constructivist framework in education is *knowledge as we know it,* for as an expression of the broader postmodern *Weltanschauung,* constructivism highlights the contingency of knowledge and knowing, and thus, in a very real sense, threatens the entire educational enterprise. In other words, taken to its logical conclusion, constructivism deprives us of the foundations on which Western education rests.

Constructivist educators, wedded as we are to a basically social scientific framework of knowledge production, find ourselves in a bind: we genuinely wish to adapt a constructivist model of cognition to our pedagogy while exercising our prerogatives in determining the nature of the real world for our students. We have avoided this dilemma largely by ignoring the antifoundationalism latent in constructivism. In doing so, we have domesticated constructivism, allowing it to serve as a theoretical mascot to be trotted out so that intellectual morale can be boosted, but ensuring that it is rendered incapable of posing a real challenge to the basic educational framework with which we are most comfortable. Our success in domesticating constructivism has made its challenge insidious, but the essentially epistemological dilemma constructivism poses remains before us, for as Berlin and Inkster (1980) note, it is impossible for educators to have a theory of learning without a theory of knowledge.

THE PURPOSES OF,
AND AUDIENCES FOR, THIS BOOK

It occurs to me that one can speak of the *rhetoric of authenticity* in education in two senses and that an examination of both would encapsulate the scope of this book. As already noted, certain educational practices have the effect of rendering constructivism harmless—celebrating it for its commonsensical, as well as theoretical and politically progressive import, but keeping it safely contained within the traditional hierarchies to which we are accustomed (e.g., the clear demarcation of roles for teachers and students, textbooks' tacit support for the uncontestability of facts, etc.). Thus, the rhetoric of authenticity can refer to how language such as *authentic, real-world, genuine,* and *everyday* is used by educators to conserve comfortable epistemological assumptions while linking pedagogical innovations to a more constructivistic intellectual framework. In this first sense, then, the rhetoric of authenticity is about how and why the *desideratum* of authentic learning is used as a central trope in the contemporary educator's vocabulary.

However, in a second and perhaps more technical sense, a *rhetoric of authenticity* can refer to the way in which the real, and thus, the authentic, can be seen as an outcome of rhetorical processes. As constructivists have argued for the constructed nature of reality, I ask how a rhetoric of authenticity, in this second sense, can be made to work for educators. That is, how can those of us who teach make peace with epistemological instability, and in doing so, reconcile ourselves to the constructivism we wish to embrace? Furthermore, in light of this, how do current conversations and research programs both constrain and further such reconciliation in fields such as educational technology?

If I had to identify, in terms of a recognized academic undertaking, what I am attempting here, the best response might be that my project is a kind of *rhetoric of inquiry*—the study of how discursive practices constitute and sustain human understanding with special reference to academic investigation. This response might be best because my own disciplinary roots lie in rhetoric and writing, and the manner in which I frame questions and offer answers cannot help but reflect this. Yet, in significant respects, this answer is unsatisfactory. First, it is such because the rhetoric of inquiry literature is often content to serve as a metaframework, a sort of intellectual Archimedean point from which commentators observe the manipulation of symbol systems within the academy. This is a point unavailable to me. My motive for writing is not to bring the rhetorical "word" to heathen education professionals or technologists, for as an educator and subscriber to scientific method myself I am not only an observer of educational rhetoric, but an avid user and consumer of it.

A second, and more weighty reason the rhetoric of inquiry label ill-suits this book is because it forecloses on the broader audience that the topic of authenticity merits. This book was originally intended to stimulate constructivist thinking in educational technology, a field whose efforts to accommodate constructivist theories I have observed with interest for several years. However, as the book progressed, it became clear to me that my audience is not so much educational technologists qua technologists, but educational technologists as educators, and that the issues surrounding authenticity are issues faced by constructivist educators in every field.[1] Thus, while educational technology serves as the backdrop for this book, I have tried to broaden the scope in such a way that educators from a number of disciplines will find a discussion of authenticity not only relevant, but self-evidently so. Obviously, there are dangers in trying to write out of, and to, more than one discipline: at certain points, the discussion is bound to more explicitly address the concerns of one or another disciplinary audience rather than bring them together on common ground. To avoid this, I have tried not to situate myself too deeply in the minutiae of one disciplinary conversation at the expense of others and, in the spirit of interdisciplinarity, import as little jargon as possible and stipulate my definitions where appropriate.

OVERVIEW OF CHAPTERS

It is more than a little presumptuous to write on a subject that draws on discussions of Dewey's legacy, activity theory, pragmatism, educational technology, rhetorical tradition, radical pedagogy, and other topics about which so much is currently being written and microanalyzed. A monograph of this length offers only the quickest gloss of many of these topics and I am well aware how far short I have fallen from comprehensiveness. Yet, superficiality has certain charms, one of which being the bird's-eye view of these diverse literatures that keeps our attention on constructivism's "big picture" and avoids getting bogged down in the intricacies of any particular disciplinary or localized dispute. If the rhetoric of authenticity and the constructivist metatheory that feeds it are to be understood as potent forces within education, they must be appreciated for the heterogeneity of their origins and the flexibility of their application. As getting a satisfying and useful handle on authenticity poses stiff organizational, as well as conceptual and interdisciplinary challenges, the reader may find a brief overview of the chapters useful in plotting how each of them contributes to my larger argument.

Chapter One gives a brief account of authenticity's status as a potent *desideratum* in American education at the secondary and postsecondary levels. Starting with classical systems of education and continuing with what I call the *elite-idealist tradition* of education, the correspondence of school learning to the

---

[1]When I speak of constructivism and constructivist educators, especially after Chapter Two, I am rarely referring to an exclusive or narrow theory of cognition or its proponents. Rather, the constructivist metatheory I flesh out in the early part of this book is a rubric under which many theories of learning can comfortably coalesce—an ecumenical and eclectic approach to learning in which disciples of Montessori, Vygotsky, Bartlett, Dewey, Mead, Piaget, Geertz, and many others can all gather. Furthermore, constructivist terminology has been widely appropriated by educators across the academy even if relatively few have any interest in its psychological roots. For this reason, we might think of it as an almost pop-educational term that alludes to learners' active roles in learning and the diversity of paths to knowledge, and in the sense I use the phrase throughout most of the book, *constructivist educators* are the rule rather than the exception.

world outside of school prompted little interest. In fact, as Western education took on an increasingly academic cast, real-world learning, such as that provided by apprenticeship, became the system against which "genuine" education defined itself. The rise of the disciplines provided an added impetus to elite idealism by creating a cult of expertise and abstracting learning domains even further away from extracurricular (and now, interdisciplinary) contexts. Authenticity becomes a force to be reckoned with in education only with the rise of democratic and commercial ideals in Europe and the United States and the corresponding efforts at deploying education in the service of training an informed and economically productive citizenry. Still, elite-idealist habits die hard, and it is not until the late nineteenth century that the carefully cultivated impracticality associated with the European tradition truly gives ground and the progressivist movement arrives to capture the new American spirit in education. In the hands of able theorists such as John Dewey, authenticity becomes a valuable trope connecting lingering elite-idealistic values of traditional education to the practical, even vocational, role which mainstream education began to play in postindustrial America. The chapter concludes with some thoughts on why authenticity can be viewed as the quintessential *desideratum* of American education and how this manifests itself in contemporary educational theory.

Chapter Two traces a very different history, although it is one that is parallel to educational theory in many respects—the rise of real-world contextualization as a psychological concern culminating in constructivism and our current appreciation of cognition's situatedness. Beginning with the behaviorists' lack of interest in context other than as a source of brute stimulus, I briefly review how correspondence to external reality has been framed in different approaches to psychology. Early interest in how we learn is quickly taken up in Western Europe with the establishment of developmental psychology and its best known proponent, Jean Piaget. In Piaget, we see what some would call the origins of modern constructivism, though one can argue that constructivism's social cast is more clearly seen in the work of British experimental psychologists, such as Bartlett.

The chapter summarizes the evolution of constructivism through the cognitive revolution of the 1950s and 1960s (and the dissatisfaction with the ascendant information-processing models of that era) to what, in hindsight, looks to be the fairly natural resurrection of Soviet sociohistoricism. It is the sociohistorical perspective initiated by Vygotsky and his colleagues in the 1920s and 1930s that creates the conceptual space in psychology necessary for the treatment of everyday context. This is accomplished via the *quotidianization* of learning—that is, by looking to everyday situations and activities as the primary source of learning rather than at deliberately structured learning episodes or learning acquired in school under formal conditions. The recent interest in situating cognition can be seen as a response to the information-processing tradition's narrow focus on individual mentation in well-structured problem spaces and thus, is both heir to the sociohistorical tradition and the most recent manifestation of what we can now appreciate is a rich and multifaceted constructivist metatheory.

Chapter Three begins by returning to the issue of education, for as the recent history of constructivism illustrates, authenticity attains its currency in psychology circles largely as a reaction to formal schooling. A sense that traditional schooling is incapable of providing the authenticity learners require is often given voice in the literature of educational technology, and this field provides a good vantage point from which to study both constructivism and the concern for authenticity. A variety of what might be called *mediating theories* has arisen from within the ranks of education and educational technology and includes theories of apprenticeship, collaboration, and cognitive flexibility. I suggest how educational technologists have used these mediating theories as frameworks within which real-world learning can be best facilitated, and the remainder of this chapter briefly reviews the rationales behind some of the most widely used features and environments developed to respond to constructivism's mediating theories. This review highlights the putative contribution of features such as interactivity, hypertext, and multimediation to the authentication of learning.

Certainly, an environment that allows for the attainment or use of these characteristics may have salutary cognitive consequences for the learner, but in Chapter Four, I ask the reader to consider whether these innovations really embody the lessons of constructivist theory. Using technology to engender vivacity, complexity, accuracy, and interaction in learning, technologists claim that a variety of newly developed environments promote the kind of learning that occurs in the real world: for this reason, I identify their objective as that of *preauthentication,* or presenting students with environments and specific tasks predetermined to correspond to tasks as they exist in the real world. Although constructivist theory identifies the student's own prior experiences and cultural assumptions as critical to building knowledge, I suggest that preauthentication appears to circumvent this and pull education back into line with those earlier epistemological and pedagogical frameworks that we claim to have abandoned.

While few educators are preoccupied with epistemological questions, constructivism has obvious implications for our working theories of knowledge, and thus, both this chapter and the next try to clarify how seemingly arcane discussions, usually relegated to philosophical debates, have a direct bearing on applying constructivism to education. Logically, the proposition that educators cannot preauthenticate problems for those whose real worlds may be very different from their own (and are continually evolving) is self-evident. The fact that we continue to speak of pedagogical innovations in terms of their ability to present authentic problems or create authentic environments is rhetorically interesting because it foregrounds the historical, discursive, and methodological issues that draw our attention away from the antifoundational threat that does not lie far beneath the surface of constructivism and theories of situated cognition. In the second half of Chapter Four, I review some of the reasons why the literature of educational technology has finessed the contradictions inherent in preauthentication and sidestepped the epistemological baggage constructivism carries. The problem educational technologists confront in designing authentic learning environments reflects the basic dilemma every constructivist educator faces when importing epistemologically destabilizing notions into what remains a fairly conservative conception of education.

Chapter Five provides the means for handling this dilemma. First, I suggest how the metaphor of education-as-argument provides a kind of rationally pragmatic foundation that may be more appropriate to education than the ethically or politically pragmatic responses to constructivism evinced in educational technology and other education-related disciplines to date. In addition, rooting learning in argument and persuasion permits us to turn to the task of sketching a rhetorical framework within which we can deal more comfortably with the constructive processes of education.

Rhetorical and constructivist frameworks share many features—for instance, both are preoccupied with an interest in how representations of the world are constructed and modified. However, the rhetorical tradition usefully distinguishes itself in its focus on the affective dimensions of thinking and knowledge-making and in its long experience with context-dependence. For these and other reasons, it is argued in Chapter Six that reframing the traditional constructivist challenge as a rhetorical challenge permits educators to reconsider a variety of assumptions and specific practices that result in preauthentication. Just as educational technology is used to illuminate the problems educators face in applying constructivist principles, it also provides a disciplinary framework for clarifying my proposed reconceptualization of education as an explicitly rhetorical process. Drawing largely from contemporary work in rhetoric, many of the lessons educational technologists have drawn from constructivist theory are modified and reformulated. In the latter section of this chapter, I suggest that a rhetorical view of education is already beginning to take hold in many corners of the field, and especially in a recent artificial intelligence (AI) tutoring approach known as *knowledge negotiation*. I also offer an example of my own current project in educational software to make my recommendations for rhetoricizing education more concrete. The subsequent brief chapter that serves to conclude this book ties my major arguments together and anticipates some of the difficulties we face in taking what many in the academy are calling the "rhetorical turn."

REPRISE: AN INTEREST IN THE AUTHENTIC

Wading into the issues surrounding constructivism in education, one is afforded numerous starting points; in this introduction, I attempted to explain why my chosen entrée is that of authenticity. As illustrated in the scenario with which I began, talk of the real world, the everyday, and the authentic is one clear sign of constructivism's impact on educational discourse. Following up on constructivist insights into issues such as learner centeredness, the contingency of knowledge, and the importance of social, cultural, and material context, educators have rejected the sterility of transmission assumptions, untouched, as they are, by accounts of real people confronting problems in their day-to-day lives.

Nevertheless, the triumph of constructivism brings with it a certain irony: just when the importance of the real world has finally made itself felt in education and psychology, the postmodernity that furthers the constructivist cause has cast the realness of the world into doubt. As the reader undoubtedly already appreciates, the inconsistencies surrounding the discussion of real-world learning, revealed in the anecdote that opened this introduction, are not limited to discussions conducted within the confines of that seminar room, that university, or that discipline. Perhaps part of the problem is that the language we use to talk about authenticity in education has been so comfortable and unacademic. Had we designated the *desideratum*, "scholastio-quotidian isomorphism" instead of the homely, "real-world problem solving," or "authentic learning" we would, no doubt, think twice about what we were saying. Yet, the term *authenticity* and its synonyms lull us into the belief that we do not need to explain ourselves. Thinking back to my colleague's complaint that discussion of authenticity gets "religious around the edges," I find the phrase an especially apt one; for in the absence of rational and critical vocabulary we do, in fact, fall back on faith— faith that what seems real (and thus, authentic) to me, seems real (and thus, authentic) to my students, faith that everyone knows what I mean when I talk about real-world problem solving, faith that students will respond appropriately to my preauthenticated learning environments and pedagogical techniques, and faith that, however porous my sense of authenticity may be, it is surely an improvement on the insularly academic perspective it replaces.

Yet, if we are wedded to both the principles of authenticity in education and to the essentially constructive nature of learning, a more theoretically satisfying appreciation of authenticity seems to be of critical importance for education in general, as well as for the technologies we deploy in the classroom, in order to contextualize learning. We can start with the commonsense recognition that real life is messy, that the problems we confront in everyday life are what earlier cognitivists labeled *ill-structured*—that is, they are open-ended, multifaceted problems in which solutions are equivocal. We can also recognize that cultural, social, and behavioral practices and material conditions play an enormous role in enabling and constraining problem solving. Ultimately, by interrogating authenticity, we can better understand the obstacles we face in designing genuinely constructivist learning environments, obstacles that may be obscured by our often facile references to "student-centered" pedagogy, to "everyday" problem solving and "contextualized" learning, and to the "real world."

ONE

Under, Alongside, and on the Table: A Brief History of Authenticity in Education

> *... school must represent life—life as real and vital*
> *to the child as that which he carries on in the home,*
> *in the neighborhood, or on the playground.*
> —JOHN DEWEY (*Pedagogic Creed*, 1897)

THE STORY OF authenticity's rise to consciousness in the minds of educational theorists, and its pervasiveness in theories and models of learning generally, has gone untold in the literature of education. This is so for good reason; with few exceptions, direct appeals to the "authentic" or the "real world" in education are rare until the latter half of the nineteenth century (and even then, we might question their actual significance). In classical treatises on education, it seems that the relationship between school learning and work-a-day activity was not problematized on any level. The notion of authenticity in education is the creation of a mostly twentieth century sensibility that has arisen in response to twentieth century theories of learning and knowledge. As such, authenticity almost certainly has significance for us in a way that we could not expect it to have had for educational reformers such as Isocrates, Ramus, or Pestalozzi.

In this chapter, then, I offer a highly abbreviated history of the idea and the ideal of authenticity with the intention of showing how the Western educational tradition has culminated in the contemporary and widespread view that school learning should rightfully, and nontrivially, correspond to the world outside of school. By relating this history, I mean to suggest that authenticity is not a natural objective of education, but the result of a confluence of socially and culturally informed choices. Let me be clear from the start that, because a concept of authenticity in education is noteworthy, largely for its historical absence, it would be a mistake to suggest that earlier educators' tacit notions of authenticity in education were lacking or that earlier educational systems were inauthentic.

SOME PRELIMINARY CLARIFICATION

To begin this history requires an attempt to stipulate what one commonly associates with the term "authentic learning." At one level, of course, a definition can be easily provided: Webster's Third International dictionary suggests we call something authentic when it is "worthy of acceptance or belief by reason of conformity to fact and reality." While this definition may be adequate for some purposes, if it were all we had to go on, we could easily mistake its significance in education. So to begin looking for the rise of authenticity as an educational *desideratum,* and in doing so, understand the construct's current potency, I open this chapter with some suggestions for how we might distinguish our usage of *authenticity* from that of other terms with which it might be misleadingly conflated.

One such conflation is with *relevance.* All systems of education are constructed and perpetuated for a purpose, and certainly our histories of educational systems across time and space presume that the system under consideration was intended to serve the needs of at least some groups in the societies that produced them. Of course, education has always been designed to be relevant, advance the purposes of a social order, and somehow serve society, even if issues such as whose social order and what society might remain open. While relevance lies at the core of any education system, it would be a mistake to use *relevance* and *authenticity* interchangeably. For education to be relevant requires only that it be useful, and utility and authenticity are very different things; learning to type may certainly be useful in achieving certain real-world objectives, but we would probably think it odd if someone were to associate typing skills with authentic learning. The suggestion that education should be authentic implies that there should be a correlation between the forms and formats of education and those forms and formats as they exist outside the classroom. Though relevance can be considered a given attribute of whatever system of education evolves within a society, systems must choose authenticity from among a number of options.

Similarly, I think it is a mistake to conflate authenticity with the *isomorphism of certain component skills,* or the fact that some mechanical elements of larger problem-solving routines are directly transferable to everyday tasks (cf. Anderson et al., 1995). For instance, formal training in the mechanics of filling out a spreadsheet and forming letters of the alphabet is isomorphic to the mechanics of filling out spreadsheets and forming letters of the alphabet outside of school. Sitting down to calculate 5% of 73 in the classroom exercises the skills we find useful when we calculate those numbers in the auto dealership or with a stockbroker.[1] Yet, as a rule, we do not bother to proclaim that when we teach spread-

---

[1] At this point, we are speaking in terms of skills' seeming context-independent rather than any cognitive similarity. In the next chapter, we see that many researchers have suggested that while

sheet mechanics, the alphabet, or division, our teaching is authentic, for the badge of authenticity has generally been reserved for the learning of a nonmechanical, context-dependent content. So, while some argue that genuinely mathematical reasoning requires what we call an "authentic context," it seems clear that the algorithms of arithmetic do not (Cobb, 1994b).

Of course, the line separating what appear to be context-independent skills from more evidently context-dependent skills is often blurry, and at some point in a given curriculum, we may suspect that authenticity will become a consideration, especially when discrete information is embedded in an extracurricular social or cultural milieu. This suggests an important criterion for raising the issue of authenticity: that of socially viable learning. To take the subject of writing as an example, the development of writing abilities is generally considered hierarchical and progresses from the learning of orthography to the rules of spelling and punctuation, then to fundamentals of composition, and in some cases, on to technical writing, journalism, or some other highly context-dependent and socially informed practice. It seems reasonable to assume that issues of authenticity will arise in this later training, whereas it probably would not in the context-independent instruction that preceded it. Whereas writing may be something we believe lends itself to authentic learning, one must acknowledge that elements of writing (again, such as knowledge of the alphabet) remain outside the realm of the authentic. In short, when we speak of authenticity in education, we are only speaking of the instruction carried on at a certain (usually advanced) level and we generally mean to exempt the learning of skills that appear to be mechanistic and context-independent in favor of those higher order skills that are usually plied in social contexts.

This isomorphism suggests a final problematic conflation: *accuracy.* Such conflation occurs when we label as *authentic* tasks that require technical veracity or that have some empirical basis. The distinction between factual accuracy and authenticity is one that is commonly elided by many in education. Yet, as with the isomorphism of component skills, lack of any distinction between authenticity and accuracy would lead us to label certain teaching practices "authentic" when thoughtful usage suggests otherwise. For instance, memorizing the configuration of a faithfully reproduced control panel of a space shuttle, writing down the dietary preferences of water buffalo, placing round pegs in round holes, or rhyming nonsense words may all be tasks on which we might commend a student for his or her accuracy without consideration of the task's authenticity.[2] Thus, while authenticity includes the learning of relevant things, isomorphic skills, and accurate information, it goes beyond these attributes to

---

the product of cognitive processing devoted to a particular task may be identical—whether performed in school, out, or by different individuals—the underlying processes may vary greatly.

[2]Later, we see that Salomon and Perkins' (1989) notion of *low-road transfer* makes much the same point—that there are certain kinds of learning and tasks that lend themselves to automatic performance without any deeper comprehension.

encompass the context in which such skills and information are appropriately applied to everyday life. Although we have neither defined authenticity nor exhausted a list of the senses in which a task may mistakenly be called authentic, this clarification may be sufficient to permit us to proceed with a general sense of authenticity's lineaments.

EDUCATION BEFORE AUTHENTICITY

Boyd (1947) suggests that, prior to our own century, theories of education encountered their greatest transformations in the Classical Era, the Renaissance, and in the era following the French Revolution. It is at periods of such cultural upheaval that questions of how schooling serves a society are brought to the foreground and these might therefore provide chronological markers for our present discussion. In terms of authenticity, for instance, the Classical Era might be seen as one in which the authentic was not on the table, so to speak. Instead, what one might call an *elite-idealist* notion of education, characterized by its overt hostility to the vulgarity of the vocational, was established. I suggest that the elite-idealist tradition was furthered and formalized during the Middle Ages and the Renaissance until the French Revolution, and, more specifically, the democratization of education as manifested most fully in the United States. Such democratization set in motion a social and philosophical dynamic that makes authenticity an important educational *desideratum*.

The Classical Era

Western conceptions of what it means to be educated, as well as our sense of what sort of institutions schools should be, are remarkably stable throughout history. We find the beginning of a recognizable system of formal education in the West in the seventh century BC (Smith, 1955). In Classical Greece, education was rarely intended to be practical or vocational and its stated purpose was rarely to train young people for the world of work. In fact, Barclay (1959) explains that "anything which was designed to enable a man to follow a trade or a profession for the Greek was not education at all" (p. 79). Many of Socrates' contemporaries thought so little of the vocations that they argued that tradesmen should be treated no better than slaves, and similarly, denied citizenry. Isocrates, perhaps the most famous educator of Greece's Golden Age, dissociated himself from other, more vocation-minded, sophists of his time by emphasizing that education should be designed with the generalist in mind rather than the professional (Clarke, 1971, p. 29). Plato (1926) has the Athenian Stranger articulate a similar position in *Laws:*

> The education we speak of is training from childhood in goodness, which makes a man eagerly desirous of becoming a perfect citizen, understanding both how to

rule and be ruled righteously. This is the special form of nurture to which, as I suppose, our present argument would confine the term "education"; whereas an upbringing which aims only at money-making, or physical strength, or even some mental accomplishment devoid of reason or justice, it would term vulgar and illiberal and utterly unworthy of the name "education." (p. 643E)

Hellenistic educational theory also demonstrated little concern for the relationship of the educational process to the educated product, indicating just how separable a concern for relevance can be from an interest in authenticity. Whereas the educated man would be practical, his education need not be. Just as recitation of the epics did the soul good and instilled a sort of mental discipline necessary to be a culturally worthy person, there was no real assumption that recitation in itself had value beyond this goal. Like the Greeks, Romans saw the educated individual as the vessel in which tradition was first poured and then carried to future generations. Children inducted into trades and crafts as apprentices were not being educated, they were being trained—something few Romans or Greeks would confuse. To the extent that Classical education lay any claim to providing its charges with real-world experience, it was in experience in litigation and political participation. Yet even in these arenas, authenticity, in the sense of correspondence to the real world, was not a common concern or an objective.

Although Classical educators, no doubt, would have insisted on their tuition's practicality and relevance, its cornerstone was a particular type of intellectual exercise in which correspondence to the real world played a very little role: declamation. Declamation served as a sort of mental calesthenic that was appreciated despite its utter separability from any correspondence to real-world causes and effects (Clarke, 1971; Marrou, 1982; Smith, 1955) and it is the practice of declamation that reveals most clearly the classical attitude toward authenticity in education. In the Roman version of the practice (derived from the Greek), there were two sorts of declamatory exercises: *suasoria* and *controversia*. When engaged in *suasoria*, the student–orator gave advice or recommended a course of action to a historical or mythical personage at a critical point in time. A *controversia*, on the other hand, simulated a legal case whereby the student was assigned to argue one side of a given argument or the other. As in *suasoria* exercises, these cases were usually drawn from myth or history (and largely Homeric history at that). Themes for both varieties of declamation were generally melodramatic: capture by pirates, tyrannicide, or treason provided a canvas for an imagination as fanciful as the student could muster.

As Cicero's Crassus tells us in *de Oratore* (1921), declamation excercises had a highly structured progression:

> We must begin by winning the favorable attention of our audience; then we must state the facts of the case, then determine the point at issue, then establish the charge we are bringing, then refute the arguments of our opponents; and finally in our

peroration amplify and emphasize all that can be said on our side of the case, then weaken and invalidate the points which tell for the opposite side. (Book I, p. 138)

Certainly, declamation as a pedagogical mainstay had its detractors in both Greece and Rome, but critics such as Suetonius seem less concerned with its unsuitability for real-world application than for its "show biz" aspects that seemed to reduce education to mere spectacle; "indeed, men who exalted genius, originality, the arts, and the beauty of genteel living could find no pleasure in the scholastic emphasis on pedestrian logic and on arguments one could just as well prove as disprove" (Ulich, 1965, p. 59). Clarke (1971) is also clear on the matter of declamation's inauthencity:

No attempt was made to reproduce the atmosphere of the courts. Each speech was self-contained, delivered on one side or the other and answering only imaginary objections. Even in Republican times Cicero remarked that most students of rhetoric learned little more than verbal fluency from their school exercises. (p. 43)

As Seneca (1990) notes, both varieties of declamation were intended as oratory for its own sake rather than as preparation for actual advocacy in actual courts for, indeed, it was quite possible to be an esteemed declaimer and a poor advocate.[3] Just as Quintilian would describe the ideal orator as "a good man, speaking well," the educated leader in Classical society was an articulate person ennobled by education, but not necessarily someone who had learned to apply knowledge to everyday situations. Unquestionably relevant from the perspective of its practitioners, Classical education qua education was not expected to mirror the outside world.

Elite Idealism and the Authentic

Although the West's image of education has undergone numerous reformations, if required to find a thread that runs throughout these shifts in emphasis, the thread would be that of elitism mingled with a sense of education's civilizing misson and a faith in the possibility of the accurate transmission of knowledge from teacher to learner. A shorthand for this might be called *elite idealism* as the term connotes both exclusivity with regard to those who are deserving of education, as well as the disdain for mere practicality—features which characterized conceptions of education in the Classical period and retain a powerful presence in our own day.

---

[3]As the study of argument and persuasion, Classical rhetoric had developed sophisticated theories of context-dependence centered on issues of audience and occasion (or *kairos*). Clearly, its early theorists were interested in why people accepted informal arguments in the everyday world rather than in formal deductive logic. Yet, the fact remains that the disjunctures between rhetorical theory and its technical applications (such as pedagogy) was little cause for alarm or even comment among the Ancients. Aristotle is typical, perhaps, in his suggestion that there was something almost inexorable about the process of persuasion (if done correctly) and that, presumably, solid declamation would lead to effective argument.

As is well known, in the European educational tradition, only a select number of individuals were considered deserving of higher learning—meritorious
in the sense that either they were socially deemed worth educating or somehow
they found a forum in which to demonstrate superior abilities.[4] The vast majority of individuals were left outside the education system and were thus considered uneducated even though they may have attained advanced skills in trades
and crafts by means of apprenticeship. What we might now call "vocationalism"
was probably not consciously cast as a real alternative to education as much as a
default arrangement for those who could not be educated. Still, in the Middle
Ages we see apprenticeship becoming a poor relation, but a relation nonetheless, of legitimate education. This happens without much fanfare, of course, and
the view of vocational training as something of an educational booby prize was
gradual. Apprentices did things rather than thought things. The idea of physically performing practical tasks is one that still did not belong in any self-
respecting educational system, and this disdain of manual labor carried over to
practical education in any form. Naturally, European systems of higher education from the Middle Ages onward were also concerned with producing what
we think of as professionals—lawyers, doctors, politicians, and of course, other
academicians. Yet, professional training retained a elite-idealist aire of inauthenticity in important respects. First, the professions for which students were
trained were largely theory-based. As scientific method was quite rudimentary
at this time, recuperation of Classical theory, rather than research, was the primary academic enterprise. Even in areas such as medicine, where one might expect to find an abiding concern for how treatments worked in the real world,
autopsies were performed to provide support for theory rather than to find information to cure similar cases, illustrating the extent to which men of advanced
learning were expected to live in the realm of ideas.

More so than in the Classical period, education centered around the relationship of a learner to the written word. While a polished Roman or Greek declaimer demonstrated a command of prior stories, legends, and conventions,
early Christian scholars were wholly preoccupied with the interpretation of
sacred text. Scholars debated translations of particular words and phrases and
argued for interpretations of Biblical and other religious passages by citing more
authoritative scholars and written sources. Although universities from the late
Gothic period and throughout the Renaissance redirected their hermeneutic
efforts to include more secular texts, such redirection did little to shift the focus
toward the worldly. The world of texts continued to be the only world over

---

[4]To the extent that the individuals chosen to receive an advanced education were intellectually
gifted, they were only coincidentally so, but I would suggest that the conflation of elite status with
native intelligence is critical to the spirit of elite-idealism in its obviation of authenticity (see Boyd,
1947; Clarke, 1971). That is, if one accepted that education should be reserved for the formation of
superior intellects and nobler souls, one could just as easily accept that education does not need to
correspond to anything as mundane as everyday experience.

which a learner had to demonstrate mastery, reinforcing the elite-idealist values of abstract speculation and mimetic agility.

Within the ongoing framework of elite idealism, the impact of the Enlightenment initially brought with it enormous changes in education, but left the issue of authenticity largely undisturbed. For one thing, Descartes shared with Plato an abiding distrust of experience and a faith in human reason independent of contextual influence. A second contribution to the elite-idealist framework to which Cartesian rationalism lent itself was a project taken up earlier by the French educational reformer Peter Ramus: the disciplinization of knowledge. With the division of disciplines into distinct areas of inquiry and corresponding methodologies comes the departmentalization of knowledge and its separation from everyday experience. Education's neglect of the real world was reinforced as areas of inquiry became rationalized into carefully delimited spheres of arts and sciences and then splintered into smaller subfields. Certainly, this was the view of Giambattista Vico, an early voice calling for what we might think of as authenticity in education (Mooney, 1994). In his early eighteenth-century treatise "On the Study Methods of Our Times," Vico derided Cartesian method for its poor appreciation of social interaction and its hyperrationalization (Vico, 1965). He criticizes the "modern philosopher" (i.e., the Cartesian) for idealizing human reasoning rather than seeking to explain how we think through problems as they actually exist in the world. He urges educators to use everyday experience as a resource, for "just as knowledge originates in truth and error in falsity, so common sense arises from perceptions of verisimilitude" (cited in Bizzell & Herzberg, 1990, p. 717). Yet, as Vico himself acknowledged, his call for authenticity could do little to slow the elite-idealist juggernaut that now aligned itself with rationalist suspicion of day-to-day experience.

Nevertheless, other countervailing influences were at work, destablizing the elite-idealist status quo ever so slightly. With the Enlightenment came the rapid growth of science and scientific method, along with the early stirrings of the Industrial Revolution, all of which complicated the distinction between theorical and practical training.[5] Science-oriented scholars became more intimately involved with the use of instruments and mechanical devices which took them out of the realm of text and into the real world. For the most part, however, the link between education and mental, rather than physical, activity (a hallmark of elite idealism) continued to be firmly cemented in the European psyche. This ideal is embodied in Jeremy Bentham's often-noted architectural plan for schools in which windows were placed so high above the ground that there would be little fear of students looking at the world outside rather than devoting themselves to the world of learning taking place within those walls.

---

[5] As the Industrial Revolution wore on, it became a greater and greater force for making learning practical at the secondary school and university levels; early in this process, however, the scope of industrial change initially had little impact on formal education and instead fed into the established dichotomy between education and vocationalism (cf. Cornbleth, 1987; Douglas, 1921).

In short, the European elite-idealist approach to schooling is important in understanding authenticity as an educational *desideratum* if only because it was largely bereft of it. Histories of European thought on the subject suggest that formal schooling was rarely viewed as an extension of everyday life. Indeed, an elite-idealist education was valued precisely for its otherworldliness. To be an educated individual meant distinguishing oneself from the masses and the workaday world. Educated persons were expected to make use of the opportunity afforded them to pursue extraordinary ends—ends that stood in stark relief to the mundane, the vulgar, and the everyday.

The Rise of Republicanism

Prior to independence, America's own elite-idealist tradition was firmly entrenched and there was little sense that education should be brought to the masses so much as that the masses should have a chance to participate in the elite-idealist tradition (Button & Provenzo, 1983). In Benjamin Franklin's view, education was a way for the lower classes to rise out of their station. He accepted that changes in education should result in the replacement of an educated aristocratic elite with a monied elite whose claims on education were not based on high birth but rooted in wealth. Thus, the opening of education that republicanism signaled was more an opening of educational opportunity. While the belief that "if ignorance was the deadly enemy of democratic government; education was its bulwark" (Best & Sidwell, 1967, p. 102) remained the best expression of American educational ideals, there was hardly a rush toward implementing these ideals on a large scale. Higher education, especially, seemed wedded to European models of scholarship and most intransigent in the face of republican efforts to democratize educational opportunity. For instance, Ulich (1965) notes that at the outset of the nineteenth century, Yale University's ferocious advocacy of traditional elite-idealist education could not have been surpassed by the universities of Oxford or Paris (p. 101).

Enlightenment and republican ideals, as well as their subsequent refinement in American and French Revolutionary thought, did, however, set in motion a significant departure from education's elite-idealist baseline and began the process by which authenticity as a goal of learning entered into education's vocabulary. Along with the recognition of the natural rights of man came the separation of religious and secular life, social egalitarianism, and, perhaps most important for education, the belief that all other democratic values rested on the ability of citizens to make intelligent decisions in regard to their own governance (Chambliss, 1968). A growing sense that education could not be denied to people that were otherwise created equal seemed only reasonable. In his essay on republicanism and education, Rush (1798) identifies five salutary effects of learning for the free citizen. First, it promoted religious tolerance by removing "prejudice, superstition and enthusiasm" just as it provided its second benefit by favoring liberty; according to Rush, decentralization of knowledge dissemination and the eradication of superstition was the only way a representative form of government could be made to work. Third, learning propagated democratic ideas and informed the masses on matters such as justice and the legal system. The fourth benefit harkens back to the traditional elite-idealist idea of creating a culturally refined populace for it appears that republicanism, no less than oligarchy, appreciated the fact that education promoted "the pleasures of society and conversation." Finally, Rush lauds education's implications for economic advancement, and more specifically, for agriculture. He argues that agriculture would remain the basis for wealth and that, as a science, only formal schooling provided the appropriate environment in which young men could stabilize the economic foundation of the new nation.

In Rush's enumeration of benefits, we can simultaneously detect both the revolutionary ideals of mass education and the traditional, elite-idealist ideals of service to society and moral betterment, of *noblesse oblige*, and spiritual aristocracy. Nowhere are these two aspects illustrated more clearly than in the writing of Thomas Jefferson. In his essay "To Diffuse Knowledge More Generally," Jefferson (cited in Ford, 1904) proposes a system by which the financially disadvantaged could participate more fully in public affairs. The core of his proposal is a system by which examiners would "chuse [sic] the boy of best genius in the school, of those whose parents are too poor to give them further education, and to send him forward to one of the grammar schools . . ." (p. 61). From among those exceptional boys graduating from grammar school, the "geniuses" would again be selected to continue studies for six years ("and the residue dismissed") at which time another selection would be made. This process was to continue through college. As Jefferson puts it, "by this means twenty of the best geniuses will be raked from the rubbish annually . . ." (p. 61). While we might disapprove of Jefferson's phraseology, his system efficiently accommodates the dualistic nature of the challenge facing republican education: it had to make gestures toward the enfranchisement of the common man, while upholding the traditional elistist assumptions adopted from the European elite-idealist model, which remained, after all, the only real model of education Americans could emulate. Although pressures induced by republicanism persisted, they were met with counterpressure from those elite idealists who feared that too democratic a framework for education would cheapen the entire enterprise. Douglas (1921), for instance, notes that when Northern states passed slavery abolition acts in the late eighteenth and early nineteenth centuries, the work performed by former slaves "naturally" filtered into the apprenticeship statutes in force at the time, accentuating the cultural status accorded to vocational training relative to formal education (p. 21).

This imbalance notwithstanding, however, throughout the nineteenth century vocationalism was also on the move. Many have written of the implications of industrialization for education (e.g., Bantock, 1963; Floud, 1973; Popkewitz,

1987a, 1987b) and a common theme in many of these studies is the rise of *homo technicus* to the detriment of the gentleman–scholar (Sampson, 1973). The corporate culture industrialization spawned was one in which narrowly trained technicians were skilled in the latest managerial and clerical techniques. The political and economic environment brought on by the industrial revolution, abetted by the disciplinization and quantification of heretofore humanistic enterprises (e.g., psychology and sociology), tacitly recommended a type of education that was more efficient and standardized (Cornbleth, 1987; Popkewitz, 1987a). In the United States, Scrimshaw (1932) could confidently declare that the institution of apprenticeship was reborn, that its value was "everywhere recognized" (p. 4). At the turn of the century, American universities such as MIT, Harvard, Georgia Tech, and Cincinnati, began to supplement their regular offerings with vocational interships that were accorded academic credit. In the latter half of the nineteenth century, the president of Emory College could speak of his desire to "raise up a race of men who shall be fitted for the pulpit or the plow, the court or the camp, the Senate or the shop" (cited in Young, 1994, p. 5). Even though Emory's prescribed curricula of Greek, Latin, theology, philosophy, political economy, forensics, and history seem weighted toward the pulpit, court, and Senate side of the equation, it is significant that gestures toward the real world were nonetheless made in the United States at this time. One can scarcely imagine an Oxford don or an American college president a quarter of a century earlier having made even a rhetorical nod to the plow, camp, or shop.

In Europe, as well, Georges Friedmann (1950) was arguing for the theorization of vocational training—that is, for teasing out the abstract principles underlying the technical skills in their real-world application. Thus, in both Europe and the United States, it became less and less plebian to be a skilled expert and more and more archaic to lead the contemplative life. The elite-idealist tradition was able to evolve somewhat to meet this challenge insofar as training in the classics was recast as training in accuracy and precision rather than as unabashed belletrism; as had been the case in China for centuries, refined learning was appreciated for a rigor that was believed to be appropriate to civil bureaucrats. Yet, the elite-idealist tradition never succeeded in melding itself into a populist view of education and the finest schools continued to produce the kinds of cultivated elites society could admire, if not always use.

AUTHENTICITY IN THE TWENTIETH CENTURY

Until the middle of the nineteenth century, the options facing learners seemed strikingly similar to those proposed by the Ancients: one could be educated or one could be trained. One could be socially and intellectually bettered or one could be productive. Until this point, we have had to infer the significance of authenticity largely from the shape of its absence. For most of the Western experience, education had been associated with Greek ideals, such as *paideia* (the harmonious balance of physical and intellectual maturity) and *phronesis* (practical wisdom) or with the training of an elite to move into positions of administration and governance required by empire. In these educational contexts, the goal of education was clearly not vocational, but, in my stipulated sense, elite idealist. So, the question remains: From whence did the *desideratum* of authenticity arise? While no date, reform movement, or individual can be identified with the genesis of authenticity, a plausible account of authenticity's birth as an aim of education can nonetheless be given.

Progressive Education

The American continent was the site where the elite-idealist European notion of elite education met the republican ideal of mass education, creating the need for a theoretical readjustment.[6] For higher education to be suitable for the people, it was required to resonate with something other than the cultivation of superior intellects and sensibilities (Lee, 1965). On the other hand, as we have seen, the very notion of education, and especially higher education, required relevance to something other than a trade or profession. Thus, the challenge facing American educational theorists of the late nineteenth century was to create a theoretical bridge that could mediate these twin constraints. This bridge was found in the goal of authentic learning. In a nutshell, the commitment to authenticity in education is the result of an uneasy and still imperfect reconciliation of two antagonistic impulses: the political and economic desirability of making schooling available to the masses and the retention of schooling's aura of intellectual elitism. Without a continuing commitment to elitism, education would be reduced to vocationalism, while without democratization, education would continue in the constraining elite-idealist tradition—one that clearly could not be reconciled to republican ideals. The rhetoric of the Progressivist movement in education of the late nineteenth and the first half of the twentieth centuries was the force that enabled (and still enables) this balancing act.

The move toward a progressive educational framework was neither quick nor clear, but the origins of the movement in the United States may be traced to Francis Parker who, in the 1870s and 1880s, called attention to the fact that traditional learning suffered from a certain kind of irrelevance. Parker (cited in Best & Sidwell, 1967) gives the example of the prototypical scholar, "the model of his class, persistent and alert, possessed of a powerful verbal memory. . . . But [who

---

[6]Although it lies outside the scope of this discussion, it is interesting to consider that in the middle of the nineteenth century, European colonial administrators were considering the relevence of Western education to colonized peoples in a way that recalls issues of authenticity (Vishwanathan, 1989). It is, perhaps, the degree of the cultural gap between Britain and India that the irrelevance of classical training should be noticed and decried there before the same critical eye toward relevance was turned on Western elite idealism within the West itself.

at the] the first spear-thrust of reality shivers his panoply of empty words, and leaves him defenceless before the rigorous demands of an uncompromising world" (p. 298). Parker also remarks on the unethical aspect of cramming "the heads of our children with the unusable pages of text-books and then lead[ing] them to suppose that they are gaining real knowledge." This situation, he believes, created an educational environment that was painfully inadequate to contemporary circumstances and by simply asking his audience to give sustained thought to the issue of relevance, Parker was instrumental in setting the stage for a serious critique of the elite-idealist tradition.

Rather than Parker, of course, the Progressivist movement is more closely associated with American's preeminent philosopher–educator, John Dewey, and in terms of aligning American education with the value of authenticity, Dewey's influence is impossible to overstate. The combination of his amazing capacity for synthesizing the best of continental and Anglo-American philosophical traditions, his eloquence in giving voice to American democratic ideals, as well as his sheer longevity—born in 1859, he was on the educational scene for most of his adult life until his death ninety-six years later—made Dewey almost synonymous with American educational thought for millions of educational practitioners in his day and our own. Whatever the complexity of the situation in his own time, by the end of the twentieth century, it seems evident that our essentialization of American educational philosophy centers on Dewey and his role in integrating education with the everyday realities and needs of the common man.

As part of a triumvirate alongside Peirce and James, Dewey's more formally philosophical thinking was a central contribution to the American pragmatist movement, which was rooted in the assumption that the ultimate significance of an idea is to be found in its consequences when applied in the real world. In other words, pragmatists ask the question, "What sort of knowledge is useful?" Pragmatism provided Dewey with the philosophical grounds for rejecting the elite-idealist–vocational dichotomy, for he argues that this schism is not only psychologically unacceptable (as it supports the transmission model in which learners play the role of blank slates on which knowledge and information are accurately inscribed), but that it reflects a faulty epistemology as well (Brubacher, 1950).

Earlier in his career at the University of Chicago, Dewey (1961) subsumed his disciplinary interests in philosophy into the broader enterprise of education. If education was "the process of forming fundamental dispositions, intellectual and emotional, towards nature and fellow men," philosophy might be considered ancilliary to this goal (p. 328). For Dewey, learning was not a formal activity to be reserved for the deserving and performed in appropriate settings—as it had been in the elite-idealist tradition—but a natural part of life. In the Chicago Laboratory School of the 1890s, Dewey sought to integrate students' curricular and extracurricular lives, seeing each as extensions of the other— each relying on the other for support. The wall erected between schooling and real life, a wall that defined not only an educational site but a social order, was definitively dismantled by Dewey and has resulted in a legacy of educational philosophy that would be difficult to overstate.

To fully understand authenticity within the progressive framework requires an appreciation for the centrality of experience in Deweyan thought and an acknowledgment that the traditional conception of schooling had failed to understand—that school was but a small part of a student's larger learning experience. In his words, "The solution of this problem requires a well thought-out philosophy of the social factors that operate in the constitution of individual experience" (Dewey, 1938, p. 21). Because school learning had traditionally not been integrated into everyday experience, the lessons could not be said to be relevant or truly educational. In order for education to serve the needs of both the learner and society, he wrote, it "must be based upon experience—which is always the actual life-experience of some individual" (p. 89). Thus, that which is authentic, in a Deweyan sense, is that which brings together not only the material and social conditions that shape one's world, but also one's beliefs about the world. For this reason, Dewey argues that we learn best by doing. Instead of imposing knowledge and methods on the learners, the learners must be put into learning environments that permit them to generate their own theories and understandings of knowledge as it operates in the world around them. Unlike traditional education whose artificiality created needless complexity, Dewey argues that progressive education is simpler because it is more natural and because it harnesses the power of the learner's everyday existence. Dewey sees the educator's role as one that put the student's real-world experiences into fruitful dialogue. The tasks given to students should not begin with some academic subject such as geography or biology, but instead should grow out of the student's lived experience and be worked on by both teacher and student in the laboratory of the world outside of school (Perkinson, 1987). Only in an authentic context, Dewey suggests, can the complexity of problems be appreciated and real learning transpire. Such an approach to education is not merely motivational, he argues, but reflects the ethical relationship between the knowledge and the knower as school could be a microcosm of society, not just as society is, but also how it could be.

The belief that all genuine education comes about through experience does not mean that all experiences are genuinely or equally educational. On the contrary, Dewey (1938) suggests that the wrong kind of experience, or the poor arrangement of experience in the learner's memory, may stymie intellectual growth. He notes that "experiences may be lively, vivid, and 'interesting,' and yet their disconnectedness may artificially generate dispersive, disintegrated, centrifugal habits. The consequence of formation of such habits is the inability to control future experience" (p. 26). Traditional schooling, he felt, did little to encourage the right sort of experience processing and, by the turn of the century, educators such as Gertrude Buck (1901) were already drawing on Deweyan commonplaces to speak of the real occasions for learning in the classroom and to lament their scarcity.

As Vico had been two and a half centuries earlier, Dewey was wary of the inauthenticating effects of disciplinary specialization. With the fragmentation of inquiry into increasingly smaller and more distinctive areas of expertise, consequences of understanding became increasingly removed from the actions and activities that produced them. Unlike Vico, however, Dewey seems to have accepted that such fragmentation was inevitable and even necessary, although this did not mitigate his concerns.

> His primary concern was that the demand for efficiency and the need for specialization tended to support schools where specific skills were first abstracted from some real, concrete purpose and then taught in separation from any meaningul personal relationship. The result is a "purified" subject matter such as geography, which is then taught as if it had no significant relation to the way men live or think. (Feinberg, 1975, p. 81)

Dewey was greatly impressed with accounts of primitive education that, he believed, made the distinctions between applied and theoretical knowledge appear arbitrary and unhealthy and he wrote critically of the ways in which the notions of *apprenticeship* and *vocationalism* were used to demean the intellectual efforts of the working masses. In his expressed interest in authenticating learning, as well as his lack of elitist bias against the laboring classes, Dewey brought the elite-idealist and the vocational traditions closer than they had ever previously been.

From Point of Contention to Conventional Wisdom

Long before Dewey's death, there was something of a backlash against his formulation of progressivism. For one thing, progressivism's link to philosophical pragmatism was a source of the elite-idealist distrust of practicality as the end of education. For instance, if history is only studied for its usefulness in understanding the present, many would argue that we have lost a deeper appreciation of history; disciplines become reduced to tools to achieve narrow ends rather than rich fields of inquiry that coincidentally, rather than intentionally, provide the real benefits they afford. We continue to hear such arguments to this day.

One of Dewey's staunchest and most influential critics was British literary scholar G. H. Bantock. Bantock (1963) personifies the elite-idealist tradition when he writes that Dewey's vulgarization of education and his introduction of "the ethos of 'mass man'" into the traditional curriculum, threatened to overturn the very foundations on which the entire tradition of European scholarship stood. He goes on that "whatever in the American scene may excuse or justify Deweyism," it was not a model for any European to emulate nor did he find it especially positive, even contained in the United States (p. 55). According to

Bantock, "Dewey is essentially the philosopher of 'rootless,' urban man; he is unable to see, as Arnold saw, that even the capacity to appreciate the extent and nature of social action depends on the quality of mind brought to the situation . . ." (p. 55). In Bantock's view, Dewey's prescriptions were a recipe for mediocrity, a system that made a virtue of social egalitarianism at the expense of the individual, and especially, the talented individual.

Continuing in a conservative vein, but from a very different perspective, Dewey was also faulted for encouraging subjectivity and making genuinely practical learning impossible. His inefficient focus on child-centeredness and experientiality without regard for the usability or economically viability of knowledge is, it is argued, disadvantaging (Karier, 1986). By linking learning to the student's real-world experience, the necessary regard for social structure and guidelines are not instilled in the student and, in the hands of some teachers, education may dissolve into a solipsism, whereby learners are free to learn nothing of constructive value. The reason for this, many conservative writers conclude, is that Deweyan thought (problematic to begin with) has often been reduced to a series of platitudes and slogans that ill serve students and society. In short, they argue that Deweyan education values the free thinker over the productive worker.

Dewey's detractors are not only found on the right, however. Goodman's *Growing Up Absurd* (1962) best illustrates some of the subtle currents running against Dewey's perceived bias toward vocationalism. These currents were fueled by the 1960s rejection of conformity and its perceived denigration of individual expression. The backlash invokes many of the same elite-idealist ideals of the European experience. Although writing historian and theorist James Berlin (1987) suggests that this sort of elite idealism was largely a spent force after the 1930s, the rhetorical appeal of well-roundedness and liberal education remains with us today. Whereas the new elite idealism is no longer rooted in the sort of crass elitism of a century ago, the idea that education is not about being trained for the world of work, but about nurturing a humane and socially conscious citizenry, is still with us and is still compelling. To some, therefore, the move to make learning real may sound reactionary rather than liberatory. One can anticipate an argument against the value of authenticity, making the point that if education is intended to correspond to the world as it is, it dooms us to neglect the world as it could be. Certainly, this is an argument leftist and radical educators have given that sounds remarkably neoelite idealist. Yet, seen in another way, the political import of multiculturalism, feminism, and other sociocultural agendas common in the humanities attests to the tacit belief in education's need to reflect everyday realities. The idea that appropriately liberatory pedagogy directly affects students' material conditions (and, in fact, it is this purported outcome that many identify as its most compelling attribute) suggests that even seemingly idealized outcomes can profit from the rhetoric of authenticity.

What is significant in these and other responses to Deweyan progressivism is the fact that even as Dewey comes under attack, the attack proceeds under the banner of authenticity. No longer exclusively tied to progressivism's star, authenticity's rhetorical potency is preserved by its ambiguity. Conservative proponents of the view that education should serve the needs of the national economy easily accept the importance of authenticity, for, they can argue that the world of work is the real world. Further along a sociopolitical spectrum, neo-Deweyans can, of course, subscribe to the blurring of the academic and the vocational in the name of correspondence to everyday life. Neoromantics enlist the language of authenticity in their own cause, by arguing that students' lives are multifaceted and that preparing them to deal theoretically with the world necessitates the distancing of the learner from the narrow concerns of the professional world. Radicals can speak of authenticity in a quasi-Nietzschean sense, suggesting that authentic education is that which resonates most closely with the learner's inner life.

A better, if somewhat circular, way of understanding learning as authentic is as counterposed to "that which is not artificial," for arguments for authenticity in many educational circles often are, at heart, not arguments for anything in particular, but arguments against artifice (Frymier & Shulman, 1995). Even in an area as seemingly speculative as ethics, Covey suggests that "teaching students what John Stuart Mill said doesn't drive home the reality of the situation, and you can't teach ethics without imparting that reality" (cited in Mastracci, 1991, p. 28). One could argue that the continued existence of many humanistic disciplines in our career-oriented schools is tied to a rejection of artifice (or the embrace of authenticity) and the belief that knowledge of everyday beliefs and practices is not only useful in guiding our intellectual lives, but has a real impact on the way we live and function in society. In a subtle yet politically and conceptually significant way, progressivism ensured that authenticity has not merely been put on the educator's map, but has become the compass with which the map is navigated. *Progressivism* itself no longer refers to Dewey's theories as much as to twentieth-century American educational thought. Student-centered learning, discovery learning, my engineering colleague's emergent model of learning, and (as we will see) constructivist learning are each variations on a progressivist theme.

CONCLUSION

This chapter has not provided a clear definition of authenticity in education. Rather, my objective was to trace, however briefly, the way in which the multifaceted construct of authenticity as a *desideratum* generally has surfaced in the Western experience. In doing so, I began with a point that may initially seem minor, but, in fact, raises a number of issues for educational theory: that a desire for authenticity does not inhere in just any educational undertaking, but instead is the result of political and economic choices and conditions that warrant making schooling correspond to the real world. Authenticity can be seen as the rhetorical move that both created and was created by the progressivist trend in education and continues to make contemporary American education distinctive from the educational culture of many other countries.

While the verdict on Dewey seems destined to fluctuate with the vagaries of educational politics, I would argue that his lasting legacy is an abiding, almost unquestioned, sense of the need for learning in school to prepare one for the real world, even if the precise meaning of the phrase remains vague. This is not to say that, in practice, education has ever succeeded in this regard, or even that efforts to make learning authentic have always been sincere or carefully planned. Yet, as Wolff (1969) suggests, the first line of attack for reformers of secondary and higher education is almost always the demand for "relevance" and the complaint that "Whenever possible, the real world is ignored. Where it cannot be entirely suppressed, it is embalmed by the academic undertakers and laid out for observation, looking quite lifelike but safely dead" (p. 76). Clearly, according to Tansey (1971), if the real world were not too complex, difficult, or dangerous, we would prefer to conduct education there, for the natural superiority of the real world to the classroom is unquestioned (an assumption that would have been highly contentious in mainstream education only fifty years ago and unheard of a century ago).

The fact that the rhetoric of authenticity is often employed on occasions when the user is addressing a broad public without making any substantial recommendations is due, in part, to the indeterminacy of the notion. Yet, we may also take it as proof of the largely unchallenged consensus that education should have relevance for the everyday lives of learners. With the report of the America 2000 Commission (1991), authenticity has become an official educational objective. The commission notes that "the most effective way of learning skills is 'in context,' placing learning objectives within a real environment rather than insisting that students first learn in the abstract what they will be expected to apply" (p. 4). In fact, the entire thrust of the America 2000 initiative centers on the reintegration of school with everyday living by focusing not only on school reform, but also on community reform. Communities, the Commission argues, have to be awakened to their responsibilities for education and their potential for making the distinction between school–out-of-school learning less stark.

The commission's final report neatly illustrates the concept of authenticity's steady movement from irrelevance to suprarelevance, but this is not the whole story. As an aim of education, and especially higher education, authenticity is not only a remarkably flexible fixture, but one that is beginning to carry some theoretical weight. With the reintroduction of Vygotskian and early constructivist theories of cognition into American psychology circles and an educational environment in which the notion of situated learning has taken root, authenticity reemerges, not as an inchoate *desideratum*, but as a cornerstone of a social scientifically informed theory of learning and education. In this manner, authenticity in learning has moved from pious platitutude to a logical pedagogical response to findings in cognitive science—the subject of the next chapter.

The Cognitive Evolution

. . . theory has something to say about what people do in real, culturally significant situations . . . if it does not have what is nowadays called "ecological validity" it will be abandoned sooner or later.

—NEISSER (1976, p. 2)

AUTHENTICITY HAS PLAYED an important rhetorical role in educational reforms and debates for most of this century. It has often offered a theoretical basis from which to critique the ideas of others and to launch one's own pedagogical innovations. Progressivism in education may have first created the theoretical space in which the desideratum of authenticity could arise, but, in this chapter, I wish to explore a parallel history of the construct, for if the progressivist value of authenticity emits a kind of low-level radiation that infuses educational theory, it is contemporary psychology that brings issues of authenticity into relief in a more rigorous way. This permits the trope of authenticity to set aside its merely rhetorical role and take on a social scientifically viable dimension.

But illuminating authenticity through "contemporary psychology" poses challenges of its own. Although the study of mental functioning has been a subject of perennial interest in the West and elsewhere among the ancients, the discipline of psychology can perhaps only be traced back as far as the late 1800s, prompting the German psychologist Hermann Ebbinghaus to remark that "psychology has a long past, but a short history" (Cole & Cole cited in Luria, 1979, p. i). Of course, there are many excellent accounts of the history of modern psychology with special reference to cognitivism (e.g., Baars, 1986; Bruner, 1990; Danziger, 1990; Dember, 1974; Gardner, 1985); indeed, this chapter heavily draws upon most of them. Rather than a general history, however, I draw attention to the role of real-world contextualization, and thus, authenticity, generally in psychology, and specifically, in the cognitivist tradition. It can be shown that tracing the theme of authenticity and the role of everyday context does much to explain the evolution of psychological thinking throughout this century.[1] Ultimately, my objective is to demonstrate why a broadly construed constructivism has become the metatheoretical choice of many cognitivists interested in human learning.

A final introductory hedge: The evolution in constructivist thought owes a great deal to research and theory in disciplines other than psychology, especially linguistics, anthropology, neurosciences, computer science, education, and philosophy. Notions of culture-boundedness, linguistic determinism, and epistemological instability have infused these and other fields with a greater sensitivity to the social and cultural situatedness of phenomena that had, heretofore, been studied as primarily mentalistic or individual. Contemporary cognitive science, in particular, is heavily influenced by anthropologists, neuroscientists, and linguists working both within and outside the field of psychology. While I mention some of the theoretical debts cognitivism owes other fields, I minimize references to other disciplines' impact on constructivism (a story well told by Gardner) because education has traditionally drawn from psychology's appropriations of these other disciplines (cf. Burgess, 1993).

THE REAL WORLD AND OTHER IRRITANTS:
BEHAVIORISM AND THE
INFORMATION-PROCESSING PARADIGM

What is often referred to as the "cognitive revolution" has so completely changed the face of psychology that Costall and Still (1991) can say, "psychology has become cognitive psychology" (p. 1) with little fear of contradiction. As recently as thirty years ago, this was not the case, but to begin relating the story of authenticity's rise in cognitivism, we might back up even a bit further to Wilhelm Wundt's creation of an experimental study of the mind in Germany in 1879, a study that came to be known as the *New Psychology*. Prior to Wundt, the

---

[1] I have chosen, as this chapter's organizational principles, chronology coupled with locale and I review authenticity first in the context of American psychology before moving on to the European. While the principle is satisfying for its narrative quality, one should note the danger of what logicians would identify as the *post hoc ergo prompter hoc* fallacy: that which is prior causes that which comes after it. Clearly, the cognitivist tradition in psychology cannot be so neatly summarized. To take Vygotskian thought as an example, though a strict adherence to chronology would dictate that coverage of his sociohistorical thought come earlier in this chapter, I believe most American psychologists would agree that his real influence has come about largely through the efforts of researchers working in the 1980s. Likewise, Piagetian developmental theories have had a history of unevenness in influencing cognitive thought for over sixty years. Psychologists such as Jerome Bruner and Ulric Neisser perhaps best embody the mechanism by which earlier thought continues to crosspollenate contemporary thinking, they have played a major role in resuscitating earlier theorists.

old psychology was a rich, untidy aggregate of insights, questions, and hypotheses that had accumulated in the West over the course of two and a half millennia. Also called "commonsense psychology," this assortment of observations about memory, consciousness, perception, and the effect of emotions on thinking provided a de facto definition of the domain. Although they sought to distance themselves from commonsense psychology's haphazardness, Wundt and his followers continued to view psychology's mandate as nothing less than the study of the real world as revealed through consciousness.

While there were a number of research techniques at their disposal, one that early psychologists embraced was *introspection*, a method by which a researcher attempted to become hypersensitized to his or her own perceptions and sensations and then reported on the thoughts that rose to consciousness with as little interpretation of causes and effects as possible.[2] A revealing metaphor New Psychologists used suggested that they were attempting to discover the atoms of consciousness. Naturally, such atoms were elusive, and introspective techniques quickly got a reputation not only for scientific unreliability, but also for impracticality. Neisser (1976) notes that even perception and memory were interpreted in ways that made little contact with everyday experience, and it is "not surprising, then, that it was abandoned in favor or more promising ideas" (p. 3). One such promising idea was the largely American tradition of behaviorism. Behaviorists championed the scientific and experimental spirit of the New Psychology but jettisoned both its generally shoddy method with its dependence on self-report, as well as its seemingly idealistic and unproductive focus on consciousness.

Perhaps the most distinctive plank of the behaviorist platform was a complete rejection of the idea that psychology is the study of the mind per se, and the claim that a proper science must limit itself to observable phenomena without resort to speculation. Unlike New Psychologists, then, behaviorists rejected commonsense psychology's core assumptions. In essence, behaviorists subscribed to the belief that humans, like animals, have observably systematic reactions to stimuli in their environment and that strict adherence to scientific method can uncover these basic stimulus–response episodes that eventually lead to a generalizable theory of human behavior. The unapologetic and thoroughgoing scientism of behaviorism leads to a number of necessary corollaries, principal among these being a premeditated ignorance of ideas such as feelings, intentions, and images—any unobservable dimension of context—to human experience.

Accusing behaviorists of a lack of interest in context would have sounded odd to many of their early critics who complained that context was the entirety

---

[2]Accounts of early psychology disagree on the significance of introspection to Wundt's work. Baars (1986) seems to suggest that it was a combination of certain behaviorists' self-serving revisionism and poor translation that tied the New Psychology to introspection (a view that seems to be shared by Cole & Engeström, 1993), whereas Gardner (1985) seems to accept the link.

of the behaviorists' concern, and in a very limited sense, this was true. Behaviorism and the methodological framework of stimulus–response is rooted in the belief that organisms are largely passive receivers of external forces who are buffeted by their environment: A given stimulus produces a given response. To a behaviorist, however, *environment* is only comprised of the physical stimulus delivered by an experimenter within the controlled confines of the laboratory. This highly circumscribed notion of context is reflected in statements such as the following, which reports on a typical behaviorist study done in 1980: "Subjects [in this experiment] prefer contexts in which shocks are reliably predicted by signals to ones in which shocks are not preceded by reliable signals" (Balsam, 1985, p. 7). Balsam's use of the word *context* as a synonym for an experimental condition is consistent with behaviorist usage dating back to one of the founding fathers of the movement, J. B. Watson.

In terms of the behaviorist's attitude toward real-world contextualization, it is useful to consider that the subjects used in the vast majority of behaviorist studies were rats, pigeons, and lower primates—animals whose social lives were relatively unknown and who possessed limited experience manipulating symbols or using tools. Watson was committed to the view that humans were merely advanced animals and, therefore, basic findings involving rodents or birds could be extended to humans without much difficulty. Animals were not seen as poor substitutes for humans or as a merely convenient starting point, but as ideal subjects whose relative simplicity made them easy to work with, but in no way diminished the experimenter's ability to generalize findings to *homo sapiens*.[3] Denial of the importance of uniquely human experiences of culture and social interaction speaks volumes for just how deep an antipathy for real-world context was demonstrated by the behaviorist tradition. As an aside, we might find it all the more ironic that Watson had been one of the first to rail against the methodological shortcomings of introspection.

It is easy to deride behaviorist excesses and, in several fields, the adjective *behaviorist* is more often applied as an epithet than a description. Yet, educationally, behaviorism exercised and continues to exercise an enormous influence on everyday pedagogical practices. Its emphasis on conditioned response translates into reinforcement procedures that may be as mundane as grading or as elaborate as theories of classroom discipline (Amsel, 1989; Steinberg, 1980). As Neisser (1976) argues, despite its obvious inadequacies, behaviorism was one of the first real psychologies in that it strove to predict, and subsequently, intervene in, actual human responses. Ascribing behaviorism's faults to its historical occurrence at a time when psychology was most eager to prove its empirical worth is, no doubt, a reductionism we impose on a movement that is rich in personalities, internal struggles, and remarkable insights. Still, the behaviorists' obsession—

---

[3]Earlier, this view had infused much of New Psychology, as well, with Wundt conducting some of the first recorded psychological experiments using animals (Steinberg, 1980, p. 16).

and indeed, it seems to have been an obsession—with scientism and methodological purity goes far to explain the theory's evident inadequacy to the task of understanding human psychology and its complete lack of interest in the context of everyday living—a topic to which we will return later.

The Information-Processing Paradigm

In the United States, the first shots fired in the cognitive revolution are often identified as the beginning of behaviorism's end, although cognitivism's split from behaviorism was the result of a two decades long, incremental process rather than any sudden realization. While some histories date the beginning of the cognitivist Long March from the Hixon conference of 1948, more significant steps away from the behaviorist framework occurred in the late 1950s and early 1960s, (e.g., Miller's, 1956, publication of "The Magic Number Seven, Plus or Minus Two" and Chomsky's, 1964, review of Skinner's *Verbal Behavior*). Early cognitivism in the United States coalesced around a number of computational metaphors and assumptions causing it to be known as the *information processing paradigm*.[4]

A concise definition of the information-processing paradigm is provided by Langley, Simon, Bradshaw, & Zytkow (1987):

> The human brain is an information-processing system whose memories hold interrelated symbol structure and whose sensory and motor connections receive encoded symbols from the outside via sensory organs and send encoded symbols to motor organs. It accomplishes its thinking by copying and reorganizing symbols in memory, receiving and outputting symbols, and comparing symbol structures for identity or difference. . . . The brain solves problems by creating a symbolic representation of the problem (called the problem space) that is capable of expressing initial, intermediate, and final problem situations . . . (p. 8)

As this suggests, the metaphors and methods of information processing emphasized the brain as an isolated unit. Linguistically, what has been called the "correspondence" (or "copy") theory of language articulated by the early Wittgenstein in *Tractatus* (1961) neatly complemented an unproblematic view of sensory input and mechanistic processing. This theory posited a three-way correspondence among objects in the external world, the language used to encode

---

[4]Naming the framework that dominated early cognitivist thinking and continued to command the allegiance of many cognitive scientists is difficult as there have been a number of different emphases in this phase of cognitivism's evolution. Certainly, there are clear distinctions to be made among the variously named perspectives (e.g., the stored schema, computational, information-processing, symbol-processing, or just the traditional paradigm.) Throughout this book, I follow the usage that is most commonly employed to describe this framework. I approve of Baars' (1986) caution that if we are not to do violence to the Kuhnian concept of paradigm, that it should be deployed sparingly and that the information-processing variety of cognitivism may not conform to any strict use of that term.

these objects symbolically, and subsequent *representations* of these objects in the brain.

The explanatory power of representation for practically any endeavor can hardly be overstated, for our perceptions of the world, of who we are, and of our abilities to effect change are wholly dependent on ways in which the world is projected onto our mind's inner theater. As Anderson (1990) notes, we are exposed to an immense volume of sensory information at any given moment (p. 58). The challenge we face as rational problem solvers is to process this great volume of information in such a way that the environment makes sense and to enact this processing as naturally and efficiently as possible. The idea of representation as the coping mechanism that allows for this sense making has perhaps done the most to divide the cognitivist tradition from the behaviorist tradition. As Hacking (1983) suggests, the ability to conceptualize—to create representations—may well supersede mankind's ability to use language in its quintessential humanness.

In resurrecting the commonsense psychological notion of representation, the information-processing paradigm, in its simplest early form, viewed thinking as an entirely mentalistic phenomenon in which the brain draws on the senses to construct symbolic representations of the objects sensed, as well as those intangibles the senses cannot perceive directly. This permits us to speculate on everything from the existence of intelligent life elsewhere in the universe to tomorrow's dinner plans. Importantly, the correspondence of this brain-generated symbol system with the external reality it presumably models is reasonably close, but even if it is not, the gaps in correspondence are just that; a question of incomplete data rather than multivalenced data that might be interpreted differently. In other words, issues of perceptual stability and interpretabilty were not the subject of much attention in the information-processing tradition. In this view, informational inputs exist or they do not—different inputs create different problem spaces and task representations, but issues of perceptual accuracy are largely sublimated to those of the data's adequacy.

Although arguments over what representations really are (in neurophysiological terms) inconclusively rage on, what they include and how they include them continues to interest cognitivists in many fields. Of the many concepts related to the issue of representation that have been discussed at length in the cognitivist literature, one of the most common has been that of *problem* representation—the way in which an individual represents to himself or herself the parameters of a problem or task that delimits a problem space. Within this space the problem solver defines "goals, rules, and other aspects of the situation—[it is] some kind of space that represents the initial situation presented to him, the desired goal situation, various intermediate states, imaged or experienced, as well as any concepts he uses to describe these situations to himself" (Newell & Simon, 1972, p. 59). In short, one's representation of the problem space determines the possible courses of action a person may take to resolve the problem.

An important distinction some early proponents of information processing made between types of problem spaces is that of well-structuredness and ill-structuredness. An extremely well-structured problem is one that lends itself to a relatively algorithmic solution; its parameters are finite, the necessary subgoals are evident, and perhaps, most important, its resolution is testable. Marvin Minsky (1961) has suggested that a well-structured problem is one with which we are presented (or at which we can arrive) in a systematic manner and one whose solution is unambiguous. Such well-structured problems were those confronted by cognitivists in the beginning stages of investigation into artificial intelligence and information processing. Classic examples of well-structured (though complex) problems include those involving chess playing (de Groot, 1965; Simon & Simon, 1962) and math (Collins, Brown, & Newman, 1989). Using Minsky's definition we can see that both types of problems are well-structured for they culminate in an unequivocal result: arriving at checkmate or the mathematically correct answer.

On the other end of the spectrum, an ill-structured problem geometrically increases the complexity of the problem-solving process required. Reitman (1965) and many others have suggested that most problems we confront on a daily basis are ill-structured in that contingency permeates the task environment and solutions are always equivocal. The idea of "getting it right" gives way to "making it acceptable in the circumstances." In Reitman's words:

> To the extent that a problem situation evokes a high level of agreement over a specified community of problem solvers regarding the referents of the attributes in which it is given, the operations that are permitted, and the consequences of those operations, it may be termed . . . well-defined with respect to that community. On the other hand, to the extent that a problem evokes a highly variable set of responses concerning referents of attributes, permissible operations, and their consequences, it may be considered ill-defined. (p. 151)

The nature of ill-structuredness is also distinguished from well-structuredness in that there is a wide range of schematic interactions that are simultaneously brought to bear on the problem as well as the fact that "the pattern of conceptual incidence and interaction varies substantially across cases nominally of the same type . . ." (Spiro, Feltovich, Jacobson, & Coulson, 1992a, p. 60). In other words, ill-structuredness means that problems that appear to share salient characteristics and might thus be categorized as similar problem types are, at root, fundamentally and unpredictably different. Unlike well-structured problems, ill-structured problems may require disparate, often competing, goals that demonstrate sensitivity to the uniqueness of the context within which they must be solved and provide an opportunity to deal with the contingencies that real-world problems present.

Many critics have argued that the entrée into the real world that the ill-structured–well-structured distinction provides has been ignored by the information-processing movement. The computational metaphor is largely blamed for this. Coulter (1983), for instance, states that "There are many [artificial intelligence researchers] for whom theoretical questions about 'cognition' are less relevant, interesting or important than endogenous programming and hardware problems generated by attempts to construct simulations of complex tasks of whatever kind" (p. 5). We are thus reminded that the rise of cognitivism, in the United States at least, was a byproduct of the advent of the computer rather than the other way around (cf. Papert, 1979). The first simple computers received data that was encoded symbolically. They then recognized and classified these symbols, stored them in a memory bank, and retrieved them largely at the command of mathematicians and engineers. The computer was not originally intended to model human intelligence artificially, but came to be adopted by psychologists as a plausible metaphor for thinking and quickly took on mentalistic attributes. Because of the computer's metaphorical and heuristic value, the computer revolution was appropriated by psychologists as their own revolution, and the ways in which data flowed through an elaborate mechanism became a rallying point for those disgruntled with behaviorism's evident failings (Hamlyn, 1990).

Norman (1981) has problematized the role of everyday context in the information processing movement in the following manner:

> The human is a social animal, interacting with others, with the environment and with itself. The core disciplines of cognitive science have tended to ignore these aspects of behavior. The results have been considerable progress on some fronts, but sterility overall, for the organism we are analyzing is conceived as pure intellect, communicating with one another in logical dialogue, perceiving, remembering, thinking when appropriate, reasoning its way through well-formed problems that are encountered in the day. Alas that description does not fit actual behavior (p. 266).

More succinctly, Ceci and Ruiz (1993) note that the information-processing tradition has looked on everyday context as noise that, for purposes of experimentation, required elimination. Yet, this was done at the cost of "slavishly sanitizing their experiments of all meaning and motivation" (p. 183). For this reason, an inability to deal with what we have been calling authenticity is widely considered the Achilles' heel of information processing. Elsewhere, Norman (1993) gives three interrelated and authenticity-related reasons for why an adequate understanding of human cognition has eluded the information processing tradition. First, the density of information required to deal with the world—the "enormity of the database" in his words—is a difficult obstacle to overcome (p. 2). Related to this is the interaction of our limited sensory input with the complexity, unpredictability, and dynamism of the world. Finally, an understanding of how we think in everyday environments escapes us, Norman concludes, because of the "impossibility of observing all the relevant aspects of human cognition" given the methodological and computational tools available to us (p. 2).

It is easy to concur with Hutchins' (1995) contention that over the course of the last three decades, cognitive science (in the guise of the information-processing paradigm) has indeed attempted to remake the person in the image of the computer (p. 363). No sooner than cognitivism had been defined as a movement than Neisser (1967) observed that "a number of researchers, not content with noting that computer programs are like cognitive theories, have tried to write programs that are cognitive theories" (p. 9). Gardner (1985) calls the idea that the information and knowledge we possess in our heads bears significant correspondence to the knowledge we externalize in the forms of pedagogy or computational models, the *identity hypothesis*.

One is tempted to accuse critics of straw-manning the information-processing paradigm by associating it too fully with the identity hypothesis. To be sure, several writers have leveled precisely this accusation (Hoppe, 1993; Sandberg & Wielinga, 1992; Vera & Simon, 1993). They insist that the metaphor of the mind as computer has always been understood to be just that—a heuristic intended to enable cognitivists to test theories of cognition and to account for behavior rather than models intended to bear close resemblance to internal mechanisms of the brain. Yet, it is hard to overstate the centrality of the computational metaphor to information processing, and it must be said that most cognitive scientists have, in fact, presumed that the computer analogy was not entirely metaphorical, but rather quite neatly mapped onto internal representational structures and processes. Gardner (1985) argues that there is indeed a "faith" in cognitivist circles "that central to any understanding of the human mind is the electronic computer. Not only are computers indispensable for carrying out studies of various sorts, but more crucially, the computer also serves as the most viable model of how the human mind works" (p. 6). Clancey (1993) insists that, contrary to what defenders of the information-processing paradigm claim, "many, if not most cognitive scientists have claimed that cognitive models map onto an internal level of representational structures and processes, not just behavior" (p. 7). The identity hypothesis necessarily removes context from the study of mind—at least context in terms of those subliminal cultural and ideological forces that operate on each of us as well as the affective dimension of thinking that we would readily identify as critical to our real world.

In sum, then, the face cognitivism first presented to the American academy was largely the face of the information-processing paradigm, which offered psychology a chance to return to some of its traditional commonsense concerns, such as representation and memory. After the sterility of the behaviorist framework, a concerted interest in representation seemed to make discussions of the real world possible in a way they were not possible before. While this may have paved the way for a return to a renewed respect for commonsense psychology, behaviorism's studied ignorance of the real world was not the rallying point for the information-processing view of cognition. Rather, the advent of the computation had opened up the black box to make talk of knowledge and understanding respectable once again, a necessary but insufficient condition for renewed interest in the real world. Instead, the information-processing paradigm may remain best understood and appreciated for its significant loosening of the intellectual straitjacket imposed by behaviorism and for its enormously productive entrée into the world of computation—even if it did not provide a viable window to the everyday processes of human thinking.

Late into the information-processing revolution, Neisser (1976) was still able to observe that "the study of information processing has momentum and prestige, but it has not yet committed itself to any conception of human nature that could apply beyond the confines of the laboratory. . . . There is still no account of how people act in or interact with the ordinary world" (pp. 6–7). In its migration from calculatory sciences to psychology, one expert system was simply replaced by another: an expert problem solver whose virtuoso performance could be considered paradigmatic.

ACCOMMODATING CONTEXT: THE EARLY CONSTRUCTIVIST TRADITION IN EUROPE

Both behaviorism and information processing were largely American responses to Wundt's call for a New Psychology. With the exception of conditioned reflex work in Eastern Europe, the response of Europeans heeding the call was thoroughly dissimilar. Several decades before cognitivism would overtake behaviorism in the United States, a very different cognitivist tradition, one that might be called "early constructivism," made itself felt on the continent and in Britain. Instead of presuming the "value-neutrality" of inputs, European psychologists such as Vygotsky, Bartlett, and Piaget focused instead on individuals' *constructive* processes, the way in which we individuals actively piece together meaning from information in accordance with prior experiences and understandings. Like other Early European movements in psychology (e.g., Gestalt and psychoanalytic approaches), cognitivism was isolated from the behaviorist and, to a lesser degree, the information-processing paradigms, not only by the obvious linguistic and/or political and logistic barriers, but more significantly, by methodological barriers, for several major European psychologists were less interested in experimental rigor than their American counterparts and were often willing to base far-reaching theories on scant empirical grounds.

Sociohistoricism

One of the early constructivist threads of psychological research can be traced to the work of Soviet psychologist Lev Semenovich Vygotsky and his collaborators (most notably, Alexander Luria and Alexei Leontiev). Moll (1990) and others have labeled the movement they established the *sociohistorical school of psychology* for the tenets of the school center on the ramifications of culturally and historically situated activities for thinking and learning. As Wertsch (1985) explains it, Vygotskian thought works from three general assumptions. The first, and perhaps least distinctive, assumption is that a developmental approach to cognition is required to understanding human learning, for it makes no sense to view the mind as fully formed irrespective of age and experience. Second, and more originally, Vygotsky argued that an individual's mental functioning is derived from social interaction; that is, a learner's cognitive behavior is an internalization of the social practices he or she has experienced. Finally, sociohistoricism is closely tied to the belief that social practices are mediated practices that are dependent on the physical and mental tools and symbols that the learner uses to engage in them.

The sociohistoricists' project can be seen as groundbreaking in many senses. Vygotsky worked with his colleagues in the 1920s and 1930s in challenging the Pavlovian paradigm based on conditioning and reflex. Speaking to the Second Psychoneurological Congress in 1926, Vygotsky initiated his brief career in psychology by condemning the Pavlovian school for its avoidance of consciousness. Vygotsky's principle reason for rejecting conditioned reflex and behavioralistic approaches to learning was that they conceived of learning as passive. These approaches also presumed that humans came into the world with learning mechanisms already in place and that the environment merely shaped these mechanisms rather than contributed to their creation. Instead, Vygotsky pointedly abandoned the behavioristic assumption that primary functions (e.g., perceptual ability to distinguish among letters of the alphabet) accumulated to eventually constitute higher functions (e.g., reading a bus schedule).

Yet, the way in which Vygotskian theories becomes central to the work of educators (and central to our discussion of authenticity) lies in their very conscious breakdown of traditional barriers among types of learning. Conceptually, the sociohistorical school was working on a radical assumption when it "quotidianized" learning by highlighting the mundaneness of cognitive development. In psychology's short disciplinary history prior to Vygotsky, experimentalism necessitated a model of learning that clearly delimited a start and end of the learning episode; it required that the learning under study be made discrete from both pre-existing and collateral knowledge and lent itself to use in replicative studies regardless of subjects' other experiences and background (behaviorism, of course, ensured that this formalization was perpetuated in most American learning theory for decades subsequent to Vygotsky and other early constructivist theorists). In the Piagetian framework as well, Vygotsky (1978) believed that the focus on ontogenetic development independent of learning similarly served to cleave learning from everyday cognition (p. 80).

Vygotsky maintained that, as knowledge is situated in culture and within a historical context, meaning is the result of participation in social activities. The larger objective of his sociohistoricism accounted both for the ways in which social arrangements provided the tools necessary to structure learning as well as how these tools were acquired by children and used appropriately. The second half of this objective provided the greatest focus for Vygotsky's work, and observers have commented that Vygotsky was less the social theorist (as he is sometimes presented in communication studies) than a developmental psychologist who paid a great deal of attention to the authentic environment within which cognitive development tasks take place.

From Vygotsky's (1981) perspective, the interaction of social and cognitive functioning was impossible to overstate. In an often-cited passage, he argues that:

> Any function in the child's cultural development appears twice, or on two planes. First, it appears on the social plane, and then on the psychological plane. First it appears between people as an interpsychological category, and then within the child as an intrapsychological category. This is equally true with regard to voluntary attention, logical memory, the formation of concepts and the development of volition.... [I]t goes without saying that internalization transforms the process itself and changes the structure and functions. Social relations or relations among people genetically underlie all higher functions and their relationships. (p. 163)

Thus, whether at an abstract cultural level, an institutional level, or an interpersonal level, the child's construction of knowledge depended on his or her internalization of these social relations. These relations not only provided information and raw data, but also functioned to help the child assimilate the information as knowledge. Although physical objects can be used as tools for learning, Vygotsky argues that social tools, such as language and other sign systems, play the most central role in development and learning.

In his best known work, *Thought and Language*, Vygotsky (1962) collapses the mental and the social by positing two levels of mental functioning: the higher and the lower functions. Cultural, higher functions of learning occur at two stages: they first develop as a result of interpersonal (i.e., social) contact and then later become internalized within the child. Internalization is accomplished with mediational tools that link higher and lower mental functions: most notably, language. Thought and speech, thus, become inextricably bound together, just as the Sapir-Whorf hypothesis was suggesting to American linguists at about this same time and as Vico had argued centuries earlier. In his focus on the higher functions and their origins in social interaction, Vygotsky takes pains to distinguish himself from his contemporaries (most notably, Piaget) who, he believed, incorrectly privileged the autonomous cognitive capabilities of the individual.

Certainly, Vygotsky's most widely applied idea is that of a *zone of proximal development* (ZPD)—the cognitive zone in which children can work with "more knowledgeable peers" to perform tasks that they can go on to perform independently. Moll (1990) suggests, "the zone must be thought of as more than a clever instructional heuristic; it is a key theoretical construct, capturing as it does the individual within the concrete social situation of learning and development" (p. 4). Within the ZPD, children act as apprentices, guided toward greater proficiency in performing tasks by mentors who are more experienced participants in the activity than the learner. The idea of a ZPD is also one in which we may read Vygotsky's interests in making schooling correspond more closely to everyday life. Spencer (1988) suggests as much when he writes that "In the real world, children have access to older children and adults to help them solve their problems, and so [Vygotsky] argued that we should take into account the capacity of a child to profit from help that others can give when assessing a child's potential" (p. 176). Properly trained teachers and older students, Vygotsky suggests, can provide the same cognitive scaffolding for the student that siblings, parents, friends, and coworkers provide for the young person as he or she engages in everyday problem solving.

Furthermore, sociohistoricists—especially Leontiev and Elkonin—believe that episodes of play provide children with some of the most productive learning opportunities (Cole, 1985). As children use their imaginations to create scenarios that require the assignment of roles and categories, as well as both implicit and explicit rules, play creates learning situations that are invaluable in permitting children to practice organizing skills. While most psychologists had relegated play to the margins of learning, Vygotsky saw play as absolutely critical to mental development and the development of higher order thinking skills. Play also functions to create the zones of proximal development, for in play, children create constraints and then learn to work within them or devise ways around them with the assistance of more practiced playmates. In fact, Leontiev (1978) argues that from the ages of 3 to about 6, children do not learn without play.

In short, one of sociohistoricism's most significant contributions to cognitivism, and certainly the one with which this book is most concerned, is its embedding of learning in everyday cultural practices. To be sure, most sociohistorical research was done in schools (Luria and Leontiev, more than Vygotsky, developed the links between formal and informal learning), but Vygotsky insisted that school was only one site of activity among others and that life outside of school was every bit as important a learning environment. For Vygotsky, school promoted social interaction that could be seen as paradigmatic of cognitive development, but such interaction was intimately connected with the child's life outside the classroom. As did Dewey, the sociohistoricists sought to re-envisage the relationship of the rarified world of school to the world of learning in a broader sense and create educational opportunities that drew from both.

Bartlett and Piaget

Although we have ample reason to view sociohistoricism as the most direct antecedent of modern constructivism, convention leads us to look to other parts of Europe. The two most prominent psychologists who recognized, early on, the centrality of constructive processes to thinking were Frederic Bartlett and Jean Piaget—known for their interest in how learners use schemata to construct meaning (an interest that has long been accommodated within the information processing paradigm as well). A *schema* functions as a type of memory unit that stores information in associated webs and assists in interpreting incoming information by judging what seems to be relevant and what can be ignored as irrelevant. Despite the concept's admitted "mushiness," Fiske and Linville (1980) believe that the idea of schemata, embedded in a broader theory of cognitive processing, accounts for many commonsense observations about association and memory. The concept of schema is very important to the move toward authentic learning because, like progressivism in education, it places everyday experience at the center of both memory and learning. If memory is encoded in schemata that are abstracted from experience, we begin to build a basis for the argument that thinking is largely related to living rather than to formal training: an unremarkable bit of commonsense psychology, perhaps, but one that was buried under behaviorist and early information-processing methodology as well as the elite-idealist pedagogical tradition.

While the basic outline of schema theory is attributable to Kant, it is Bartlett's notion of schema, as well as his overall research approach, that has had perhaps the most direct effect on the contemporary constructivist tradition. His book *Remembering* (1932) reports on a number of experiments in perceiving, imaging, recognition, and recall that hold up remarkably well. Bartlett's importance to psychology lies in no small part in his accessibility. His writing style and patterns of argument are models of forthrightness and clarity and his discussion of social constructivism in *Remembering* (especially pp. 274–280) remains, to my mind, the definitive primer on the importance of social interaction in cognition—a discussion that continues to be discovered by cognitivists and one that few modern theorists can do much to add to or detract from.

Bartlett's experiments in recall repeatedly confirm the dominant role social influence plays in memory. He argues that human understanding could not be adequately described as a mere series of reactions or as the mere arrangement of images and ideas that logically cohere. Memory, he argues, is encoded in accordance with expectations, prior knowledge, and what he calls "conventionalization"; the ethnological process of giving perceptions cultural relevance. This is the foundation of what Bartlett terms *social construction* (a point worth considering when we discuss more fully constructivism's epistemological dimension in Chapter Four). An appreciation of the importance of authenticity in psychology is revealed in Bartlett's careful, yet pointed, criticisms of contemporary psychology (by which he meant other early strains of New Psychology best exemplified by Ebbinghaus) that attempted to account for memory in terms of stimulus and response using nonsense syllables. Bartlett was bothered by such methods' isolation of memory performance from a larger, everyday context, and in his own studies, he sought experimental tasks that most closely resembled memory tasks "commonly dealt with in real life" (p. 12).

The other major force in early constructivism, Piaget, also expanded our understanding of how schema functions, but unlike Bartlett, Piaget was interested in the *ontogenesis*, or the developmental progression, of schema formation and cognitive abilities. In some respects, the very notion of developmental psychology, with its focus on children's accretion of cognitive abilities as a result of experience in the world, can conceivably be seen as a move to situate cognition in authentic environments.[5] Although sociohistoricists were also interested in children's cognitive development, Piaget differed from them on many counts, most notably, perhaps, on the subject of the distinct developmental stages children passed through on their way to becoming reasoning beings.

The child acquires logical structures, Piaget argued, through his or her interaction with objects in the external environment. Piaget emphasized that children were actively involved in the construction of their physical environment rather than passive perceivers of objective reality. As learners, they explore and experiment with their operations on objects (including other individuals) to move from sensory–motor stages of development to advanced, representational stages. Piaget, like the sociohistoricists, also saw play as an essential part of the progression from the sensorimotor stage to pre-operations and on to concrete operations (Tudge & Rogoff, 1989). To Piaget, children were little scientists using the real world as a laboratory in which they experimented with their surroundings and structured learning. Like his American behaviorist contemporaries, Piaget was vitally interested in physical context, though unlike them, he was willing to concede that the complexity of the material conditions in which children learned could not be faithfully replicated by experimental studies (Donaldson, 1978).

Like Bartlett, Piaget focused on the cognitive assimilation, accommodation and adaptation of schemata. He argued that schematic development is triggered by *perturbation* and that problem solving (and generally, thinking) is motivated by the individual's sense of disjuncture between information previously schematized and new information. Such perturbation is often the result of social interaction with others, which leads the learner to accommodate the conflicting information in a modified schema. According to Piaget, each individual's ability to accommodate and act on new information is unique insofar as no other

---

[5]Though one should note that developmental psychologists within the information-processing school assume that development is largely, perhaps entirely, a function of neurocognitive maturation and individual effort rather than exposure to social contexts.

learner occupies a particular space in the universe physically, historically, or mentally. In a sense then, Piagetian theory, like that of Bartlett and the socio-historicists, centers on the development of cognitive abilities in children acquired through quotidian experience rather than through formal episodes of learning, although as we have noted, Vygotsky vehemently objected to Piaget's inattention to social and cultural forces. Confrey (1995) suggests Piaget "invites us to witness and participate in the ways that children build their knowledge from their interactions with objects and the resolutions of perturbations experienced in goal-oriented activity," while Vygotsky draws our attention to the intensely social contexts that produce learning and reminds us that all learning is culture- and history-bound (pp. 222–223). Piaget, to a greater degree than any of his predecessors, sought to explain how schemata change by incorporating new information and adapting to their environment and Elkind (1979) contends that the rhetorical strength of Piaget's writings lie in the fact that "he portrayed recognizable children, children who spoke, behaved, and thought as did children in our own everyday experience" (p. 7).

Given the very different agendas and commitments of theorists such as Vygotsky, Bartlett, and Piaget, it is understandable that what hindsight permits us to label "early constructivism" never attained the theoretical cogency that behaviorism or information processing possessed. Unlike those American frameworks, early constructivism raised knotty issues that the relatively atheoretical paradigms of behaviorism or information processing had been able to avoid. Still, early constructivism made it possible for psychologists to engage many of the commonsense concerns traditionally associated with psychological inquiry, such as purpose, emotion, meaning, and motives; it thus went far to inject a fuller and more satisfying concern for contextualization that nudged the cognitive paradigm closer to an appreciation of thinking in authentic situations.[6]

CONSTRUCTIVISM'S SECOND WAVE AND THE MOVEMENT TO "SITUATE" COGNITION

Early Western European constructivism first called our attention to the "ungivenness" of knowledge and the role of the learner in constructing informa-

---

[6]Vygotsky's relatively late appearance on the American scene, compared to Piaget and Bartlett, may be due, not only to the fact that Soviet science was generally slighted in the West, but to his own relative obscurity in the Soviet Union from the time of his death until the arrival of Gorbachev and perestroika (Davydov, 1995). A committed Marxist, Vygotsky—always open to psychological thought from Western theorists—was posthumously accused of "bourgeois pseudo-science," which ignored Marxist objectivist ideals. A 1936 decree from the Party forbade any teaching or researching of child development, including developmental psychology, and effectively marginalized sociocultural thinking as Vygotsky's erstwhile collaborators quietly shifted the focus and methods of their research to bring it more in line with political conditions. This decree was not rescinded until the 1980s, making a complete examination of his work possible both inside and outside Russia.

tion. Soviet sociohistoricism complemented this by highlighting the influences of social and material culture as well as activities on both perception and learning. Although these early movements with their talk of schema and socialization could be used to reinforce and extend the critique of behaviorism, for a long time they had relatively little impact on psychology in the United States because Americans were busy refining the information-processing framework. Yet, as we have already seen, at the height of that framework's influence, Neisser (1976) sounded a clear note of dissent and proposed that cognitive psychologists take a "realistic" turn. By this, he meant four things:

1. Cognitive psychology had to make greater efforts to understand thinking "as it occurs in the ordinary environment and in the context of natural, purposeful activity."
2. Psychologists should pay closer attention to the "real world in which perceivers and thinkers live."
3. Methodology must accommodate the complexity of real-world thinking by moving away from its traditional dependence on inexperienced subjects performing novel and meaningless tasks.
4. Cognitivists must accept and examine the implications of the "fundamental" questions it raises about human nature (pp. 8–9).

Gardner's (1985) formulation of this same challenge is encapsulated in what might be called the *computational paradox*—the fact that computers have helped us understand just how unlike computers we are. He notes that:

> . . . the kind of systematic, logical, rational view of human cognition that pervaded the early literature of cognitive science does not adequately describe much of human thought and behavior. Cognitive science can still go on, but the question arises about whether one ought to remain on the lookout for more veridical models of human thought. (44)

Availing itself of the information-processing paradigm's success and standing on a now secure cognitivist foundation, a "second wave" of constructivists responded to the concerns of Neisser and Gardner and returned to the once marginal literatures generated by the Vygotskians and early constructivists to gesture toward a theory of mind capable of accounting for the real world.

A major strain of this reinvigorated and expanded constructivist movement argues for situated cognition. As James Greeno (1989) puts it, *situated cognition* promotes the view that "thinking is situated in physical and social contexts. Cognition, including thinking, knowing, and learning, can be considered as a relation involving an agent in a situation, rather than as an activity in an individual's mind" (p. 135). "Situated" cognitivists argue that everyday learning (i.e., learning that occurs as a function of being in the world) always takes place within a socially and culturally informed context; it is this context, this situation, that shapes both knower and knowledge. Such a view eliminates the distance between a learner and a subject matter, by emphasizing, as Vygotsky did, that "learning is a way of being in the social world, not a way of coming to know about it" (Hanks, 1991, p. 24).

What might be called the "situationist" movement covers a variety of interests and possesses a number of disciplinary precursors. Psychology, linguistics, philosophy, anthropology, and rhetoric, have all, at various times, highlighted the importance of context for thinking. Although certain writers have pushed the notion of situated cognition to the forefront of many cognitivist discussions, many of the movement's basic premises have been around for decades, and even (as Vico illustrates) centuries.

According to Greeno and Moore (1993):

> It may not suffice to say that cognition is influenced by contexts. In the view of situated cognition, we need to characterize knowing, reasoning, understanding, and so on as relations between cognitive agents and situations, and it is not meaningful to try to characterize what someone knows apart from situations in which the person engages in cognitive activity. (p. 100).

Proponents of situated cognition reject the assumption that thinking is exclusively the mental manipulation of static representations or that knowledge can only be derived from what is encoded and stored in schemata. They also reject the identity hypothesis and its mind as machine metaphor so central to information-processing models. Unlike earlier constructivists such as Bartlett, whose studies suggested that the propensity to construct information was a propensity to distort information, contemporary situationists' arguments tend to cast constructivism not as a problem so much as a fact of learning to be accepted rather than remediated. The difference is noted less for its substance than for how it reflects why one might consider situationism more in tune with the epistemological ramifications of constructivism that researchers in Bartlett's time may have found more difficult to accommodate.

Two notions that may best represent the interests of contemporary constructivists in the real worldliness of learning are neither recent nor exclusively constructivist. The first is the notion of *activity* and the second is the idea of cognition's *distribution*.

Activity

My earlier discussion of sociohistoricism glossed over one of its key conceptual contributions to a notion of authenticity: a theory of activity (cf. Wertsch, 1981). Developed, in large part, by Vygotsky's collaborators after his death, the concept of activity has gained prominence as a cornerstone of second-wave constructivist theory.[7] Kuutti (1996) broadly defines activity theory as "a philo-

---

[7]Kozulin (1986) argues that activity theory, attributed to Leontiev, but often considered as part of the Vygotskian tradition, was, in some essential respects, a fundamental departure from Vygotskian thought. He identifies Leontiev's insistence that "the development of the consciousness of a child occurs as a result of the development of the systems of psychological operations, which, in

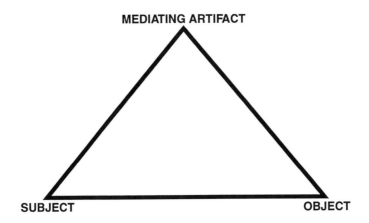

FIG. 2.1.   The basic mediational (activity) triangle.

sophical and cross-disciplinary framework for studying different forms of human practices as development processes, with both individual and social levels
interlinked at the same time" (p. 25). He points out that activity theory is neither
interested in *activity* in the usual sense of the word, nor is it really a theory in any
strict sense. Russell (1995) suggests that while activity theory is open and developing, there are key constituents of activity that most theorists focus on, including activities' historical development, their mediation by tools, and the idea that
they are collaboratively and interactively structured (p. 54). In accordance with
Hacking's (1983, p. 17) observation that "reality has more to do with what we
do in the world that with what we think about it," the notion of activity directs
our attention away from cognition as purely mentalistic to the idea that thinking
is a complex interaction with the world through the use of symbolic and physical tools.

The idea of human cognition's implication in activity systems is represented
in the simple tripartite model shown in Fig. 2.1. Its constituent parts include a
subject (or agent), an object (a goal or task that can be manifested physically or
in the abstract), and the mediational means or tools that the subject may apply to
the object.[8]

---

turn, are determined by the actual relations between a child and reality" (p. xliv) as the principle
that divides the two collaborators' theories. The close correspondence of external activity and internal mental processing (in some respects, a variation of the identity hypothesis for which information-processing cognitivists are routinely criticized) led Leontiev's group to a more experimen-
talist and more materialist framework than Vygotsky might have endorsed. This framework left
out much of the distinctively phenomenological flavor of sociohistoricism. If Kozulin is correct, it
is a Leontievian variation on activity theory that has become central to current discussions of situated cognition (e.g., especially in the work of Engeström), and Vygotsky's influence over current
situationist thinking may be less direct than is commonly assumed.

[8]The basic model of activity developed by Leontiev has precursors in other theoretical traditions. Kuutti traces activity theory back to Kantian philosophy through Hegel, Marx, and later

An activity perspective can be detected in Pylyshyn's (1989) account of symbol manipulation:

> Consider an abacus. Patterns of beads represent numbers. People learn rules for transforming these patterns of beads in such a way that the semantic interpretation of before-and-after pairs corresponds to a useful mathematical function. . . . What makes the rules useful for doing mathematics is that we are assured of a certain continuing correspondence between the formal or syntactic patterns of beads and mathematical objects (such as numbers). (p. 56)

Commenting on this, Hutchins (1995) notes, "there are no hands or eyes in this description . . . Pylyshyn . . . is not interested in what the person does or what it means for a person to learn, to 'know' or to apply a rule. Rather, he is interested in the properties of the system enacted by the person manipulating the physical beads" (p. 366). As with other contemporary constructivists, Hutchins' situationist perspective draws attention to the material as well as mental dimensions of perception and understanding. To the situationist, thinking is not the abstract manipulation of purely symbolic data, but a process embedded in our physical interactions with the world and, thus, relationships among the constituents of an activity are always products of mediation (Davydov & Radzikhovskii, 1985). For instance, an instrument mediates between a subject and his or her objective, and that objective, depending on its actor and the instrument that actor uses to achieve it, also undergoes transformation. Artifacts too have been created and transformed during the development of the activity itself and carry within them the social and historical residue that gave rise to their creation. As dynamic processes, activities undergo changes as they unfold, as actors' motives shift, as tools become available or unavailable, and as objects and objectives form and reform. Of course, subjects and tools have capabilities and limitations (which naturally shape the objects they attain), but these capabilities and limitations are also in flux.[9]

---

to the Vygotskians. More interesting, perhaps, he also calls our attention to the fact that several strands of Anglo-American thought have much in common with activity theory, most notably that of Deweyan pragmatism and Mead's symbolic interactionism. Readers from rhetoric-related disciplines may recognize the striking similarities between an activity system and Burke's (1945) notion of a dramatic pentad that adds the elements of *scene* and *act*. When one considers that the sociohistorical perspective presumes the centrality of *scene* (the historical and material conditions in which any action occurs) and that the entire system is meant to delimit an act, Burkian and sociohistorical models become virtually indistinguishable in many respects. This observation becomes more relevant in Chapter Five when I suggest that second-wave constructivism and rhetoric have both evolved to share a single object of inquiry. It may also be worth adding here (and developing later) the fact that Burke regretted he had not incorporated the element of *attitude* in the pentad. This addition would have highlighted the important affective dimension that a rhetorical perspective is in a special position to offer situated constructivism.

[9]Engeström (1987, 1990, 1993) and his collaborators have perhaps done the most to popularize and develop activity theory; the summary given here provides only its barest outline.

Distribution of Knowledge and Thinking

I suggested earlier that the New Psychologists had an appreciation for the real world—one that is lacking in either behaviorism or information processing models of thinking. This appreciation, I argue, was rooted in their concern for consciousness. I also noted that early constructivists and sociohistoricists extended the cognitive arena to include the social and cultural environments in which learning occurred. But an element of the real world that these efforts at contextualization lack is a fully elaborated awareness of the role played by other entities in the world for an individual's thinking. Of course, constructivist and especially sociohistoricist understandings of learning as a product of social interaction assume that interpersonal and social relationships are enormously important to cognition, but both Piagetian and Vygotskian perspectives highlight the social influence on the more (in Piaget's case) or less (in Vygotsky's) self-contained cogitator. Piaget made a clear separation between the social individual who availed himself or herself of tools and other people in order to learn and the individual as an autonomous thinker. While sociohistorists emphasized the social means of learning with few reservations, theories such as that of the ZPD suggest that the more competent peer interceded in, but was not really an extension of, the cognitive processes of his or her less competent counterpart. In other words, in the sociohistoricist's methodological framework, the learner retained a degree of autonomy in key respects; while the self was receptive to (and even permeated by) social forces, it nonetheless remained distinct from them.

And so while second-wave constructivism is beholden to its predecessors for many of its central tenets, it does not fully capture the spirit of movements, such as situated cognition, only to note their exploration of the social influences on autonomous individuals. A second, and to some researchers, more important, dimension of the move to situate cognition has been its exploration of "shared" or "distributed" cognition (Hutchins, 1995; Lave, 1991; Moll, Tapia, & Whitmore, 1993; Nardi, 1996a; Pea, 1993; Perkins, 1990; Resnick, 1991). In the diagram shown in Fig. 2.2, Coles and Engeström (1993) amend the basic mediational triangle to accommodate other people, social rules and norms, and the division of labor among the actor and others.[10]

Second-wave constructivism is more explicit than its precursor in its insistence that other entities not only shape cognition, but are a part of it. We use artifacts in myriad ways to identify problems, structure problem solving, and assess solutions. Objects around us contain affordances that promote particular uses and encode information in their very existence. Artifacts can be as material as maps and landmarks or as conceptual as number systems and alphabets, but

---

[10]A very different approach to distributedness is reflected in the work on parallel processing exemplified by McClelland and Rumelhart (1986) and others working within the information-processing framework, which, naturally perhaps, has viewed distribution nonsocially.

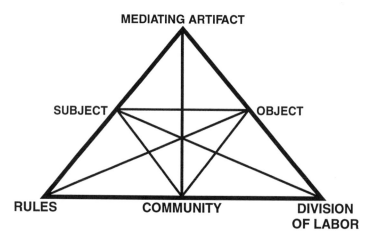

FIG. 2.2. The amended basic mediational triangle. From Cole & Engeström (1993). Copyright 1993 by Cambridge University Press. Reprinted with permission.

all of these creations are united in their symbolic significance for humans as well as the fact that each is a product of prior thought and thus comes to us with intelligence already inscribed. This prompts Pea (1993) to suggest that "intelligence is accomplished rather than possessed" (p. 49).[11] Just as sociohistoricists take the focus off the isolated thinker and demand that we consider our everyday interaction with others as a source of information, the notion of distribution of intellectual resources among people and things requires us to attend to the fact that we think in conjunction with our environment. What is considered by many to be an extreme view of distributed intelligence is sometimes called the *ecological* or *perceptual* approach of Gibson and Brunswick, which has been more recently advocated (and legitimated, in the minds of many) by Neisser. Essentially, the ecological view holds that entire processes within the cognitive system may be bypassed by an individual's unconscious awareness of spatial relationships and object significance (e.g., when we see a door, we know, without thinking, that it is for passing from one space into another).

What might be considered new in the more recent treatment of distribution is its destabilization of the assumption that the individual is the unit of cognitive analysis. Tools and other beings not only inform our cognition, but also extend it. In this way, the real world becomes not so much a resource that the individual

---

[11]Pea (1993) makes an important distinction in choosing to speak of distributed intelligence and not of distributed cognition (and presumably, shared cognition), for cognition, he argues, is a clearly human mental activity, whereas intelligence lies in the relationship of objects (social as well as material) to objectives.

information processor draws on, but part of a larger cognitive network of which he or she is but a node. In light of this, Perkins (1990) suggests that we abandon metaphors that suggest autonomy, and instead, conceive of the self as the "sum and swarm of participations" (p. 24). In a nontrivial sense, the mind becomes part of the everyday world, a node in a web of links connecting (and blurring) representers and the represented. Psychologists investigating an individual's cognition are thus actually confronted with a rich web of social and material interactions and only capable of inferring the larger activity matrix from the performance of a particular entity within this web (i.e., the individual). They are, in short, confronted with the real world in all its complexity.

For the remainder of this book, I wish to employ the terms *constructivism* and *constructivist metatheory* to connote a broad range of contemporary cognitive and educational frameworks that have the *desideratum* of authenticity at their center.[12] Readers may wonder if we pay too high a price by collapsing so many distinctive approaches to cognition into a constructivist metatheory. Certainly, if we were discussing a conventional psychological topic, such as the neurology of perception, memory, or even the role of representation, such conflation costs more than it buys us. Unlike these other topics, however, I ask the reader to consider that the *desideratum* of authenticity in education has grown out of a century-long, intellectual progression rather than from any single framework attributable to any single movement or individual. Our professional interest in the "real world" is not traceable to any particular constructivist theorist, but to a general dissatisfaction with transmission models of learning, instructivist modes of teaching, and theories of mind that preclude context. Thus, the collapsing of distinct strands of cognitivist thought is not intended to erase the considerable differences between Piaget and Vygotsky or Bartlett and Lave, but is intended to blur them. By doing so, I mean to suggest that, given a sufficiently distant vantage point, we can comfortably speak of a sizable group of scholars within the cognitive sciences and education, who share with Dewey the premises that we construct our knowledge of the world from prior knowledge and experience, and that knowledge and learning are derived from participation in activities that are distributed across social, cultural and material dimensions.

---

[12]More careful distinctions among socioculturalism, sociocognitivism, constructivism, and radical social constructivism have been laid out in the education literature (cf. Confrey, 1995; Duffy & Jonassen, 1992; Phillips, 1995; Shotter, 1991; Smith, 1993). In a discussion on human–computer interaction, Nardi (1996b) compares and contrasts activity theory, theories of situated action, and theories of distributed cognition. While, as she argues, there are useful distinctions to be made among these, in the next chapter dealing with educational technology, we see that educators often collapse perspectives that may be described more narrowly as progressivist, sociohistoricist, early constructivist, or situationist into a single metatheoretical body of principles. Because of this, I ask that for heuristic reasons we adopt *constructivism* as a shorthand for this metatheory.

THE RECEPTION OF CONTEMPORARY
CONSTRUCTIVISM AND THE ROLE
OF METHODOLOGY

Gergen (1995) voices the view of many in psychology when he argues that constructivists are not necessarily psychologists, but social theorists deeply concerned with matters such as "negotiation, cooperation, conflict, rhetoric, ritual, roles, social scenarios, and the like" (p. 25). Although Gergen intends his statement to be laudatory of constructivism, the evolution toward integrating cognition into the everyday world has not been unanimously welcomed by the broader cognitive science community. In Gergen's statements, some psychologists find confirmation of their suspicions that constructivism lies outside the accepted parameters of cognitive science. Like Dewey's early formulation of progressivism, constructivism has not lacked critics.

To some of these critics, accounts of learning provided by "strong program" constructivists—such as Lave and Wenger, Suchman, and Hutchins—seem to suggest that learning entails the adaptation of a learner to a situation by means of tools and other externalia rather than through mental processing. The charge of neobehaviorism is leveled at this view because it denies the possibility of knowledge independent of external stimuli in the form of context (Anderson, Reder, & Simon, 1995; Coulter, 1983; Palincsar, 1989).[13] Suchman (1987) uses her work on photocopiers, for instance, to basically reject the notion of planning as a prior mental activity, an idea held dear by most information-processing cognitivists. The traditional psychological view of planning, she argues, ignores the opportunistic ways in which learners interact with tools around them, formulating and reformulating plans as the circumstances permit or demand.

In response to Lave's assertion (1988, p. 1) that "'Cognition' observed in everyday practice is distributed—stretched over, not divided among—mind, body, activity and culturally organized settings which include other actors," critics of contemporary constructivism also complain that the representational level so central to both information-processing and early constructivist frameworks is ignored and perhaps even denied. At a more philosophical level, the strong constructivist program, critics fear, undermines basic notions of individual agency and relegates the individual to the status of mere mouthpiece for an underspecified society or situation. Sandberg and Wielinga (1992) find in the recent constructivist literature, a "danger of reductionism, that is, reducing the mind to a simple organism interacting with its environment and producing com-

---

[13]Garrison (1995) reminds us that Dewey and Mead accepted the label of *social behaviorist*. Because progressivists, like modern constructivists, were eager to reject modernist or *correspondance* theories of language, they have emphasized the dialogic nature of meaning and thus, privileged the social over the cognitive and made little reference to individual agency.

plex behavior through the application of simple behavioral rules" (p. 137). Finally, Prenzel and Mandl (1993) note that another issue that causes the information-processing cognitivist to be wary of situationism is that of transfer. Within the information-processing framework, skills and knowledge are contained in the individual independent of the contexts within which they were acquired, thus permitting application of learning to any similar context. If one maintains a situated constructivist view, the argument goes, the possibility of transfer seems less likely as no two situations are identical.

Ironically, many of these same critics are eager to dismiss the constructivist metatheory as common sense (Anderson et al., 1995; Dillenbourg & Schenider, 1993; Hoppe, 1993; Sandberg & Wielinga, 1992; Vera & Simon, 1993; Wineburg, 1989). From an artificial intelligence (AI) perspective, critics argue that the constructivist view, if it could be enacted, would have little discernable impact on the design of artificially intelligent tutoring systems. Dillenbourg and Schneider's (1993, p. 42) claim that "systems have already moved in some direction [toward appreciation of context] and that this evolution can be explained without the situationist framework" is another way of saying that the modern avatars of constructivism are nothing special—experience-based learning has long been a feature of traditional AI and educational psychology. And Hoppe (1993), for instance, rightly concludes that situationist calls for authenticity are not unlike the discovery learning of Bruner (1961) and Ausubel (1968) or Weil's notion of *enracinement* in which knowledge is rooted in concrete experience. He contends that the idea that learners should be led directly to the phenomena under study (before any teacher mediation structures the experience) is hardly news.

Constructivists have not been deaf to such criticism. Greeno and Moore (1993), Salomon (1993), and Bredo (1993), for instance, caution fellow constructivists not to indulge in any postrevolutionary excesses by negating the role of the individual in learning. They appear sympathetic to critics of constructivism who fear that this turn in psychology goes far beyond merely valorizing social inputs and constraints; indeed some proponents of situated cognition do seem to relegate the individual to the status of a passive container through which cultural forces flow. And yet Pea (1993) identifies desire as the uniquely human contribution to intelligence, noting that "unlike other species, such as Simon's (1981) ant on the beach, whose complexity of behavior is determined more by the shape of its environment than by its mental contents, humans have desires that lead them to recraft their environments to carry out aspects of reasoning, to make reminders for action, and to get help from others" (p. 49). Far from passive, human desires regulate choices and create relationships among symbolic artifacts and systems in accordance to their objectives. In my view, most constructivists, like Pea, have been appropriately engaged in thorny issues such as agency, transfer, and motivation. Many acknowledge constructivism's looseness and warn against any complacency when adopting what they admit remains a theory in progress; certainly the constructivist metatheory still offers more questions than answers (cf. Agre, 1993).

In other respects, however, much of the criticism of constructivism seems undiscriminating and overblown. The absence of a concern for representation (the club with which constructivism is routinely beaten) may apply to some ecological fringes of the metatheory, though not to its sociocognitive core. Although Gibson hoped "to explain activity purely in terms of the structure of the environment; all hypothetical explanatory constructs (including 'schema'!) seem [to Gibson] dangerously mentalistic" (Neisser, 1976, p. 53), it is hard not to see representation implicated in every page of Vygotsky's *Mind in Society,* Bartlett's *Remembering,* or even in Hutchins' *Cognition in the Wild* and Lave's *Cognition in Practice.* Clancey (1992) and Salomon (1993) are especially explicit in their arguments that while situationism certainly casts issues of representation in the shadows, it does not deny the essential representational level of cognition. Most constructivists are appropriately careful in separating the somewhat anticognitivistic notion of affordance from their broader metatheory; Neisser, for instance, has been much more forthcoming than most ecologists in identifying and delimiting those areas in which perception may obviate representation and cognitive processing.

While most participants in constructivist conversation subscribe to the notion of representation, they emphasize (though less carefully than early constructivists did, perhaps) that representation does not make direct reference to external reality. Thus, the constructivists' seeming lack of interest in representation may be, as Hayles (1993) suggests, not so much a denial of a mental theater that processes information using prior schemata, as it is a rejection of that theater's correspondence with the external world. In their eagerness to highlight the intersubjective and activity-based nature of cognition, many constructivists have indeed adopted what sounds like a quasi-behaviorist rejection of individual processing. This is unfortunate, for such constructivist rhetoric, intended perhaps to get our attention, does so at the risk of appearing antirepresentational and, thus, anticognitive. Yet, it is difficult to see where such a blanket rejection of a representational level has actually been explicitly stated or defended (cf. Clancey, 1993; Suchman, 1993), although the idea that perceptions passively mirror an external world is rejected by most contemporary constructivists. The centrality of representation to cognition remains as firmly entrenched in the modern constructivist movement as its roots in Piaget and Bartlett would lead us to expect.

In summary, while a few radical constructivists may have overshot the mark and projected a kind of constructivism that lends itself to caricature, one can easily argue that contemporary constructivism is the next logical step in our cognitive evolution. Although it has perhaps fixated on the ill-structured end of the ill-structured–well-structured spectrum, modern constructivism might best be seen as an advance on, rather than as a rival to, information-processing models of human learning. In Norman's words, "psychology has become a mature discipline. It's so mature, in fact, that some people feel that its days are over—that information-processing psychology is no longer the appropriate view. . . . But to me, the new [situationist] paradigms are well within the same spirit" (Baars, 1986, p. 382). Thus, it is easy to understand the constructivist metatheory as both a radical departure from computational models of mind (and thus, all the talk of shifting paradigms) as well as a logical outgrowth of early movements (and thus, possessing a sound cognitivist pedigree).

From Experiment to Ethnography

One of rhetorician Kenneth Burke's most cited adages is: "A way of seeing is a way of not seeing." This certainly applies to methodological frameworks: they cannot help but obscure even as they illuminate. Scattered throughout this chapter have been allusions to the role method plays in determining the relationship of research frameworks to their accomodation of real-world contextualization. I want to reiterate and extend these points a bit more systematically, for an appreciation of the methodological values enforced by various movements in psychology goes far in explaining how the forces for authenticity in cognitivism have gathered steam. Put more forcefully, it may not be possible to tease out from our methodological commitments the desire for an understanding that is in better accordance with our experience of the world.

From the beginning, the role of experimentation proved to be seriously contentious in modern psychology. The fact that experimentation carried with it the constraints of the laboratory and a de facto limitation of the phenomena psychologists hoped to investigate was worrisome to many. Such constraints cleaved the discipline, such as it was, into separate spheres of science (i.e., the New Psychology) and armchair speculation. It is not difficult to understand the allure of the former, as scientism was exerting enormous influence throughout society and producing undisputed technological achievements in the hard sciences. The most paradigmatic science, perhaps, was Newtonian physics which provided the seventeenth century model that many twentieth century social sciences sought to emulate. Newtonian materialism set out the mechanistic worldview that held that objects, including organisms, were machines—fabulously complex machines in the case of humans, but ultimately reducible to a system of wheels and pulleys or cogs within an elaborate clockwork. Physics was a model of certainty, methodological and theoretical clarity, and what appeared to be an undeniable force for positive change.

It is no wonder, then, that psychologists would want to follow in physics' footsteps. As Danziger (1990) notes, the New Psychology arose, in part, out of a justified criticism of groundless theorization that was never given over to any systematic investigation (p. 194). He adds that psychology's rapid embrace of experimental method had the unfortunate effect of promoting a certain blindness toward the limits of those methods whose fundamental structures were unable to account for what centuries of psychological speculation had determined to be of obvious importance. Ironically, it was also for methodological reasons (i.e., suspicion of introspection) that early behaviorists dissented from the New Psychology, treating observers in the early half of this century to the sight of the tail of experimental method wagging the dog of psychology.

As we have already seen, for Watson and his followers, the New Psychology was insufficiently rigorous, and so, in its search to remake itself in a more physics-like image, behaviorism gave no quarter to anything that could not be expressed in material terms, externally observed, and replicated in laboratory environments. Because of its methodological affinities with the physical sciences, Bartlett (1932) observed that:

> It is no wonder . . . that experimental psychology began, either with direct studies of special sensorial reactions, or with attempts to determine a measure of relations between physical stimuli and various apparently simple forms of resulting human reaction. . . . Moreover, it is easy to see why attempts have constantly been made to control variations of response and experience by known variations of stimuli, and to explain the former in terms of the latter; and why it has been thought that reactions must be reduced to their "simplest" form and studied in isolation from the mass of responses to which, in everyday life, they related. (p. 2)

Like the rest of Newtonian matter, behaviorists insisted that the brain played a largely passive role, responding to external stimuli. Just as the telos of the physical sciences was bound up in the invention and production of practical methods and objects, so did it seem clear to newly white-coated psychologists that any truly worthwhile study would have as its objective the discovery of the means by which behavior could be predicted and directed toward useful ends. In this way, the advent of behaviorism announced a radical shift from viewing the outcome of psychological theory and research as a humanistic contribution toward a better self-understanding (as traditional psychological speculation and the New Psychology had undertaken them) to the view that research should, like physics, be a science that could intervene in the world and extend human control over it.

The positivistic study par excellence, behaviorist psychology focused exclusively on demonstrable facts and refused to admit into its study ill-formed constructs such as intention, affect, and creativity. For this reason, in the behaviorist literature one almost never reads of any reference to *mind,* and only grudging reference to the brain (neurophysiology has played surprisingly little role in behaviorism for most of its history). True experiments (i.e., laboratory-based experiments permitting random assignment of subjects to conditions) undertaken by behaviorists did not, therefore, account for many of the contextual variables contemporary educational psychologists consider commonsensical. Instead, environmental variables that were manipulated were those that could be expressed in physical terms (such as pressure, volume, or pitch) and thereby operationalized. George Miller vividly illustrates the highly stipulated behaviorist understanding of context with his observation that B. F. Skinner "never even looked at a pigeon; he looked at the trace on the cumulative record. Who cared whether the pigeon was pressing the bar with his bill or tail!" (cited in Baars, p. 206).

In much the same way that authenticity was "off the table" for most of the Western educational experience, behaviorist assumptions completely looked past issues of contextualization in a bid for experimental cleanliness. As true experimentalists, behaviorists could not investigate phenomena as they occurred, but as they were induced to occur in laboratory conditions. As one of the first heirs to the New Psychology's claim to social scientism, behaviorists, fully wedded to a particular methodology, held that real-world context was precisely what needed to be gotten rid of, for the most elegant and convincing behaviorist study was that which controlled for contaminating effects. Baars (1986) starkly contends that behaviorism "sacrificed the psychology of everyday life" in order to attain scientific respectability (p. 397).

Although behaviorism largely gave way to cognitivism in the form of information processing, the shift in paradigms did little to overturn methodological constraints on the real world. Certainly, the cognitive rehabilitation of knowledge and information pulled psychology away from its rigid positivist moorings that would not admit linguistic data as real data, but in a significant sense, the information-processing paradigm with its basis in computational models of mind that could not accommodate *meaning* opened up psychological method in only limited ways. True experimentation remains the information processor's method of choice and, when all is said and done, a machine, rather than the real world, is the ultimate arbiter of a theory's adequacy. Without questioning the enormity of the shift between the two frameworks, the information-processing paradigm did not break with behaviorism's commitment to experimental method and concomitant neglect of everyday context. As a result, the success of information processing did little to stimulate discussion of authenticity.

Conversely, in the interest of moving toward a more theoretically, as well as commonsensically, satisfying description of human learning, early constructivists and sociohistoricists began the risky business of permitting speculation to outpace empirical findings. Although Vygotsky rejected the arbitrariness of experimental psychology and its utter dependence on direct evidence, he was equally impatient with what Kozulin (1985) called the *phenomenological approach* to consciousness taken by philosophers and humanists. Throughout his career, Vygotsky was determined to find some middle-ground—a third way—between experimentalism and pure speculation that would produce a viable scientific foundation for psychology. As mentioned earlier, a critical distinction made by Vygotsky (1962, 1978) was that between higher and lower mental functions. The higher functions were those specifically human functions, such as language, that mediate social interaction, while the lower functions are those associated with traditional cognitive issues of memory, perception, and attention. Kozulin

(1985) maintained that, for Vygotsky, "the building blocks of higher behavior seem absolutely materialistic and can be apprehended by ordinary empirical methods" (p. xxv). Thus, while the situational matrix within which thinking was embedded might not lend itself to experimental manipulation, Vygotsky reserved a place for scientific inquiry that could be complemented by speculative theorization only as long as those theories sought consistency within an empirical framework. He sought to ensure this by limiting his empirical efforts to appropriate objects of study, such as ontogenetic comparisons that permitted relative ease of investigation (Wertsch & Toma, 1995, p. 161).

However, the more experiential, introspective approaches to cognitivist research (rejected by Vygotsky) have not been met with as much skepticism by second-wave constructivists, who found what is called the *naturalistic paradigm* more to their liking and have sought to escape what they consider to be an inauthenticating emphasis on experimentalism. Although they have not rejected empirical inquiry, much of the work in situated cognition has gradually turned away from true experiment and even quasi-experimental research toward more qualitative study (e.g., Lave, 1988; Newman, Griffin, & Cole, 1989; Suchman, 1987), which makes less pretense of the external validity of its findings. Almost by definition, second-wave constructivists deal largely with *found cognition* (that is, thinking as it unfolds in natural contexts) and thus, are highly skeptical of data produced by controlled studies. They are unwilling to accept that because certain contextual dimensions cannot be satisfactorily operationalized or even defined, these dimensions have no place in an adequate theory of human cognition.

The fact that constructivists find little use for computer modeling of intelligence puts them at a distinct methodological disadvantage compared to their information-processing counterparts, but this disadvantage is liberating in some ways because it pulls psychology away from the formalisms that afflict theories constrained by extant hardware and software. Instead, many constructivists subscribe to Lincoln and Guba's (1985) view that:

> In order to provide some (persuasive if not compelling) evidence in favor of the claim that the hypothesis is true, it is necessary to eliminate the possibility that plausible rival hypotheses could be at work. "True" experimental designs . . . are "true" precisely because they . . . unambiguously rule out all such plausible rivals. But . . . it is often not possible to mount such true designs in practice. Perforce, one falls back on "quasi-experimental" designs that, while better than mere guesswork, may yield inauthentic results because they are exposed to the 'threats' of certain common plausible rivals. (p. 295)

The naturalistic approach adopted by many contemporary constructivists is undeniably problematic, relying as it does on the importance of narrative and its often politically advocative dimension. Regardless of their own cogency or future success in commanding the allegiance of researchers, naturalistic methods germane to much of contemporary constructivism have generated a very powerful critique of experimental and quantitative methods that cannot be ignored. In Nardi's (1996a) words, "There is a new kind of post-postmodern voice struggling to speak clearly here; it is polyvocal and dialogical, to be sure, but also committed to social and scientific engagement" (p. 15). If our thoughts about everyday thinking cannot be permitted to entirely break free of the methodological constraints, we can at least be satisfied that a conceptual space has been made that permits us to consider dimensions of human cognition that may not lend themselves to narrowly empirical exploration.

Similarly, Cole and Engeström (1993) attribute recent interest in distributed cognition to a methodological crossroads in which authenticity plays a key role. They suggest that such interest is due, in general terms, to the widespread belief that:

> the positivistically oriented social sciences, with their notion of cognition firmly located inside the individual, are inadequate for the task of grasping the essential nature of human experience and behavior . . . we are replying in new terms precisely the same debate in which Wundt, Munsterberg, Dewey and the Russian cultural-historical psychologists formulated competing versions of psychology that unite the natural and cultural sciences. (p. 42–43)

Thus, we are left with a very old question: is the world "out there" and thus, is cognition merely the neurology of physical perception and calculation, or is the world "in here" and, therefore, an entirely mental construct? Or (the real issue, perhaps), in what gray area does our gray matter combine both constructions and perceptions of the world to produce the everyday world in which each of us participates? While such epistemological issues were ignored by behaviorists and sidestepped in the early information-processing tradition, there seems to be something of a revival in contemporary cognitivism and a renewed sensitivity to the relationship of epistemology to method and authenticity. While it may indeed be the case that the basic tenets of situated cognition and constructivism can be accommodated within an extended information-processing paradigm, the fact remains that it has been left to the constructivist metatheory to draw attention to the real world: the social, cultural, and material circumstances in which individuals find themselves, and the activities in which they engage.

CONCLUSION

Elkind (1979) has made reference to *zeitgeists* in developmental psychology in which earlier thinkers (or contemporary but obscure researchers) are drawn into the mainstream conversation. I think the trajectory of cognitivism is less ethereal than the term *zeitgeist* implies. Over the last century there has been, within psychology, a steady march toward a utopian understanding of our mental lives that accounts for the totality of our experience. As Pea and Brown (1993) concluded:

The situated nature of learning and remembering through activity is a central fact. It may appear obvious that human minds develop in social situations, and that they come to appropriate the tools that culture provides to support and extend their sphere of activity and communicative competencies. (p. ix)

As with the history of most areas of inquiry, the story of cognitive science is one of evolution rather than revolution. In searching for a catalyst and theme for this evolution, I think one cannot do better than attribute it to the search for understanding thinking in authentic contexts—Geertz's *outdoor psychology,* Lave's *cognition in practice,* or Hutchin's *cognition in the wild.* Even if our current fascination for "socialness" wanes in the cognitive sciences (as it no doubt must), it hardly seems possible that we could return to either the reductive behaviorist version of context-as-brute-stimulation, or the information-processing tradition's ignorance of cognition's situatedness. An account of human cognition that squares with what we believe we know about the real world is one that is not likely to recede.

I end the telling of cognitivism's evolution with modern, messy constructivism cast as the moral of the story. Though it is by no means a unified theory of cognition, it offers a hope to many that the multiple dimensions of the mind can comfortably coexist within a single metatheoretical framework. Thinking back to the last chapter, the move to situate cognition in psychology parallels, in several respects, the historic trend in education that began when progressivism harnessed the trope of authenticity to strike a balance between the undemocratic character of the elite-idealist tradition and the unacademic nature of vocationality (cf. Bredo, 1994). The largely speculative and socially motivated movement toward authenticity, described in Chapter One, has been joined, legitimated, and expanded by many of the central figures in cognitive science, giving the argument that real-worldliness is a critical, perhaps the critical, *desideratum* in contemporary educational theory even greater warrant. As knowing inheres in situations and everyday practices learning cannot be bifurcated from those practices, and thus, any distinction one makes between learning and authentic learning dissolves into tautology. As a fitting bookend to the epigraph opening this chapter, then, we might conclude with Neisser's assessment of the general cognitivist enterprise, given in an interview with Baars: "So we've freed ourselves from a certain set of unreasonable strictures. We're trying to think about interesting problems, but we've only gone a step. The step was towards the real world . . ." (1986, p. 283).

THREE

Constructivism and the Technology of Authentication

Situated learning occurs when students work on "authentic tasks" whose execution takes place in a "real-world" setting. It does not occur when students are taught decontextualized knowledge and skills.
—WILLIAM WINN (1993, p. 16)

As THIS BOOK is being written, educational psychology has come to rest on a cognitive framework for human learning that is more theoretically open and less disciplinarily pure than it has been for most of this century. Ironically, the speculative, commonsensical, and uncodified study of mind associated with Aristotle and Kant—the baseline from which the fledgling discipline of psychology sought to distance itself—has come full circle, even though our contemporary constructivist metatheory approaches traditionally speculative questions from a grounding in social science. In educational theory especially, a new generation of constructivists has made inroads that cannot be easily dismissed. Bagley and Hunter (1992), for instance, identify constructivism as the third pillar of the educational reform in the United States alongside school restructuring and the integration of technology. Constructivism neatly complements and extends the mandate for authenticity arising from progressivism, and it is precisely on points such as the importance of authenticity to learning that we see the convergence of mainstream philosophies of education and educational psychology. While Dewey is not best known for his psychology, nor Bartlett and Piaget for their educational theories, they join Vygotsky (who is known for both) in providing a fairly smooth conceptual bridge between scientific work on cognition and theories of how educational practices should be structured to accommodate learners' constructive processes.

This chapter begins with the revisitation of an earlier issue: the juxtaposition of the world of formal education to the real world. In the earlier discussion, we saw that for most of the West's educational experience, schooling served as the privileged alternative to vocationalism, a hierarchy that progressivism moderated but did not displace. In the current constructivist literature, however, we find that it is formal education, rather than real-world vocational training and apprenticeship, that is put on the defensive. Arguing that school perverts the nature of real learning, some theorists, we will see, have used constructivist theory to make the call for authentic learning operable. The remainder of the chapter then discusses the ways in which correspondence to the real world serves as an increasingly formal criterion guiding the development of innovations in a particularly rich area of educational thought, that of educational technology.

SCHOOLING AS OTHER

It is common to label unproductive theorizing as *academic*. The success of a progressivist rhetoric of authenticity goes some way toward explaining this usage, but the phrase might merit closer investigation. Earlier in this century, Whitehead (1929) coined the phrase *inert knowledge* to describe knowledge whose isolation in memory meant it could not be applied to new problems. He believed, as had Parker and Dewey, that inertness resulted from pedagogical routines that separated knowledge from contexts in which that knowledge was relevant, leaving it incapable of being tested or "thrown into fresh combinations." Whereas Whitehead viewed inertness as afflicting a relatively minor (however worrisome) proportion of school learning, many subscribers to the constructivist metatheory suggest that inertness may be the rule rather than the exception in formal education (Hendley, 1986). As a tacit corollary, learners' representations stemming from a more mundane process of knowledge construction are often viewed as more in touch with the real world.

Early anthropological study of learning outside of formal school settings validated informal and vocational education and thus, neatly fed into the constructivist metatheory; learning was transformed in both Deweyan and Vygotskian terms from a rarified and self-conscious mental feat to simply a dimension of what people do. Vygotsky's collaborator Luria was one of the first of a series of educational anthropologist–psychologists who set out to study the ways in which formal environments structured learning. Drawing on other anthropological work in the 1950s and 1960s, psychologists continued to problematize the institution of education in a way that made special reference to the world outside the classroom. Researchers such as Cohen (1971), Luria (1976), Mead (1951), Becker (1972), and Scribner and Cole (1973) using other societies as points of reference, began to see Western education as distinctive and distinctly lacking in several respects. Observing informal learning carried out in apprenticeship situations with approval, educational anthropologists and psychologists cast a critical eye at the ways formal schooling diverged from these more natural educational contexts (Cole, 1990).

The sense that there is a disjuncture between formal education and the world outside of school is echoed by Young (1993), who argues that as learning occurs within a particular situation:

> then part of the attributes of the situation for most traditional instruction is a classroom, where learning is competitive among individuals, the subject and nature of problems change on the hour in a predictable succession, and the major, if not only, source of information is one person: the teacher. This is not a context that transfers to many situations outside the educational system. (p. 45)

Yet, Luria and that select group of researchers notwithstanding, an empirical interest in the effects of the educational context on problem-solving is relatively new. While they have been largely faithful to the thinking of Vygotsky, Bartlett, Dewey, and others, it has been left to second-wave constructivists to directly address questions of authenticity as they relate to schooling. For one thing, the sociohistoricists and other early constructivists saw their general theories as broad enough to accommodate all sorts of learning; one might imagine that the novelty and sketchiness of their observations did not encourage too narrow a focus on any particular context. Conversely, for second-wave constructivists, the context of formal schooling serves as a catalyst that reifies and magnifies the importance of authenticity latent in earlier theories.

Our tardiness in carefully examining the impact of educational context on learning might be attributable to what Scribner and Cole (1973) note is the tacit and pervasive overestimation of the continuity between formal and informal education. They argue for the necessity of distinguishing school-based learning from learning that transpires outside of the classroom by suggesting that "school represents a specialized set of educational experiences which are discontinuous from those encountered in everyday life and that it requires and promotes ways of learning and thinking which often run counter to those nurtured in practical daily activities" (p. 553). Following this lead, Lave's (1988) contrast of student behavior to that of "just plain folks" is emblematic of the dichotomy that pits school learning against natural learning. Brown, Collins, & Duguid (1989) succinctly frame the point, yet again, when they note, "Many of the activities students undertake are simply not the activities of [authentic] practitioners and would not make sense or be endorsed by the cultures to which they are attributed" (p. 34).

While sociohistoricists and early constructivists clearly sought to harness this sort of natural learning in the classroom, it seems clear that an important shift has occurred: formal schooling is less frequently considered to be the solution to educational ills as much as yet another problem to be solved. The reasons for this are varied. One of the distinctive aspects separating school learning from learning within apprenticeship contexts, and thus, one important dimension of authentic learning, lies in the realm of the interpersonal. Cohen, for instance, suggests that outside the formal classroom, individuals are socialized rather than taught. The consequences of this for learning are enormous. For one thing, the learner associates context with knowledge, and the value of information is closely related to the mentor who imparted it. According to Cohen (1971) "one of the most outstanding characteristics of socialization . . . is the high affective charge that is associated with almost everything that is learned in context" (p. 11). This association of ethos with information is one example of how the affective-motivational and the cognitive domains are fused to a greater extent in nonformal learning. Nix (1990) seconds the importance of affect in distinguishing in-school from out-of-school learning. He contends that, "in normal life, as is well known, children learn through participation in activities and thoughts triggered by their lives as humans. There is often a feeling of ownership concerning what they know. In the abnormal world of a school setting, such self-directed learning is unusual for the majority of children" (p. xi). Certainly, it is difficult to argue with the observation that students do not sense much control over their learning performance in school relative to learning opportunities they encounter on their own "turf" outside the classroom.

Another salient difference between school and extracurricular learning, according to Becker (1972), lies in the necessary homogenization of the learner from the perspective of the teacher. He notes that:

> Schools . . . process students in batches, treating them as if each were the prototypical normal student for whom they have constructed the curriculum. Being part of such a batch naturally constrains the student to behave, as best he can, as though he were prototypical; it is the easiest way to fit into the collective activity he is part of. (p. 88)

On the other hand, Cohen claims, learning situations outside of school are more commonly one-on-one with the teacher or mentor adapting instruction to the learner's personal history, motivation, and particular strengths and weaknesses.

Another general criticism of formal schooling has been its scatter-shot approach to knowledge. With the reification of expertise in both the information-processing and constructivist traditions, cognitive science has recommended that productive learning is that which embeds knowledge and skills within a specific domain. Expertise within a domain gives learners generative capabilities to solve a wide range of problems, but schooling has traditionally sacrificed depth for breadth. Thomas and Rohwer (1993), echoing Francis Parker's progressivist sentiments voiced over a century ago, argue that

> Descriptions of the capabilities of high school and college graduates portray students whose learning outcomes equip them, at best, to solve only stylized textbook problems. Confronted with problems cloaked in the garb of the real world, these students evidently lack the resources to frame the problems with reference to principled knowledge structures . . ." (p. 1)

Rather than promoting authentic learning, schools encourage a kind of gaming that may have the effect of completely obscuring the nature of learning in the real world.

Thus, the practices of genuine practitioners engaged in the culturally appropriate behaviors of their activity fields are not only misrepresented through reduction, but are distorted. Far from merely and innocuously being useless, some argue that school activities can be harmful. In this view, the problem confronting us is not that students will not learn, but that they will learn the wrong thing. According to Brown et al. (1989), "By participating in such ersatz activities students are likely to misconceive entirely what practitioners actually do" (p. 34). Reinforcing this view, Choi and Hannafin (1995) contrast the everyday cognition of just plain folks to what they call *academic cognition:* the problem-solving procedures used to accommodate curricular expectations that may disadvantage learners when they attempt to apply this learning to extracurricular tasks. As Brown et al. (1989) insist, "textbooks ask students to solve supposedly 'real-life' questions about people who do very unreal things, such as driving at constant speeds in straight lines or filling leaking troughs with leaking buckets. Students are usually not allowed to indulge in real-life speculation. . . . The ubiquitous Mr. Smith might, after all, wisely repair the hole in his bucket or fill the trough with a hose" (p. 41).

For all these reasons, constructivists argue that classroom tasks often fail to provide the sort of contextual features that permit authentic activity. Such attitudes have been read by some of constructivism's critics as a blanket indictment of the institution of formal education. They have suggested that constructivists approach school learning as a corruption of naturalistic learning and, thus, view schooling with suspicion and even contempt. Anderson, Reder, & Simon (1996), for instance, argue that the thrust of work in situated cognition has been to illegitimate school knowledge to make the political point that formal education serves reactionary power structures. They later argue that constructivism's penchant for the apprenticeship model of learning (discussed later) serves to undermine the legitimacy of school (p. 6). It would be inaccurate, however, to suggest that constructivist theorists, in general, take a dim view of schooling (and again, guiding lights such as Vygotsky and Piaget certainly did not question the value of school learning). Rather, it might suffice to say that school provides a highly particular context within which certain skills can be optimally exercised and in which certain understandings can be most easily developed. Just as clearly, even apprenticeships are riddled with episodes of mentor–learner interaction that contain formal elements, such as practice drills, explicit teaching, and disincentives for error. So the question is not whether school learning is bad, but rather, what makes schooling distinctive?

Resnick (1990) categorizes the major differences between the context of schooling and an everyday context as the following four:

1. In school, cognition is individual rather than shared.
2. In formal learning contexts, students rely on pure mentation rather than reliance on external resources.
3. Thinking in school relies to a much greater extent on the manipulation of symbols rather than objects.
4. School promotes highly generalizable learning rather than situation-specific learning.

Schools place a high value on personal achievement and individual initiative. For evaluation purposes as well, the student unit dictates, to a great extent, that success is seen in individual rather than group terms. Combine this with the stereotypically American values of individual responsibility and independence and it becomes understandable why most school tasks are designed to isolate the learner from peers who might unduly influence his or her performance. Resnick argues that, unlike the contrived didacticism of the classroom, everyday situations permit—even demand—shared cognition (i.e., group problem solving). Formal settings also differ from informal settings in that they privilege knowledge that is abstracted away from any material situation and the use of tools. Take, for instance, the fact that in many classrooms (especially in testing situations), calculators, reference books, and other externalia are forbidden. This notion of "pure mentation" is also reflected in Resnick's third point, that school learning encourages abstract reasoning involving symbols, such as letters or numbers, over hands-on manipulation of objects—manipulation that educators presumably fear would not tax the truly cognitive dimension of learning.

These fundamental differences combine to make problem solving in school a very particular kind of problem solving. Work in situated cognition seems to suggest that, in cognitivist terms, tasks in which situational variables are limited and known and solutions are predeterminable (i.e., as in well-structured problems) are the sorts of tasks that formal schooling is able to best accommodate. Because schools have to strip away interpersonal and situational contexts to get at the generalizable formulae students are expected to apply to a broad range of problems, it is not surprising that the problems considered most pedagogically sound are those with relatively unambiguous solutions as well as those whose accurate method of resolution can be taught in advance and evaluated objectively (cf. Confrey, 1990). For the same reason teachers are compelled to treat students as prototypical, school tasks have to be effectively decontextualized. Today's students are often quasi-strangers to teachers who are confronted with an enormous range of student aptitudes and attitudes and who intervene in the student's educational process for the merest fraction of the time a student spends in school. Given the logistics of modern education which have to take into account high student–teacher ratios, the mobility of families, and teacher specialization, it is clear that well-structured problems are used in formal schooling, not in spite of their limitations, but because of them.

Empirical research in humanities, such as applied ethics, is one site where the major differences between formal and informal cognition have been demonstrated. For instance, studies have shown that the ethical persona an individual projects, when questioned about how he or she would act when placed in a hypothetical situation, bears little resemblance to what that person does when put in a similar situation in real life (cf. Haan, 1975; Ville-Cremer & Eckensberger, 1985). Other research suggests that hypothetical tasks in the humanities—even when the teacher or researcher explicitly acknowledges their value-ladenness and ill-structuredness—prompt students to reason formalistically, rather than realistically (Haan, 1975; Petraglia, 1995; Potts, Elstein, & Cottrell, 1991). Regardless, then, of whether school learning is better or worse than learning in the real world, constructivists argue that we have good reason to believe that it is qualitatively different, and in educational psychology (and as we will see, in educational technology), this difference is generally expressed in terms of the authenticity of the tasks and problems learners are asked to address.

DESIGNING TECHNOLOGIES
FOR AUTHENTIC LEARNING

Wilson (1993) proposes that "authentic activity" can be "best understood as ordinary cognitive practices that are situationally defined, tool dependent, and socially interactive" (p. 77). He continues that "authentic activity therefore requires that learning and knowing always be located in the actual situation of their creation and use, not the simulations artificially constructed in schooling practices." Yet one could easily argue that the idea that learning is a byproduct of being in the world rather than the result of conscious efforts does not seem readily adaptable to the project of those of us in education who work, for the most part, with conscious efforts. In other words, declaring the authentic nature of extracurricular learning seems more like a final pronouncement than an invitation to further discussion. If, as the constructivist position argues, we learn by doing and by being in the world, and if the artifice of formal schooling is often more of a hindrance than a help, how does the professional educator respond? In tacit response to this tacit argument, educators have had two options: give up on the enterprise of school learning or make school learning approximate the sort of learning that occurs in informal settings. Not surprisingly, perhaps, we have chosen the latter alternative.

In the writing field, Clark (1995) notes that "when students interpret an activity or an activity-situation as unrealistic and non-meaningful, encoding, representation, and learning are likely to become reductified and narrowly school-focused" (p. 259). Having identified the problem, he proposes a solution put forth by many constructivist educators: "Full contextualization combats such tendencies; students realize that complex, multidimensional problems are much more endemic to real-world activity and that flatly unidimensional problem-situations exist only in school environments" (p. 259). Real-world contextualization is offered, then, as a way of remediating many of the deficiencies that have plagued formal education and especially those deficiencies that are rooted in problems of motivation and transfer. However, it is one thing to understand learning in everyday situations and entirely another thing to capture the dynamics of that learning and then set them in motion on cue. Although educators may appreciate that contemporary theories of cognition have created a social scientific basis for valuing learning that mirrors everyday life and complements our cultural attachment to authenticity, this remains a largely descriptive endeavor. Authenticity in the social scientific tradition, as suggested in Chapter Two, has not been a debate about what ought to be, but what is: learners learn in the context of everyday activities. The task facing educators, has been to turn what was a description into a workable prescription by creating the sorts of curricular environments that permit authentic learning to take place.

Choosing the Focus on Educational Technology

The move from the constructivist metatheory to practice is a move closely followed by theorists and practitioners in a number of fields; as Phillips (1995) notes, across the broad spectrum of educational theorists and researchers, we see that constructivism has become something of a secular religion (p. 5). In looking for a field in which to observe authenticity's pedagogical challenge to best advantage, three alternatives readily spring to mind. One especially prolific literature in authenticity is that of second language learning and testing. This is where the authentic assessment movement, which has spread to other areas of education, first got its impetus if not much in the way of rigor. As the name suggests, the idea that we can only accurately assess a language learner's performance in the actual contexts in which language skills are used is reflected in current second language learning and in may theories of genre (cf. Ellis, 1990; Krashen, 1982). Yet, an observer of the authentic assessment movement gets it right when she suggests that "'authentic' has almost come to mean 'anything that isn't multiple choice'" and that many proponents seem to have missed the central thrust of both constructivism and the meaning of "authentic" (Valencia, Hiebert, & Afflerbach, 1994, p. v). Owing more to Dewey than to Vygotsky, perhaps, the idea of authenticity, in the authentic assessment movement, is not so much a constructivist term of art, but a commonsense expression with little theoretical basis. For this reason, the vast literature on authentic assessment, however important, may not be the most interesting field from which to glean insights into constructivist education.

Continuing on to a more rigorous disciplinary candidate for an "authenticity case-study," Moll (1990) suggests that "no other researchers have been as concerned with 'authentic' or socially meaningful educational activities as those associated with a 'whole language' approach" (p. 8).[1] This approach, although indeed a valuable source for the literature and theory of authenticity, is largely limited to very young students, and as I suggest in Chapter Six, the nexus of age and authenticity is a special topic—one that may make elementary education a less suitable vantage point from which to observe the issue of authenticity in education more generally.

Therefore, in this chapter, I examine authenticity through the lens of a third disciplinary alternative: the field of educational technology. For one thing, educational technology is perhaps the most cognitive psychology-driven enterprise of the three options, making an analysis of authenticity both easier and more cogent. A second reason is that the importance of real-worldliness is very salient in educational technology; whereas in some other fields, authenticity's role is pervasive yet obscured, the literature of educational technology actually devotes a good deal of space in its journals to discussions of authenticity and learning's correspondence to the real world. Finally, educational technologists, more than any other specialists, perhaps, have taken on themselves the challenge of literally constructing contexts for learning and accept the burden of making their ideas material. For all these reasons, the ways in which educational technologists have grappled with authenticity in education can be seen as both representative of the challenge faced by constructivist educators generally, as well as relatively transparent in that technologists design material environments that they believe embody their constructivist principles.[2]

Educational technology's theory is most explicitly derived from the literature explored in the previous chapter—that is, from the body of psychological work that suggests the centrality of contextualization to thinking. What is often made less clear, however, is educational technology's indebtedness to the general desideratum of authenticity outlined in Chapter One. That is, in staking claims to the constructivistic soundness of their innovations and their abilities to

---

[1]Briefly, a whole-language approach proposes that subject matters across the curriculum should be integrated with the language arts. This, whole language proponents argue, encourages "nonreductionist" learning and encourages collaboration and immersion in authentic environments (Godman & Goodman, 1990).

[2]In identifying educational technology as the site for an investigation of authenticity, it may remain unclear to whom I am referring as an educational technologist; this is a rubric that can be used to refer to a broad group of individuals, united by no more than their common interests in electronic and/or computer-enhanced learning. As such, educational technology academicians may be found in departments ranging from psychology, computer science, and education to English, linguistics, and, of course, departments of instructional technology. Within these departments, people may identify their interests as more specifically related to human–computer interfacing, instructional design, artificial intelligence, and so on. For the remainder of this book, then, my stipulated community of educational technologists are those who participate in its professional fora—especially those who write in the journals devoted to the subject of technology and education (e.g., *Educational Technology, Journal of Artificial Intelligence in Education, Communications of the ACM, Educational Technology Research and Development,* etc.)

authenticate learning, educational technologists are working not only from the educational psychological theories of learning invoked in their literature reviews, but also from a deeper progressivist commitment to real-world learning. Because we understand authenticity both as a cultural value as well as a social scientific finding, educators avail themselves of a wide variety of rationales to support their pedagogical innovations. Perhaps more to the point, educational technologists' efforts cannot be solely understood as a natural outgrowth of new trends in cognitive theory, but as the yoking of constructivist tenets to an ongoing evolution in cultural attitudes about education.

Mediating Theories

Educational technology has not always been as attuned to cognitive science as it presently is. Vosniadou (1994) notes that the field has been historically driven by advances in technological "do-ability" rather than by an appreciation for the psychology of human learning. Pioneers, in applying computers to the job of education, often possessed only a nodding acquaintance with social scientific theories of learning, for their initial mandate was to develop aids that plausibly enhanced extant pedagogy; envisaging technology as something that could fundamentally alter the learning process would have to wait because it was not perceived as creating entirely novel pedagogical opportunities (cf. Zucchermaglio, 1993). Educational technology movements in the 1960s and 1970s, such as computer assisted instruction (CAI) and instructional design (ID), for the most part reflected the transmission model of learning to which they were harnessed. The learner was cast as a passive receiver of information whose objective in learning was the accurate assimilation of data as it was presented. Zucchermaglio (1993) calls these *full technology approaches,* for they assume that the technological environment contains all the knowledge to be learned and that the aim of the environment is solely to facilitate the transmission of that knowledge.

As a concern for contextualization evolved into a central theme in educational psychology, however, technologists, like educators generally, became increasingly critical of reductive learner models that filtered out the complexity of the real world. These models also had the effect of reinforcing a teacher-centered approach to learning that ignored the learner-centeredness educators had come to appreciate. In place of these technologies and these models and in response to the constructivist metatheory that now dominates educational technology, a variety of what might be called *mediating theories* have arisen and come to occupy a space between constructivism and its pedagogical application.[3] Mediating theories play an important role in the movement from con-

---

[3]One should note that just as constructivism is not a bandwagon all cognitivists have climbed aboard, so too does constructivism in educational technology have its skeptics. Hoppe (1993) and Dillenbourg and Schneider (1993) might be representative of these. Like critics elsewhere, they first point out that the basic tenets of situated constructivism are hardly news. Hoppe, for instance,

structivist learning theory to practice as they suggest elements of both, yet are flexible enough to support variations on both theories and practices. Before we consider how technologists have attempted to accommodate authenticity in their design of learning environments, it may be useful to elaborate some of these theories.

Collaborative Learning. One common response to the idea that knowledge is socially constructed is that authentic learning occurs when students are put into dialogue with others (Bruffee, 1986). Because second-wave constructivism argues that meaning is socially negotiated, education, it is thought, should promote such negotiation by facilitating the coming together of varying perspectives. Yet, the idea that students learn best in collaborative situations has had many proponents and rationales throughout this century, and these have been less propelled by their theoretical soundness or their tested effectiveness than their loric value to teachers. So, like authenticity itself, collaboration has a social and cultural history that parallels its social-scientifically grounded desirability.

The idea that learners should work together in pairs or groups is at once mundane and mildly radical. In the model of traditional education rejected by Dewey, collaborative learning was frowned on as not requiring individual learners to acquire the rigor and independence of thinking that was highly valued in both the rationalist and elite-idealist worldviews. Certain ethical issues came into play as well, given a model of authorship that conferred ownership rights on a single, inspired inventor—a model that made group effort morally suspect (cf. Ede & Lunsford, 1990). While collaboration has long been a mainstay of fields such as writing, there is plenty of evidence to suggest that collaborative pedagogy is still a new frontier in many fields outside the humanities. Although groupwork has often been a response to overcrowded classes, valuing collaborative learning for itself is only beginning across the academy.

Myers (1986) traces theories supporting the educational value of collaboration back to Sterling Andrus Leonard, who in turn grounded his work in the observations of Dewey. As education is a microcosm, according to Dewey, collaboration in the classroom induces a social order similar to that which we find in the world around us. Slightly different from its social rationale, one might say that collaboration's logistic appeal is the one to which many teachers respond: collaborative learning permits teachers to spend class time concentrating on individuals or small groups while the rest of the class interact (on task) among themselves. As it allows students to learn from people other than the teacher, it facilitates a sense of community in the classroom, and so on.

More recently, Bruffee (1993) suggests yet another practical argument for

---

points out that Pestalozzi and Montessori, among others, advocated many of the principles of real-world engagement attributed to Dewey. Furthermore, they charge, these principles have been integrated in instructional design for decades; in short, constructivism is much ado about little.

collaboration: that collaboration is important because it mirrors the dynamics of doing business in the real world—that is, in a student's future economic career, learning alongside others has been found to be a crucial skill and, therefore, collaborative learning is preparation for the world of work. In this way, we see collaboration shifting from an ideal to a description of authentic learning. Though many of these claims remain more intuitively satisfying than they are empirically demonstrated, one could argue that these commonsense arguments for collaboration are more influential to teachers than those promulgated by educational psychologists. Nevertheless, sociohistorical studies of learning and cognitive development have, in fact, given an empirical basis for the long established observation that people naturally learn and work collaboratively throughout their lives, because a fundamental tenet of constructivism is that learning and thinking in the everyday world are overtly and thoroughly social activities. Because cognition is embedded in activities, a significant aspect of those activities is that they are inhabited with mentors, experts, and advanced peers who permit us to observe and apprentice.

Having students work together in collaborative problem solving has been considered a powerful method for motivating learners. Reciprocal teaching and other student-centered pedagogical approaches share roots in the larger theory of collaborative learning. According to Brown and Palincsar (1989), the presence of other learners provides students with the means to gauge their own progress which, in turn, assists them in identifying their relative strengths and weaknesses and permits them the insight necessary to improve their own learning (p. 486). Cooperative learning enables students to share their knowledge and skills while providing opportunities for them to observe the learning process of others. Collaboration not only allows the student the chance to see learning activities modeled, but also provides opportunities to articulate one's thinking to an audience. Thus, collaboration permits the metacognitive awareness that encourages self-correction and redirection.

From the constructivist perspective, collaboration is also a powerful method by which multiple worldviews are brought into contact and negotiated by learners who are thereby explicitly led into social activities. If genuinely advanced learning requires that students understand that many different representations of an event and multiple solutions to a problem exist, collaboration seems to ensure that such representations and solutions are negotiated within a social environment similar to the ones in which variation naturally arises. Bruffee (1993) maintains that "college and university education should help students renegotiate their membership in the knowledge communities they come from while it helps them reacculturate themselves into the academic communities they have chosen to join" (p. 191). For the educational technologist, this has provided a rationale for devising environments—usually networked—that facilitate the ways in which social interaction and learning can take place—environments in which individuals can share information, problem-solving techniques, and avail themselves of the real-world mentoring of peers. The idea that authentic learning only occurs in collaboration with others has become the central pillar of constructivist orthodoxy and is the one on which practically every other principle is dependent to some extent.

Apprenticeship and Legitimate Peripheral Participation. There is a close link between theories of collaboration and notions of legitimate peripheral participation and apprenticeship. Like authenticity itself, apprenticeship has evolved from a description of learning to a prescription for the sorts of environments that need to be constructed for learning. Apprenticeship is, conceptually, an institution with which we have been comfortable for centuries. Described as a fairly elaborate legal relationship in Hammurabi's code, it is the sort of tuition delivered long before there were systems of formal education; it embodies a socioeconomic arrangement with a history of its own quite apart from the disciplines of psychology and education. Apprenticeship in some form served as the basis for most informal education in the West and continues to be the means by which professions are perpetuated in much of the world.

In a sense, part of apprenticeship's appeal may be its return to earlier and simpler educational models, whereby learning is truly a byproduct of getting on in the world. In the present context, however, apprenticeship has made the transition from socioeconomic arrangement to educational model as a result of its deep implication in theories of situated cognition. Industrial psychologists, among others, maintain that apprenticeship and learning-by-doing deserve to play greater roles in practically all training efforts. According to Lesgold, Eggan, Katz, & Rao (1992), "When people have real tasks to accomplish, motivation is less of a problem than when they simply have exercises to practice. Equally important, when knowledge is anchored in experience, then it becomes more than sentences to be memorized: the sentences have meaning for the trainee because they are rooted in his or her personal experience" (p. 49). According to this reformulation of apprenticeship, mental abilities and knowledge are deeply embedded in the apprentices' activities; apprenticeship is thus a logical manifestation of constructivist educational theory. Unlike the self-consciously artificial nature of formal schooling in which skills and knowledge are abstracted from their use, the apprenticeship relationship between masters and those who learn from them is framed by, and embedded in, the natural activities of experts. Of course, although professionals such as chefs, medical practitioners, and draughtsmen can be apprenticed in highly regimented and bureaucratic fashions that, in many respects, mirror formal education, many constructivists would point out that these apprenticeship-like practices remain very distinctive from learning in school.

A slightly different spin on apprenticeship, the notion of *cognitive apprenticeship,* has been presented by Allan Collins and his colleagues as a way of replicating the critical elements of actual apprenticeship for the learner confined to the classroom. Collins, Brown, & Holum (1991) argue that because cognitive processes are often invisible to both the teacher and the student in school, cognitive apprenticeship is one way of making thinking visible. This can be accomplished, they suggest, if the teacher (1) breaks tasks down into identifiable parts and makes these parts explicit to the learner; (2) situates abstract tasks in authentic contexts so that learners can understand the relationship of these parts to the whole; and (3) presents the learner with enough variations of the problems so that they can generalize their learning to other contexts (p. 6). The ultimate aim of cognitive apprenticeship, according to Collins et al., is to "situate the abstract tasks of the school curriculum in contexts that make sense to students" (p. 9).

The mediational role of apprenticeship has been theoretically furthered by sociohistoricists and, more recently, by the idea of *legitimate peripheral participation* (LPP): a term used by Lave and Wenger (1991) to describe the process by which novice apprentices become drawn deeper and deeper into the activities of the communities they aspire to join, a process that alters both the learner and the community. Participation is peripheral when performed by a newcomer to the activity who remains an observer of more expert, fully engaged participants. What makes this peripheral participation legitimate in the eyes of the newcomer is his or her "acceptance by and interaction with acknowledged adept practitioners." As a social psychological description of apprenticeship, LPP is often cited as the theoretical rationale for many technological enhancements of a learning environment (e.g., Brown et al., 1993).

Cognitive Flexibility.   As discussed in the last chapter, an important distinction made in the information-processing phase of the cognitive evolution was between well- and ill-structured problem spaces. Again, well-structured problems are those whose parameters are known and finite, whose subgoals are self-evident, and whose successful resolution is predeterminable. In response to this, constructivists argue that the contingent nature of human affairs permeates the task environment and solutions are thus almost always equivocal. The real world's complexity leads individuals to construct their problem spaces using different experiences and resources and embeds these spaces in socially and historically situated contexts. This suggests that there are multiple pathways through problem spaces that afford different insights, associations, and subgoals; the space itself shifts depending on the choices of the learner navigating it. Ill-structured problems that may appear to share key features are, in fact, fundamentally different and require a much greater degree of flexibility than the information-processing tradition comfortably accommodates.

When we think about the sorts of situations we find ourselves in and the many choices left to us, we have to concur that most problems we confront on a daily basis lie on the ill-structured end of the spectrum. In the literature of educational technology, a much-cited response to the ill-structuredness of everyday learning is *cognitive flexibility,* a mediating theory most closely associated with

Rand Spiro and his colleagues (Spiro, Coulson, Feltovich, & Anderson, 1988; Spiro, Feltovich, Jacobsen, & Coulson, 1992a, 1992b; Spiro & Jehng, 1990), but arguably a broader theory that has deep roots in constructivist theories of reading and communication (cf. Spivey, 1987). Central to this theory is that no single perspective is adequate to the task of representing ill-structured problems and, therefore, learners, if they are to understand problems as they exist in their full complexity, must "crisscross" the problem space in multiple passes. A *cognitively flexible* learner is one who can readily restructure his or her knowledge in response to varying situational demands. As Choi and Hannafin (1995) put it, "When dealing with real problems, learners reference their personal experiences and strategies which evolve through continuous self- and context-referencing. Students learn to use their knowledge flexibly as a tool to deal with everyday, as well as novel, situations" (p. 58).

Spiro et al. (1992a) explain that the core tenet of cognitive flexibility theory is that "revisiting the same material, at different times, in rearranged contexts, for different purposes, and from different conceptual perspectives is essential for attaining the goals of advanced knowledge acquisition" (p. 65). The reason material must be repeatedly covered is because a full understanding of any complex- and ill-structured problem cannot be gleaned from a single pass. Learners must be able to create multiple representations of information presented in a variety of contexts if they are to appreciate the interconnectedness of a problem's components. As a constructivist educator's objective is to provide a repertoire of representations from which a learner can draw when confronting an ill-structured problem as well as give learners a generative capacity to solve future isomorphic problems, cognitive flexibility, it is argued, is an important metacognitive ability we wish our learners to possess. Reigeluth (1992) and Winn (1993a) suggest that, in the face of the constructivist critique, instead of content knowledge, educators should concentrate on instilling "general skills" that transcend particular situations and can thus be applied in a variety of contexts provided by the educator. According to Winn, the potential for acquiring general skills is improved when a pedagogy is open to modification that permits students to meet unanticipated difficulties arising from problems other than those for which the environment was specifically designed. Thus, we will see that cognitive flexibility theory has given an important impetus to authentication in educational technology via hypertext and multimedia.

Technological Responses to Mediating Theories

Technological responses to the problems of authentic learning might be framed in light of two similar observations: McLellan (1994) argues that "it is important to re-emphasize that according to the situated learning model, knowledge must be learned in context. This can be the context of (1) the actual work setting; (2) a highly realistic or 'virtual' surrogate of the actual work environment; or (3) an anchoring context such as a video or multimedia program" (p. 8). Likewise, Jonassen (1992) suggests that because constructivism is based on the principle that learning is actively integrating new experience into existing schemata, "learning environments should support that process by providing multiple perspectives or interpretations of reality and enable knowledge construction in the learner through providing context-rich, experience-based activities" (p. 394). A third way of saying the same thing is that educational technologists are seeking ways to create pedagogical tools that accommodate the mediational theories of collaborative learning, apprenticeship, and cognitive flexibility.

There are several different ways in which the developer of educational technology accomplishes the goals suggested by constructivist theory, which mediating theories have tried to make more operational. A fairly comprehensive inventory of constructivist guidelines is provided by Jonassen (1994) who suggests that purposeful knowledge construction is best facilitated by technological learning environments that:

- provide multiple representations of reality, thereby avoiding oversimplification of instruction by representing the natural complexity of the real world;
- focus on knowledge construction, not reproduction;
- present authentic tasks (contextualizing rather than abstracting information);
- provide real-world, case-based learning environments, rather than predetermined instructional sequences;
- foster reflective practice;
- enable context- and content-dependent knowledge construction; and
- support collaborative construction of knowledge through social cooperation, not competition among learners for recognition.

As this list illustrates, the correspondence of instruction to the real world and the importance of the authenticity of the environment are the threads that unify the constructivist metatheory that guide the efforts of educational technologists. Dunn (1994) collapses these guidelines into three general recommendations for educators, recommendations that do much to delimit many of the efforts of technologists. First, if our realities are constructed, and thus, nothing is learned independent of a socially informed context, the instructor must do what he or she can to create environments that mirror real-life situations in all their complexity. Second, deliberate and prescriptive sequencing of objectives is ill-suited for learners who construct knowledge in accordance with individual schemata. Third, an appreciation of multiple perspectives is critical to future transfer, and thus, collaborative learning is seen as a key component of making learning relevant and realistic (p. 84).

Mediating theories rarely result in any single pedagogical application; in the same way that teacher-centeredness, objective evaluation, and the importance of native intelligence constituted a elite-idealist ecology for education within which instructional design technologies seemed to make sense, theories of collaboration, cognitive flexibility, and so on have been woven together to create a constructivistic ecology by which we gauge our sense of pedagogical progress. Although in the following discussion I tease apart elements of learning environments that technologists argue contribute to the environment's or the task's authenticity, it is not my intention to suggest that these elements exist in isolation; rather it is common for several of these elements to be combined into a single environment. The Knowledge Integration Environment developed by Marcia Linn and her colleagues (Bell, Davis, & Linn, 1995; Linn, Bell, & Hsi, in press) is a good example of this. In the literature as well, issues of what we will call problem "thickness" are recycled in subsequent discussions of multimediation and networked collaboration. Thus, in practice, authenticating elements are often mutually reinforcing rather than modularly self-contained.

Thick Problems. Early cognitivist work on problem solving is mostly directed toward mathematical or hypothetical (i.e., well-structured) problems—problems whose parameters are relatively well-defined and whose solutions are clearly identifiable. In these sorts of problems a real-life (i.e., socially situated) context is unnecessary. For example, in problems like Missionaries and Cannibals or the Tower of Hanoi, the issue of authenticity is moot, the sort of cognition entailed in such problem solving is highly procedural and (barring extensive contact with missionaries, cannibals, or Vietnamese) relatively devoid of the experiential dimension so important to situatedness. As we have seen, such tasks prompted contemporary constructivists to argue that many school tasks seem to fall short in terms of authenticity. The Cognition and Technology Group at Vanderbilt (CTGV, 1993) believe that story problems given in math classes best illustrate this problem. While the story problems may contain authentic settings (such as going to the store), the vast majority of such problems are contrived and do not really represent everyday situations in which the student might find himself or herself. Honebein et al. (1993) concur, arguing that it is uncommon for real world tasks to exist in a vacuum devoid of the "noise" that permeates our everyday lives and that establishing learning environments that approach or simulate the complexity of the real world means providing extraneous and unusable information. As we have always known, everyday thinking is crowded with constraints and opportunities determined (or at least suggested) by our sense of where we are relative to where we want to go at a given place, time, and social context and with given resources. To convey the idea of this in a more three-dimensional sense, we might go beyond the traditional label of *ill-structured* and appropriate the terminology of Geertz (following an earlier lead from Ryle) to describe such problems as *thick*. For this reason, a common response of educational technologists has been to inject fuller complexity into problem solving by presenting learners with thick problems. Two examples of how the issue of problem thickness is framed in the literature of educational technology are provided by the CTGV's notion of anchored instruction and the goal-based scenarios as propounded by Schank and others.

The CTGV (1990, 1992a, 1992b, 1993) is perhaps best known for its work in what it calls *anchored instruction*. This pedagogical approach argues that learning should be situated in thick contexts that offer opportunities to identify and solve problems creatively. In the case of the Jasper Woodbury materials that have been produced as a result of anchored instructional theory, such contexts are created using a multimedia environment that, according to Hmelo and Narayanan (1995):

> Present a situation as one would see it in the world, though it is orchestrated so that it has embedded in it all the data the students need to solve the problem. As in the real world, the presentation does not make clear which of the presented material is relevant to problem solving and which is incidental. Students must learn to differentiate between relevant and irrelevant data. . . . The problems that are used are much more complex than typical math word problems on the premise that students cannot learn to deal with complexity unless they have had the chance to experience it. (p. 2)

The CTGV (1990) also introduces a distinction between microcontexts and macrocontexts; the former focus on a specific subset of a more complex problem or domain while the latter seeks to prompt exploration of the larger framework. They note that macrocontexts find an antecedent in the Deweyan notion of theme-based learning. The terminology is important because when they speak of anchored instruction, they are referring to anchoring within a macrocontextual environment in which real-world complexity can be introduced. Macrocontexts permit the exploration of an authentic problem space for extended periods of time and from many different angles. The rich context provided by information-dense and anchored scenarios invite learners to find and define their own issues to explore (p. 3).

Goal-based scenarios (GBS) have also been put forward as an exemplary type of a learning environment particularly well suited to the issue of problem thickness. A GBS, according to Schank (1992), has three parts: a concrete goal to be achieved, a set of target skills that can be learned and practiced and which lead to achievement of the goal, and an environment suited to the mastery of the target skills and resultant goal. According to Schank, Fano, Bell, & Jona (1994), this framework shares much with Collins' notion of cognitive apprenticeship, though, they argue, GBSs place even more emphasis on the authenticity of the context. Schank et al. make a distinction from the CTGV's work as well, in that they suggest that anchored instruction generally gives the learner an observer status lying outside the task to be learned, whereas a student working through a GBS is working "on his own behalf" (p. 3).

As in anchored instruction, GBSs are particularly well suited to implementation by a computer in which resides an extensive database that may or may not be hypertextualized. One example of a computer-assisted GBS is the *Broadcast*

News program that aims to teach high school students about a variety of social studies topics. As the name of the program suggests, the concrete goal of the scenario is the production of a videotaped news show by a group of students. A student may also play the role of writer and anchor if he or she wishes, and the computer is used to guide the learner through each of these roles. In *Broadcast News* an enormous amount of actual newswire text and video footing is compiled for a single story in the recent past. The computer environment provides students with informational assistance about the roles they are playing as well as background information on the story on which they are working. The system also creates informational density by responding to the learner's choices and making suggestions, thus providing a kind of professional social environment that might be found in the world of broadcast journalism.

GBSs are predicated on a number of principles, but one of the most important of these is the *authenticity principle:* "knowledge, skills, and attitudes should be embedded in tasks and settings that reflect the uses of these competencies in the world . . . the authenticity of the learning environment ensures that the knowledge gained will be readily available in the kinds of situations they will face in their [users'] work" (Collins, 1994, p. 30). While GBSs incorporate many other authenticating features (e.g., apprenticeship elements and interactivity), the density of the informational resources available to the learner and thus the thickness of the problem is perhaps most noteworthy.

Interactivity.   Whereas nonconstructivist theories of education draw attention to the information the teacher or curriculum imparts to the student, the emphasis on individual construction has led many educational technologists to consider issues of agency and choice. A fundamental rationale linking interactivity to a constructivist account of learning is that interactivity shifts learning from the prerogative of an instructor to the needs and wishes of the learner. Interactivity, in this view, permits learners to faithfully replicate learning in everyday situations by providing them with an opportunity to determine, to some degree, the form and content of their tuition. In doing so, interactivity is a clear response to the constructivist and progressivist critique of the passive learner model, giving rise to Neuman's (1995) observation that educational technology's potential for interactivity has "become the focus of irrepressible optimism" (p. 52).

Interactivity mirrors communication in the real world in many commonsensical ways. A fundamental human activity—conversation—is perhaps the most obvious of these. In a conversational exchange, Speaker A presents an utterance to Speaker B and Speaker B responds by either signaling confusion and requesting clarification from A, building on A's utterance, refuting or amending A's utterance, or, perhaps, by changing the subject. Just as conversation is a principal way we get information from others, so interactivity in a learning environment permits the user to interrogate the environment. Contrast this to traditional educational media—print, linear video, movies, and so on—that are characterized by their inherent unidirectionality that does not permit learner rejoinders to the information conveyed.

As with hypertext, the perceived benefits of interactivity lie in the cognitive demands made on the user. The proactiveness that results from students having to select information is believed to provide a motivational boost to learning that traditionally nonsituated learning does not, for it is assumed by many educators (cf. Collins, 1994; Palincsar & Brown, 1984; Shank et al., 1994) that interactivity allows, maybe even requires, students to learn in line with their own needs and prior experience. Just as in authentic social situations, the individual learner is given more control over the pace at which information is presented. Neuman (1995) speaks for many educational technologists when he argues that individuals basically like having the option of interacting with the environment. According to him, they respond positively to "the ability to voice an opinion, to skip a commercial, to select from a diverse offering of channels, and to call up specialized data and interaction" (p. 54). Not only do users enjoy exercising such prerogatives, but more important, their excercise in interactive environments renders the problem solving more conducive to learners' natural inclinations.

Of course, the value of interactive learning is, by now, so common throughout education that it may not seem to merit continued theorization, though, as with other topics we have touched on in this chapter, one can consider such conventional wisdom as a tacit response to the *desideratum* of authenticity.

Multimedia.   The link between multimedia and authenticity is intimate, for the real world is nothing if not multimediated by the senses. Memory is generally assumed to be encoded and schematized differently, depending on whether the information comes to us visually, tactually, aurally, or affectively. In everyday life, information comes to us in these distinct forms, each of which carries with it a particular dimension that cannot be replicated by any other form. Visual information provides a spatial- and physical-qualitative dimension of information that sound cannot; textual information permits a sort of explication that cannot be done pictorially; aural input resonates with memories in a unique way, and so on. McLellan (1994) contends that the reason technology is such a central consideration in the constructivist paradigm is because "technology expands the power and flexibility of the resources that can be deployed to support the various components of situated learning" (p. 7). As an example, he cites the various recording techniques, such as video camcorders, audio recorders and computers, which provide learners with the opportunity to compare the performances of experts and novices. Replaying these performances repeatedly provides not only opportunities for reflection, but also serves as a method of coaching students within the apprenticeship framework. In the case of the CTGV's Jasper series, the video element allows a more veridical representation of events than does text alone in the sense that it is dynamic, visual, and suggests spatial relationships.

In the real world, we represent information to ourselves in several dimensions, each interwoven with the others to provide our fullest understanding of the information, but each also prompting different associations. For instance, while leafing through a travel brochure about Zanzibar, an island I have never visited, my representation nonetheless draws on the images invoked by the stories I have read about Africa's east coast, the dark greens of the topographic maps in which it is always depicted, my prior experiences in other parts of Africa which I tacitly (and probably erroneously) associate with the music, peoples and traditions of Zanzibar, and even the evocativeness of the name. Of course, educational multimedia, as it presently exists, does not fully recreate any experience or idea; it is limited to still and moving pictures, words, sounds, and perhaps in some virtual reality environments, spatial relationships. Nevertheless, educational technologists are undoubtedly correct in supposing that, to whatever degree information can be presented in a variety of media, multimedia systems provide a kind of enriched input that emulates the sort of inputs we encounter in the real world.

A good example of current educational multimedia is the videodisc *A Right to Die?: The Case of Dax Cowart* developed by Covey and Cavalier at Carnegie Mellon's Center for Design of Educational Computing (CDEC). Briefly, the videodisc asks learners to work through the real-life case of Dax Cowart, a young man involved in a gasline accident that took his sight and left him without the use of his hands. In addition, as part of his burn therapy, he is subjected to months of painful, daily antiseptic "tankings." As the videodisc recounts, Dax repeatedly demanded to have the treatments discontinued. He was, in essence, asking that he be allowed to die of the massive infection that almost certainly would have set in were the treatment withheld. As he was totally incapacitated by his condition and treatment, Dax required the cooperation of others, be they medical staff or family, to end his life. As the videodisc interviews clearly demonstrate, however, Dax's doctors and family refused almost without equivocation. Dax's situation had been videotaped from his earliest days in the hospital, and Dax, his family, and medical staff were interviewed on numerous occasions throughout the ordeal. It is this very powerful and graphic videotape from which CDEC has created its interactive videodisc. The success of the videodisc in portraying Dax's story, and its overall quality, is reflected in the fact that it is the recipient of two national awards, the 1988 industrywide University of Nebraska Merit Award, and the EDUCOM/NCRIPTAL award for Best Humanities Software of 1989.

Covey (1990) provides a common rationale for both the Dax videodisc and multimedia generally:

> computer-based multimedia can provide new channels to moral experience, adding stimuli to moral imagination, as well as new opportunities for reflection on that experience. Multimedia environments are useful for the rich data, texture, and context they allow us to import into experientially barren groves of academic

study—allied with interactive computer technology for easy control, flexible exploration, and the disciplined reflection it can induce. (p. 15)

Educational technologists, as well as researchers such as Martin Hoffman (1984) and James Rest (1984) turn their attention to ethical decision making due, in part, to the inherently ill-structured nature of the problems ethical issues present. Questions of morality, they argue, present particularly rich aggregates of affective and cognitive inputs and socially-prescribed preferences. For this reason, these sorts of dilemmas are especially ripe for multimediation, though it is clear that like interactivity, the value of multimediation has attained such commonsense status throughout educational technology circles that it seems to require less and less theoretical justification. Multimedia, then, like the thick problems they portray, provide multiple paths spiraling around a problem and offer the sort of cognitive flexibility authentic learning requires.

Hypertext and Hypermedia.   A major component in many technologized learning environments, hypertextualization provides a system of informational nodes linked to other nodes that can be easily accessed with a click of a mouse or push of a button. Words, images, icons, and entire documents can be made "hot" by an information designer (and increasingly, many of these nodes and links may be authored by the learner) who provides the links necessary to jump to associated ideas, creating a weblike structure of information readily accessible to the learner. More important, from a cognitive flexibility vantage point, the variety of paths one can choose to work through a topic provides multiple representations of the same information. Some level of hypertextualization has almost become taken for granted within educational technology in the 1990s; as with interactivity, one can more easily list the environments without hypertexual capabilities in some form than those that incorporate them.

According to Spiro and Jehng (1990), "Linearity of media is not a problem when the subject matter being taught is well structured and fairly simple," but as already noted, most of the tasks we confront do not lend themselves to such well-structuredness (p. 163). Translated into educational technology design, this is largely the rationale behind the common element of hypertextuality, an element that has found its way into most constructivists' vision of a theoretically adequate learning system. Combining the ideas that authentic learning requires learners to be introduced to informationally rich contexts for learning and to be active participants in their own learning, we arrive at the gist of hypertext and hypermedia's contribution to the goal of creating real-life learning environments.

Although hypertext's current theoretical popularity arose out of a number of very different interests ranging from calculation to narration (cf. Bolter, 1991; Conklin, 1987), it has come to be closely associated with the goal of authenticating learning via the theories of Spiro and others. This connection is perhaps best articulated by Jonassen (1992) who argues that "learners need instructional conditions that stress the interconnections between knowledge within cases as well as different perspectives of viewpoints on those cases that reflect the perceptions of different entities. Learners need flexible representations of the knowledge domains that they are studying, representations that reflect the uncertainties and inconsistencies of the real world" (p. 386). Here, we see a common claim in the literature relating to hypertext: that the associative principles that undergird hypertext mirror in some significant way the complexity of human representation. Jonassen further suggests that ". . . hypertext can convey through its node and link structures the organization of any knowledge or information processing requirements of the task. The associative structure of hypertext adapts particularly well to the multi-perspectival approach of cognitive flexibility theory (p. 393)."

Others, such as Gray (1993), also note that hypertext derives much of its theoretical potency from its links to cognitive science and its use in artificial intelligence. She maintains that the metaphor of "spreading activation," so prevalent in schema theory, which gives rise to cognitive psychologies from information processing to constructivism and connectionism, reinforces the argument that we think hypertextually. While some argue that hypertextual advances continue to lack theoretical underpinnings and are driven instead by technological doability, most educational technologists insist that as reader–learners construct their own pathways through information based on the links they wish to follow, the constructivist model of mind is more easily accommodated (Allen & Hoffman, 1993). In this same way, hypertext, like interactivity, is often heralded as releasing reader–learners from the tyranny of auctorial intention by allowing learners to construct and follow their own associative links.

Like hypertext, hypermedia connects information nonhierarchically. Going beyond simply textual information, hypermedia systems (the present World Wide Web being the most well known example of this) permits learners to link a wide array of photos, sounds, and quicktime video clips in addition to illustrations and texts. Choi and Hannafin (1995), drawing extensively on the work of Winn (1993a, 1993b) and Brown and Duguid (1994), recently tried to develop guidelines for technologists in line with constructivist thinking in which hypermedia plays an important role. Their first guidelines suggest that educators need to focus less on teaching specific information to the exclusion of everything else and instead, make a rich web of practice available, one that permits learners to avail themselves of a broad range of information as it is needed. Hypertexts and hypermedia provide such webs. Yang and Moore (1995) claim that hypermedia not only provides rich and realistic contexts for learning, but also allows learners to randomly access the available information in accordance with their own "needs, interests, or whims." They suggest that the process of searching and organizing that hypermedia requires gives "true meaning" to information and "inherently helps learners focus their attention on the learning relationships among facts" (p. 6). Just as reality cannot be isolated from contexts that produce it, hypermedia illustrates the interconnectedness of real knowledge, overcoming the sort of inert knowledge Whitehead warned us to guard against. In short, hypertext and hypermediation are ways of personalizing information's connectedness for learners and making access to unlimited information possible, again as exemplified by the World Wide Web. In accordance with the views expressed by Spiro and Jonassen, these features afford the customization of a space within which learners are free to construct knowledge in accordance to their own goals, just as they do in the world outside the classroom.

Networked Environments and Cognitive Apprenticeship. As suggested earlier, one of the central elements of technological environments presumed to authenticate learning is that of simulating the social processes learners rely on in their everyday lives. Accordingly, Brown et al. (1989) suggest that as "ideas are exchanged and modified and belief systems developed and appropriated through conversations and narratives, so these must be promoted not inhibited" (p. 40). Bagley and Hunter (1992) highlight the motivational aspects of collaboration, and argue that research has shown that technologies which foster collaborative effort increase the positive nature of students' mood states (p. 25). Whereas there is a useful distinction to be made between theories of collaboration and theories of apprenticeship, in educational technology, both ideas are often combined in environments that seek to precipitate and support the social relations that naturally surround learning.

For constructivist educators in the sociohistorical tradition and those that look to the social constructionist conversation for guidance, the importance of facilitating knowledge-building communities can hardly be overstated. As Honebien et al. (1993) put it, "one particular cognitive activity that should be promoted in the design of most authentic learning environments [is] the ability to generate and evaluate alternative perspective" (p. 92). Technologists have facilitated this activity by augmenting face-to-face communication with computer-networked opportunities for working together as well as by creating virtual communities of learners (Hooper, 1992). For this reason, some teachers recommend using the Internet to stimulate student interest in learning by providing them with the opportunity to join communities around the world that share similar interests (e.g., Bowen, 1994).

Beach and Lundell (1996) suggest that networked collaboration is a "more authentic" means of education in that it enables learners to work with peers rather than with teachers. They suggest that computer-mediated communication "creates an electronic forum or 'interpretative zone' in which participants share multiple perspectives and attitudes relative to a particular topic or issue." Furthermore, in Collins' view, mediated collaboration makes cost-effective opportunities for apprenticeship learning that could not have existed earlier. Apprenticeship structures learning in several ways. Collins breaks these into the following elements: most obviously, perhaps, in an apprentice situation, an expert performance is modeled in ways that learners can appreciate and emulate. Technology allows such performance to be broken down into processes and subprocesses in ways that books traditionally have been unable to, and even ways in which human mentors cannot. "Computers can make the invisible visible," according to Collins (1991); "they can make tacit knowledge explicit," and "to the degree that we can develop good process models of expert performance, we can embed these in technology, where they can be observed over and over for different details" (p. 125).

Within the framework of cognitive apprenticeship, technology also serves the important role of coach by locating the points in the problem-solving process where students are having difficulty and by providing as much coaching as the learner needs to accomplish the task. Such coaching functions range from providing the learner with a set of problem-solving heuristics as the situation warrants to drawing on a body of error patterns to guide a student through a task. Coaching provides the scaffolding necessary for a learner to approximate an expert performance through a series of successive approximations. Computers also offer students opportunities for metacognition, or reflection, on their performance and learning strategies. This is accomplished in several ways. Unlike traditional teaching methods that tend to obscure the learning process, computers tacitly call attention to the learning events, leading students to objectify those events and to see their performance in a computerized environment as a kind of data. This both encourages them to reflect on the performative nature of their problem solving as well as permits them to compare their performance to that of others. Collins notes that technology-based environments offer the tools that make it possible for students to articulate what it is they are doing, again prompting them to make tacit knowledge explicit. If the environment can lay the performance out in a two-dimensional form (i.e., in pictures, text, or computer models), students have an added opportunity to reflect on their learning.

The cognitive apprenticeship offered by computers also provides yet another important real-world dimension: temporal flexibility. A key element in traditional apprenticeships is the fact that learners are given time to learn, a luxury not afforded in most school curricula that are driven by factors other than the needs of the learner. By having the coaching and modeling capabilities accessible to the learner whenever they are needed, computers are actually an improvement on real-world apprenticeships where mentors may not be as patient. With computers, students are afforded the opportunity to think through problems at their own pace. For this and other reasons, the CTGV (1990) believes that their anchored instruction can actually provide a more efficient variety of apprenticeship than real-world apprenticeships that suffer from certain logistical constraints:

> One obvious advantage of anchoring instruction in videodisc-based macrocon-
> texts is that it makes the idea of transforming school instruction into apprentice-
> ships more feasible. It is easier to teach problem-solving in the context of a Jasper

video than to put a class full of students on a boat or in a plane. One advantage of the videodisc context is its compression of time; hours and days can be compressed into minutes. In addition, the videodisc allows students to revisit segments and test their memories against actual events. (p. 8)

Computers make it possible to provide the sort of individualized training masters provide for apprentices in the traditional model of apprenticeship. Collins et al. (1989) suggest that without the highly individualized elements of teacher modeling, coaching, and *fading* (i.e., teacher relinquishment of direction), apprenticeship is impossible and, thus, "appropriately designed computer-based modeling, coaching, and fading systems can make a style of learning that was previously severely limited, cost effective and widely available" (p. 491).

To recap then, Collins et al. (1989) argue that technologies that support cognitive apprenticeship can actually improve the traditional (i.e., vocational) apprenticeship model. This traditional model is inefficient in several respects, mostly due to the limitations of time and space that constrain apprentices working out in the world. For one thing, such apprenticeship leaves a lot to chance. As learning only occurs in response to the real needs that arise in the real workplace, apprentices in the real world can only play the hand dealt them. Educational technologies circumvent some of these limitations by creating learning contexts that are apprentice-like in several respects, but that permit a greater number of opportunities for self-correction and learning modification. Recording technologies, such as computers or videotapes, for instance improve traditional apprenticeship because they allow for *abstracted replay*—the opportunity for learners to view important episodes of their problem solving as many times as they need to.

A Word on Virtual Reality

A reader may expect that any discussion of authenticity, learning, and technology would extensively deal with the topic of virtual reality as the very name alludes to correspondence with the real world. Pea (1993), for instance, persuasively argues for the power of virtual reality to create visual contexts that "narrow gaps between desires and actions" (p. 59). By this, he means that the opportunities for intelligent relationship-building afforded by objects can be exploited by learners in a virtual environment. His views are predicated on what was noted earlier as the ecological cognitivist's belief that knowledge is distributed and objects contain intelligence. Yet, for the most part, the literature of virtual reality is oddly devoid of claims of authenticity. The reasons for this are difficult to determine, though one can offer some hypotheses. Most obviously, perhaps, virtual reality is still in its nascent stages of development. The fact of its technological achievement, rather than its current applications, seem to occupy much of the writing on the subject. One sign of its novelty is that, with few exceptions, virtual reality systems have been popularized only as games. Although development of educational applications are under way, issues of cost seem likely to keep this in check for the near future.

Another reason for the paucity of claims for its authenticity might be that the typical glove-and-goggle technology, to date, is about simulating physical and material environments rather than creating social contexts, which, as noted in Chapter One, are taken as the realm within which we generally speak of the authentic. Virtual reality's well-known application to fields such as aviation training are those in which the learner is taught to coordinate a variety of constraints (e.g., variables of speed, panel layout, resistance, etc.) that can be faithfully recreated. Similarly, recently publicized efforts by researchers attempting to assist sufferers of agoraphobia and claustrophobia do not seek to recreate reality in any sense other than the spatial. To be sure, flying airplanes or riding elevators are social activities, but the elements of their reality that are virtually simulated are limited to issues of eye–hand coordination, depth perception, and attention rather than performing these processes in social environments.

Text-based virtual reality systems (i.e., multiuser dungeons, or MUDs), on the other hand, are highly interactive and social, but their use is rarely promoted as authentic. Instead, the MUD simulation of a library or a writing lab is intended to connect with learners' schemata for libraries and writing labs at a purely metaphoric level. Insofar as the MUDs are "peopled" with other users and helpful wizards, one might expect that the claims for collaborative learning might also be applied to these environments. However, reviews of the literature (still limited as it is) extol the virtues of MUDs without bothering to make claims of their verisimilitude. In the case of both virtual reality and MUDs, the technologies are presently rudimentary. It is conceivable—indeed, probable— that developers are presently working on virtual reality scenarios that will be complemented by virtual social interaction, that presently graphic MUDs will be augmented, and that the claims for authenticity will correspondingly arise.

CONCLUSION

Pedagogy is the most obvious way in which we translate educational theory into practice. We learn a great deal about how constructivist theory is rendered usable by looking at how technologists have met the challenge of authenticating learning. Operationalizations of authenticity can be inferred by reviewing the previously outlined statements made by educational technologists. Were one to compile a fill-in-the-blank list of alternatives that technologists could slot into the sentence, "An important aspect of the everyday world, and thus of an authentic problem, is its _____" that list might include: utility, historical or factual accuracy, and structural isomorphism (the traditional associations with authenticity), in addition to opportunities for social interaction, learner-directedness, visual dimension, interactivity, expert mentoring, ill-structuredness and multiplicity of solutions, characteristics that computer technologies are especially well-equipped to provide. Yet, technologists would undoubtedly reject the suggestion that constructivist learning environments are the product of merely filling in such a blank. Instead, they would almost certainly argue, the authenticity of tasks and of learning environments is not captured by any single one of these characteristics, but by the convergence of all these and more.

FOUR

Constructivism Lost

*There are not two worlds—the world of past happenings and
the world of present knowledge of those past events—there is
only one world, and it is the world of present experience.*
—M. OAKESHOTT (1966, 107–108).

THE ACCRETION of several decades of inquiry into the ecology of education has drawn attention not only to the interpersonal dimension of learning,
but also to its cultural context and the material features contained therein. The
constructivist metatheory that most educators have adopted makes claims not
merely about social influences on thinking (as some information-processing
cognitivists grudgingly speak of them), but, in addition, argues that most—
perhaps all—higher level mental processing is social processing, and, as such, is
susceptible to the vagaries of everyday collaboration with others whom we
undertake to participate in the activities that comprise what we call living. For
this reason, we have seen that the metatheory, in its various guises, has been
interpreted as a clarion call for making learning authentic—a call that has been
heeded by many educators in a variety of fields and subspecialties (Jonassen,
Mayes, & McAleese, 1993). Constructivism's mandate for authenticating learning is clearly observed in the field of educational technology where even basic
technological dimensions and modalities such as interactivity, networking, and
multimedia are re-envisaged and recast as features that further the constructivist
goals of making school learning correspond, to as great a degree possible, to the
learning that results from everyday social interaction (Jones, Knuth, & Duffy,
1993).

My portrayal of the progression from constructivist theory to practice suggests that this movement is relatively seamless, yet I suspect the reader (especially one who has already read the introductory chapter) detects a certain
facileness in the shift from the sociohistoricists' quotidianization of learning to

technologists' applications of networked and hypermediated environments. I believe this is due to the fact that the capture of constructivist theory by educators papers over some very serious disjunctures. This chapter flags a shift away from historical or descriptive accounts of constructivism and educational technology and instead uses these accounts as the basis for an argument that may strike the reader as somewhat more polemic: that the efforts of educators to harness a constructivist framework for learning is fundamentally misguided, and our seeming commitment to constructivism may mask a much less genuinely progressive enterprise. I argue that in our desire to avoid the unpleasantness that a *whole* constructivism (i.e., a constructivism that acknowledges its epistemological entailments) brings with it, we have permitted the genuine lessons of constructivism to slip through our fingers. If, as the chapter's title suggests, we have "lost" constructivism, the source of the problem is not difficult to locate. It is wholly within constructivism that we find an unresolved tension between the metatheory's epistemological implications and its educational and methodological commitments.

THE EASY LEAP FROM CONSTRUCTIVISM
TO SOCIAL CONSTRUCTIONISM[1]

The lessons of constructivism for educators, filtered through mediating theories such as apprenticeship or collaboration, often result in educational prescriptions for authenticating learning. This filtering process, however, generally obscures the fact that, rather than prescribing authenticity, constructivism problematizes it. One needs only to scratch lightly on constructivism's surface to reveal underlying implications for knowledge that make present efforts at authenticating learning suspect. The title Geertz chose for his influential book *Local Knowledge* reflects the essence of the postmodern and constructivist shift away from encompassing, eternal, immovable, and demonstrable truths toward the view that knowledge of the real world is limited, contingent, pragmatic, and elusive. A commonly used label for the epistemological stance that is the consequence of constructivism is *social constructionism*. Just as I argued that constructivism is best understood as a loose amalgam of cognitivist principles relating to the activeness of the learner and the importance of social and material contexts to thinking, the social constructionist part of the constructivist metatheory is less

---

[1]For purposes of readability, I would like to identify the epistemological dimension of constructivism in some way other than social constructionism. This has not been possible, however, because both have become terms of art and figure prominently in the literatures of education, psychology, sociology, rhetoric, and philosophy where one or the other is often the subject of interest. The relationship of constructivism to social constructionism is an important theme, but once we have established this distinction early in this chapter, we can comfortably fold social constructionism back into the constructivist metatheory.

of a cogent epistemological theory than an epistemological stance that is accommodated by a wide range of theories (Bruffee, 1990, p. 145).

As a generic epistemological stance, social constructionism is hardly new. Whereas what we recognize as the scientific theory of constructivist learning is largely a product of our own century, the genealogy of social constructionism is often dated back to Vico (Baars, 1986; Phillips, 1995; von Glasersfeld, 1995) though others argue that it is possible to understand the Greek sophistic tradition as one that fully reflected social constructionist epistemology (Jarratt, 1995).[2] Indeed, constructivism's tendrils in this century were able to infiltrate cognitivism so quickly, perhaps, due to the spadework performed by the social constructionist theories in philosophy and rhetoric that preceded it. It must also be said that social constructionism is hardly obscure: in fact, Sullivan (1995) termed it the "default theory of the nineties." Entire disciplines, including the sociology of knowledge, rhetoric of science, literary theory, and most varieties of cultural studies, are so predicated on social constructionist theories of knowledge building that the term, as well as the worldview it suggests, seem almost quaint in some circles.

A social constructionist argues that knowledge is created, maintained, and altered through an individual's interaction with and in his or her discourse communities. Bruffee's (1986) essay introducing social constructionism to many language teachers, explains, "a social constructionist position in any discipline assumes that entities we normally call reality, knowledge, thought, facts, texts, selves, and so on are constructs generated by communities of like-minded peers" and that these are all symbolic entities rather than entities with a reality outside our socially induced perceptions of their reality (p. 774). An extreme, but not uncommon, social constructionist perspective denies the possibility of any world that exists independent of our socially conventionalized representation of that world. Accordingly, reality and truth are better understood as historically situated, cultural, consensus-driven, and tentative, and thus, susceptible to shifts in the social milieu in which such reality arises.

According to Bruffee (1986), "we generate knowledge by 'dealing with' our *beliefs* about the physical reality that shoves us around. Specifically, we generate knowledge by justifying those beliefs socially" (p. 777). Thus, it is the social arena that produces what passes for knowledge, not systematic, rational inquiry in the traditional sense. As Brummett (1976) argues, "reality . . . is shared meanings. Therefore truth for the individual, is the extent to which the meanings of experience (that is to say, reality) of that individual are shared by significant others" (p. 34). In sum, the social constructionist argues that knowledge arises through consensus rather than through correspondence with objective truth or in an individual's autonomous construction of that reality. For educators such as

---

[2]In the rhetoric field, this observation has been widely propounded, most recently, perhaps, in a collection of essays edited by Mailloux (1995).

myself, social constructionism seems a logical and complementary extension of constructivist learning theory especially as embodied in sociohistoricist and second-wave cognitivist schools of thought. For instance, although Bartlett (1932) was wary of the ontological or epistemological implications of constructivism, he seemed to realize their central importance. He notes first that, from a psychological perspective, one can take reality, and thus real meaning, to substitute for conventionalized meaning, rational meaning, salient or dominant meaning, intuitive or "fitting" meaning, and so on. At the end of his list, however, he notes that:

> A psychologist can take any of these types of "real" meaning . . . and state how the conditions which give rise to them come into operation or are developed. All this still gives him no basis whatsoever for deciding whether, in a theory of knowledge, "real" meanings are to be preferred to any other kind; or whether, and in what sense, "real" meanings may be related to facts that are taken to display an order of things outside psychology. These questions remain, as ever, beyond the scope of the psychologist. (p. 287)

Psychologist Kenneth Gergen (1995) notes that both constructivism and social constructionism challenge the traditional view of "the individual mind as a device for reflecting the character and conditions of an independent world" (p. 27). Tobin's (1995) introductory contribution to a listserv on constructivism illustrates the natural encroachment of epistemology and social construction on traditionally constructivist concerns. According to him, the central constructivist tenets are as follows:

1. All knowledge is constructed by cognizant beings (that is to say that knowledge does not exist independently of thinking subjects).
2. The only access humans have to an external reality is via their senses.
3. All knowledge is subjective because experience is given meaning in terms of extant knowledge and prior experience.
4. Although an external reality exists, humans can only know an experiential reality.

Accordingly, the test of given knowledge is not whether it matches an external reality that we can know in an objective way, but whether it enables an individual to meet given goals. Both constructivism and social constructionism deny the objectivist conception of a real world that is understood independent of experience, both accentuate the role activity and social interaction play in thinking.[3] Thus, both views reject the traditional transmission model of education,

---

[3]There are many more nuanced terms for the epistemological position I am calling *objectivism*. Depending on the context, one could just as easily speak (as I do later) in terms of foundationalism. I am following Lakoff's (1987) definition of objectivism as the view that "rational thought consists of the manipulation of abstract symbols and that these symbols get their meaning via a correspondence with the world, objectively construed . . ." (p. xii). As such, *objectivism* reflects the

which envisages learning as the faithful translation of external phenomenon into mental representation.

In short, social contructionism calls our attention to the epistemological dimension of a constructivist metatheory rather than offers an alternative theory. Social constructionism, like the constructivist metatheory of which it is a part, emphasizes the contingency of our perceptions of the real world; constructivists and social constructionists agree that reality (and thus, any sense of authenticity) has to do with perceptions of causation and that our notions of the real world are formed from our abilities to change and be changed by it. Hacking (1983) summarizes this view when he suggests that "We shall count as real what we can use to intervene in the world to affect something else, or what the world can use to affect us" (p. 149). Mavrodes (1964) also writes of reality as tied to implication (or what he calls *dependence*). That is, a thing is real insofar as it is prerequisite to (i.e., depends on) other things that we believe are real. When the existence of something, such as a value or self-concept, is dependent on a belief in the existence of something else, that something else takes on the character of the real from our perspective. Thus, we again arrive at the premise that much of what we know to be real is not known in any objective sense, but is believed (in the fully tentative sense of that word) to be real.[4] The task of balancing a checkbook, for instance, may be an authentic task from the perspective of a twenty-one-year-old, but we would question its "reality status" vis à vis a five-year-old. Yet, more to the point, among twenty-one-year-old students, for whom we believe the task should be real, there are many who find any given lesson in personal finance irrelevant, inaccurate, or inappropriate given their own prior experience.

From the social constructionist perspective, a task's reality is confounded by an individual's personal epistemological assumptions dictated in large part by that which commands one's attention. According to Berger and Luckmann (1967), consciousness is always intentioned; directed toward objects that we are socially conditioned to perceive as real or significant (p. 20). Authenticity lies in the learner's recognition of a situation's verisimilitude and the potential they

---

basic scientific and dualistic assumption that the world is "out there" and thus knowable given appropriate instruments of observation and a commitment to rational inquiry. *Objectivism* is also the term most frequently used by many educational psychologists and technologists as the antonym of the constructivist metatheory (e.g., Duffy & Jonessen, 1992).

[4]While I have settled on a simple distinction between the psychologists' accounts of how we construct meaning (i.e., constructivism) and a social theory of knowledge that reflects an antifoundationalist epistemology (i.e., social constructionism), it is important to note their stipulatedness, for in the discipline and subfields of psychology the meanings of the nomenclature is not always the same as used here. Harré (1986), for instance, uses both constructivism and constructionism to distinguish among developmental psychological approaches. Other writers have used the name *radical constructivist* in the sense that I am using *social constructionist* (e.g., several contributors to Steffe and Gale's, 1995, anthology on the subject) while still others fail to make the distinction at all.

perceive the task to have for implicating them. As such, authenticity is not an intrinsic property possessed by an object, but rather a *judgment*, a decision made on the part of the learner constrained by the sociocultural matrix within which he or she operates.[5] For this reason, constructivists and social constructionists are united on the principle that constructions of reality are often the result of a conscious and active process, although social constructionists would hasten to add that perhaps our most important and generative constructions (e.g., notions of family, community, education, etc.) are usually unconscious and culturally determined.

Although I argue for the ease with which one can integrate social constructionism into the constructivist metatheory (and in doing so highlight constructivism's epistemological implications), I wish to maintain their somewhat artificial separation for a bit longer. My thesis is that, at present, constructivists in education tend to embrace the latter without taking on the baggage of the former. Nowhere is this seen more clearly than in what might be called the constructivist educators' and technologists' tacit efforts at *preauthentication*.

Begging the Epistemological Question: Preauthentication

Over the course of the century, constructivists in education have formulated and reformulated two basic insights: the first establishes that one does not learn without authentic experience of a phenomenon, while the second argues that educators must provide learners with authentic experiences. Many in education have assumed that the second statement is a mere corollary of the first, but in making this assumption, we see that they are taking on certain beliefs about the nature of the real world and the possibilities of knowing. For instance, when someone labels something as "authentic" he or she is making not only a statement about that thing, but about the world of which that thing is an exemplar. The declaration of a short story's "authentic Americanness," for instance, tells us more about the speaker's notion of what the real America is like than it does about the story being described. For this reason, a notion of authenticity is clearly tied to a perspective on reality and thus ultimately, to knowledge of the real world. In educational technology we have seen that authenticity has been subject to many operationalizations and equations: authenticity lies in accuracy, is a product of complexity, arises in collaborative activity, depends on the accessibility of accurate information, and is a matter of cognitive flexibility. In each of these instances, the technologists' efforts to "make learning real" involve a feature that can be satisfactorily verified through external and independent means. Accuracy (though problematic) can be more or less factually discerned, the

---

[5]Linguistic and cultural determinists, of course, might go so far as to argue that our language and/or our social mores completely dictate our thinking and our behavior and thus the issue of agency is one that is currently the subject of much interest in education.

complexity of a problem (relative to be sure) can nevertheless be ascertained in comparison to the complexity of other problems, collaborative behavior is self-evident, and so on. Given such operationalizations, it seems safe to presume that one can, prior to entering a given teaching situation, make a problem or a learning environment authentic. In other words, one can preauthenticate.

At the heart of preauthentication lies a dichotomy separating those tasks that are authentic and those that are not. This is revealed in the very common, almost incidental, directive to provide students with authentic tasks. Consider a definition of authentic activity given by Honebein et al. (1993) that complicates a simple notion of authenticity, but clearly suggests that the ability to differentiate between authentic and inauthentic tasks is predeterminable. According to them, an authentic task is one in which three conditions obtain: the learner feels *ownership* over the learning in the sense that they must assume responsibility for establishing, monitoring, and evaluating their goals and performance with coaching from a teacher; an authentic task must be "project-based" and contribute to seeing subtasks as part of a bigger picture (e.g., "Global authentic activities might include performing a break-even analysis or designing a brochure for a business or building a deck for your home," p. 91); and the authentic task must encourage a learner to generate multiple perspectives (cf. cognitive flexibility).

It is this knowledge of the environments in which learning will be used that warrants the assumption that we can predetermine authentic tasks from those that are inauthentic independent of the learner. This view is clearly and succinctly reflected in Duffy and Jonassen's (1992) observation that ". . . the context need not be the real world of work in order for it to be authentic. Rather, the authenticity arises from engaging in the kinds of tasks using the kinds of tools authentic to that domain" (p. 9). Although Honebein et al.'s definition (and especially the first criterion) reveals some nuance, the problem is one with which any social constructionist would immediately identify: how can we authenticate a problem or issue whose reality is not a given? As Winn (1993) puts it:

> Instructional theories proceed from the assumption that students will solve problems with the same logic that task analysis uses to break them apart. It is assumed that the student will see and learn the same logical structure in a procedure or task hierarchy that the designer does . . . [but] instructional designers cannot possibly foresee all of the situations in which the knowledge and skills they teach can be applied." (pp. 199–200)

Contrast this to Bednar, Cunningham, Duffy, & Perry's (1992) assertion that "the constructivist view turns towards a consideration of what *real people* do in a particular knowledge domain and real life context *typically* do" (p. 23, emphasis added). They further suggest that it may not be possible to give a student an authentic task, but that one may simplify the task while retaining its authentic essence. One is tempted to ask to which real people they are referring. How do terms such as *typically* fit into a constructivist account, and just how do we uncover the *essence* of a task? When we consider the social constructionist episte-mological implications of constructivism, the efforts of educational technolo-gists to authenticate learning are turned on their head and what appears to be a logical and theoretically satisfying response to constructivist learning theory is shown to be neither.[6] In *Democracy and Education*, for instance, Dewey (1961) writes, "the fallacy consists in supposing that we can begin with ready-made subject matter of arithmetic, or geography, or whatever, irrespective of some di-rect personal experience of a situation" (p. 12).

To see preauthentication in action, we return to the work of the CTGV not only because it has a well-established track record in educational technology, but also because it is notable for its overt concern for the authenticity of the learning materials they produce. Consider, for instance, their development of Jasper interactive video materials, which embody their theory of anchored in-struction. Central to the CTGV's (1990) argument for the superiority of their materials is their authenticity. They note that the construct of authenticity has more than a single dimension. At one level, they claim their materials are au-thentic because they use actual facts and data. On a second level, they are au-thentic in that the tasks that individuals are asked to perform are those that they could legitimately be expected to perform if they found themselves in the actual situation. Finally, they pose a question that, at first blush, appears to be some-what more interesting: "for whom are these tasks authentic?" Further reading, however, reveals that they are not asking "who is construing these tasks as real?" but rather "who can make best use of the authenticity with which he or she is presented?" In other words, they ask the question in order to make the point that the software's user may not have sufficient knowledge, or "expertise," to profit from its authenticity. This suggests that, for the CTGV's purposes, au-thenticity is objective—the programmer made the software authentic (p. 7).[7]

---

[6]In educational technology, the word *context* is used in two senses we might distinguish as *stipu-lated* and *natural*. There are some systems intended to operate within a stipulated context. That is, it is common for the designer of a learning environment to explicitly lay out the parameters of the context within which the task operates and then assesses the learner's progress or facility with the materials on the basis of the prespecified criteria (this is commonly seen in simulation and gaming exercises). The very idea of authentic learning environments, however, is often accompanied by an overt rejection of stipulation; instead, environment designers are often concerned that the con-text be as naturalistic as possible. In practice, however, the distinction between the two is often elided because most designers of natural contexts are, in fact, delimiting the contexts within which they validate learning. Consider the following sentence: "Instruction should establish and elabo-rate a context, because information acquired in a real-world context is better retained, the learning that results is more generative, higher order, and more meaningful, and the transfer of that learn-ing is broader and more accurate" (Jonassen, 1992, pp. 388–389).

[7]We might consider how this plays out in goal-based scenarios as well. In the instance of *Broad-cast News*, for example, while its developers explicitly and repeatedly claim that the scenarios are authentic they also acknowledge that learners may have little or no background knowledge relat-ing to the subject of the broadcast (e.g., Rajiv Gandhi's assassination) nor of the role broadcasters play.

Other preauthenticating "features" are questionable as well. As we have seen, the idea that knowledge is socially constructed has been translated by theorists, such as Bruffee and many technologists, into the assumption that if students are put into dialogue via collaborative environments, they will simulate learning as it really happens. Yet, the focus on (and expectations of) collaborative effort and networked environments is at once welcome and excessive. Clearly, thinking is a social process informed by cultural assumptions and conventions governing symbol usage, but educators sometimes fail to recognize that social knowledge, in the sense in which most theorists use the term, is quite different from the knowledge that results from explicit collaborative effort.

The assumption that making students work with others replicates the natural processes of social construction demonstrates a thin appreciation for how meaning is negotiated. Yet, Clancey (1993) advances this view when he suggests replacing the individual with the group as the psychological unit of study. I argue that one can retain the individual as the unit and recognize that the individual contains the social—operationalizing *social* to mean *group* does nothing to mirror the way in which cultures and ideologies function. Criticism similar to this is voiced by Dillenbourg and Schneider (1993) when they note that, in traditional AI tutoring theory, the "mentalistic concept of metacognition [is] turned into a concrete activity" (p. 44). Like the notion that metacognition can be reduced to a series of discrete and logical procedures, the idea that social construction occurs when you have students sharing a worktable or networked computer desktop seriously diminishes the potency of the original observation. Social knowledge is characterized by both its subtlety and pervasiveness. It is also distinguished by its glacial movement across generations and social formations (witness how long it has taken us to identify knowledge's essentially social nature). Thus, a response such as collaboration does little to rearrange the essentially elite-idealist nature of education and promotes what I think is a fairly tepid response to a fairly radical reconceptualization of what it means to participate in a knowledge-building community (cf. Harris, 1989).

Similarly, the link between cognitive apprenticeship and authenticity in educational technology is problematic, for it reduces apprenticeship to a few key elements (and, not coincidentally, those elements that are emulatable with computer environments such as modeling, coaching, etc.) that can be empirically verified (again, consider Honebein et al.'s first criterion). As a number of anthropological scholars of education suggest, interpersonal relationships between learner and mentor, with its attendant-affective dimension, are an absolutely indispensable part of any notion of apprenticeship (Cohen, 1971). Without this dimension, apprenticeship is divorced from the interpersonal contexts with which Vygotsky, Luria, and Dewey were so concerned and, instead, becomes compendiums of prompts suited for human–computer interaction. I find that cognitive apprenticeship is to actual apprenticeship what computational models are to human cognition: important starting points for a conversation, perhaps, but metaphoric and highly essentialized facsimiles of the genuinely situated phenomena. The models of cognitive apprenticeship proposed by many technologists might indeed have benefits for learning, but we could not count among them the replication of real-world apprenticeship.

In much the same way, arguments that hypertextualization authenticates learning by releasing reader–learners from the tyranny of someone else's auctorial intention are also overstated. As the reader–learner constructs his or her own pathways through information based on the links they wish to follow, it is claimed, the natural constructivist proclivities of the mind are more easily accommodated. A problem with this argument, however, is that it equates release from an author's imposed linearity with the freedom to cogitate in accordance with one's own reality. Hypertext does not do this, and the idea that information connected in a hypertext parallels one's naturally occurring schema-generating processes in some significant sense, seems weak. Hypertexts are not neutral—they are constrained by a variety of factors: first and foremost, the information available for linking, which has been predetermined in most cases, by others.[8] There is also growing evidence that clicking one's way through a hypertexted document can, in fact, be disruptive to learners and stymie their intentions (cf. Spiro et al., 1992a). In other words, hypertextualization of information certainly creates easier connections among sets of information, but it does not seem to follow that it supports a learner's natural associations. Most hypertext applications do not allow instantaneous connection of concepts in accordance with the user's own associations, but instead, allow a limited freedom of movement within someone else's conceptual web and intentions (cf. Bolter, 1991).

Summary

Following the constructivist view of cognition to its logical conclusion, we arrive at the epistemological stance that suggests that it is an individual's representation of the world—a representation rooted in prior and present social interaction, rather than objective reality—that matters when we speak of what is real and of what is authentic. In keeping with the Deweyan and sociohistorical traditions, Singer (1992) suggests that knowing is a function of experience, and experience is the product of interaction with an environment because the only

---

[8]Even when users are invited to create their own connections, as is increasingly the case (e.g., as in the SemNet software), they continue to be bound by the educator's assignments and the implicit requirement that some links should be created in order to problem solve correctly. The context of the hypertext's use rarely, if ever, permits the student to learn in accordance with his or her own prior understanding. In itself, this is not a problem as the formative nature of schooling is something with which we should be comfortable. After all, what does it mean to learn or to teach if students are not prompted to rearrange prior understandings? The point is that the arguments for hypertext's facilitation of natural associative processes may be misdirected and inappropriately linked to the rhetoric of authenticity.

"ground" of knowledge lies in its utility to a knower, and a knower is always working within a specific context (p. 191). This seems to suggest that we cannot preauthenticate a problem any more than we can predetermine the precise contents of a learner's operative schemata and the range of inferences that are likely to be made from them. Again, this problematization grows naturally out of the constructivist tradition. If constructivists accept the idea that thinking is our means of coping with, rather than gaining objective knowledge of, the world and that cognition cannot be entirely divorced from the contexts in which it occurs, we must also accept that an authentic problem or problem space cannot be manufactured outside the learner's experiential framework for understanding (von Glaserfeld, 1984). In essence, this is the problem with preauthentication from the constructivist perspective: preauthentication denies (indeed, it must deny) the contingency of cognitive processing that is the very soul of constructivism. My criticism is not intended to refute any of the mediating theories mentioned earlier or to denigrate the technological innovations that purportedly embody them; almost certainly, each of these innovations might be useful in facilitating learning (which is, after all, what educational technology is supposed to do). Instead, my argument is that the benefit to be derived from having learners use these features may have little or nothing to do with their ability to create authentic environments for learning.

THE ANTIFOUNDATIONALIST THREAT TO EDUCATION

In the conclusion of his essay entitled, "The Good, the Bad, and the Ugly: The Many Faces of Constructivism," Phillips (1995) identifies constructivism's good face as "the emphasis that various constructivist sects place on the necessity for active participation by the learner, together with the recognition (by most of these groups) of the social nature of learning" (p. 11). The bad, according to Phillips, is:

> the tendency within many forms of constructivist epistemology (despite occasional protestations to the contrary) towards relativism, or towards treating the justification of our knowledge as being entirely a matter of sociopolitical processes or consensus, or toward the jettisoning of any substantial rational justification or warrant at all. . . . (p. 11)

Basically, Phillips identifies what we have been calling social constructionism as the source of constructivism's unmanagability. Although constructivism and social constructionism are two sides of the same coin, social constructionism, unlike constructivism, is not shy about announcing its antifoundationalist nature. It forthrightly proclaims that we do not have any objective or privileged foundation from which we can construct an accurate model of the world. The inaccessibility of foundations for knowledge thereby opens the door to the unsettling claim that there is no right or wrong independent of our ad hoc assessments. As Lincoln and Guba (1985) contend, "When naive realism is replaced by the assumption of multiple constructed realities, there is no ultimate benchmark to which one can turn for justification—whether in principle or by a technical adjustment via the falsification principle. 'Reality' is now a multiple set of mental constructions" (p. 295). In short, we are beset by the demons of relativism.

The threat posed by relativism is expressed in Winn's (1993a) acknowledgment that as constructivism (specifically, its social constructionist elements) implies that each individual knows the world in a different way, that there is neither a shared world about which we can teach nor any means by which to assess the effectiveness of any particular pedagogical intervention; "if knowledge is constructed entirely by students, there being no objective reality to teach them, there is nothing that instructional designers (or teachers for that matter) can do to affect student understanding and behavior" (p. 189). Elsewhere, Winn (1993b) encapsulates the problem presented by constructivism (here, expressed in terms of situated learning) by explaining that:

> The apparent incompatibility of ID [Instructional Design] and SL [Situated Learning] arises because ID assumes that what people learn is relatively stable across situations in which it is used and that people apply what they have learned in planful ways. Since proponents of SL claim that human action is dependent on the context in which it occurs, and that, by implication, it is impossible to foresee every situation in which learned knowledge and skill are likely to be applied, it is impossible to design instruction that can prepare students to act appropriately in all situations. (p. 17)

While most educators probably disavow any live interest in classical philosophical questions, in our attempts to preauthenticate learning situations, we tacitly enter the epistemological fray on the side of knowledge's ultimate knowability and teachability. Educators have good reasons for doing so.

Education's Implication in Scientific Method

Most disciplines necessitate atomizing, isolating, classifying, and quantifying in order to make sense of the phenomenon they study. Even if our disciplinary interests lie in areas such as, say, accounting or fine arts, or if we choose to excuse ourselves from social scientific conversations about our practices, most educators who claim to subscribe to constructivism at least tacitly base their beliefs on evidence gathered in educational and cognitive psychology, the sociology of education, or similar empirically based disciplines. Science, social or otherwise, provides an arena in which questions of knowledge's status are most commonly fought, at least publicly. As educators, we are deeply indebted to scientific method even when we fail to acknowledge that debt (cf. Crosswhite, 1996, p. 14). This is important because acquiescence to constructivism's antifoundationalist entailments not only undermines the authority of the teacher's personal authority, but also calls into question the very methods that produce many of our knowledge claims. For this reason, the role of social science advocate, even if one is but a consumer of social science, is one that places constructivist educators in clearest conflict with constructionism's epistemological consequences. Cizek (1995) no doubt speaks for many when he complains, "If one accepts the notion that all understanding is contextualized, if all experience is embedded in culture, and if all knowledge is a personalized construction, and so on . . . then we are not only poststructuralist, postconstructivist, and postmodernist, but probably postscientific as well" (p. 27).

In Chapter Two I argued that it is only insofar as constructivism has been able to pull away from the rigid empirical framework to which earlier psychological perspectives have been tethered that an appreciation for the complexity of everyday thinking has been able to exert itself. Yet, even as constructivism edges psychology toward the phenomenological, it steadfastly remains within the social scientific tradition and only tempers its dependence on scientific method rather than abandons it. We see this tension reflected in Bartlett's career, as he too felt compelled to choose between promoting psychology as an applied discipline and promoting it as an intensely social phenomena. In Costall's (1991) view, Bartlett was forced to push many of his own social observations to the margins of his theories (p. 39). To stay within the bounds of social science requires cognitivists to soft pedal dimensions of their theories that are methodologically inoperable, even when those elements are critical to one's full understanding.

Gergen (1985b) suggests that constructivist psychologists do not, perhaps cannot, make a leap to social constructionist epistemology as they are methodologically linked to a model of science that does not permit the taking of social constructionism too seriously, for to do so would call into question the status of psychology as a science. In his words, "In seeking objective truth . . . the cognitive researcher . . . denigrates the importance of the very processes he or she seeks to elucidate. The exogenic basis of the scientific activity undermines the validity of the endogenic theories under examination" (p. 270). Gergen contends that cognitivism has not been able to truly reject objectivism because it is objectivism that forms the metatheoretical basis of the science itself; "That is, the contemporary conception of psychological science is a byproduct of empiricist or exogenic philosophy — committed as it has been to rendering an account of objective knowledge of the world" (p. 269). To the extent that education looks to educational, developmental, and cognitive psychology as a source for intellectual legitimization (and this is to a large extent), education suffers from this same contradiction and thus the same anxieties.

Revealingly, Berger and Luckmann (1967), whose treatise on the sociology of knowledge remains one of the definitive essays on social construction, are emphatic in their insistence that they are social scientists whose "purpose is *not* to engage in philosophy" (emphasis theirs). Their introduction to the book is forthright in its acknowledgment of the odd position in which their commitment to social constructionism places them:

> To be sure, the sociology of knowledge, like all empirical disciplines that accumulate evidence concerning the relativity and determination of human thought, leads towards epistemological questions concerning sociology itself as well as any other scientific body of knowledge . . . in this the sociology of knowledge plays a part similar to history, psychology, and biology, to mention the three most important disciplines that have caused trouble for epistemology. The logical structure of this trouble is basically the same in all cases: How can I be sure, say, of my sociological analysis of American middle-class mores in view of the fact that the categories I use for this analysis are conditioned by historically relative forms of thought, and that I myself and everything I think is determined by my genes and by my ingrown hostility to my fellowmen and that, to cap it all, I am myself a member of the American middle class? (p. 19)

Without the slightest hint of irony, Berger and Luckmann continue, "Far be it from us to brush aside such questions. All we would contend here is that these questions are not themselves part of the empirical discipline of sociology" (p. 19). Here, the echoes of Bartlett's earlier handling of constructivism's epistemological entailments can clearly be heard.

Nagel's phrase "a view from nowhere" has been coined to articulate the positivistic ideal that the observer should avoid implication in the phenomenon under study; in fact, such nonimplication forms the basis of scientific method, but this manifests itself in ways other than purely methodological. For instance, Levine (1994) remarks on scientists' general lack of interest in their own constructive processes and the fact that the stories scientists relate are usually about natural phenomena rather than about their own past. We see this in the central importance accorded periodicals, rather than books, to the practice of science, as periodicals reveal the last word in inquiry, whereas books have an archival function of relatively little use to practicing scientists. Thus science lives in the present, with posterity reserved for the preservation of past understanding on which its current success rests. Levine provides a reasonable list of the other tenets the scientist must accept; according to him, science is distinguished by the following:

1. The seeming objectivity and rationality of its procedures (and as a corollary, the disinterest of its practitioners).
2. Its commitment to the replicability and verification of results.
3. The external validity (i.e., context independence) of its conclusions.
4. Its claims to represent an essential reality that is not a human construction.
5. Its commitment to a progressive (i.e., cumulative) theory of knowledge

whereby we learn more and more about the real world by virtue of observation and experiment.

6. Its insistence that these scientific procedures can, in theory at least, be developed into a body of natural laws.

Having to fit within the parameters of these constraints, Levine observes that "unlike literature, the results of science are not affected by rhetorical manipulation of arguments (which would produce an element of irrationality) nor by the social contexts from which it emerges . . ." (p. 68). In short, to be a scientist means not being a rhetorician—a finding only counts as a product of science if it can withstand the charge of being sullied by experimenter bias or social influence and misrepresentation. In this view, scientific findings accurately correspond to the world as it is and the responsible scientist seeks to present them as accurately (and unrhetorically) as language permits.

As Fodor (1972) wryly observes, however, "Psychologists have not been able to stop doing philosophy . . . [even though] they have often managed to stop noticing when they are doing philosophy . . ." (p. 84). While many psychologists allude to epistemological issues, they do so in a distinctive and telling manner. Piaget (1970, 1979), for instance, extensively wrote on *genetic epistemology* and argued that the project of psychology was largely epistemological in nature (Brief, 1983). Yet, it is clear that he was not using the term as a philospher would, but more as a description of the adaptive nature of organisms' cognitive function to their environment—much as any scientifically oriented constructivist would (Wartofsky, 1983). For an example of how large this difference is, we might turn to the part of *Genetic Epistemology* where Piaget (1970) complains of philosophers' lack of interest in verification and their unproductive reliance on thought experiments. He argues psychology could be much more helpful to philosophers if they took it seriously, for many of the claims epistemologists make are, at root, he believes, psychological claims and that such questions of fact "should be approached not by speculation but by an experimental methodology with its objective findings." He further suggests that "when a question of psychological fact arises, psychological research should be consulted instead of trying to invent a solution through private speculation" (p. 9).

Of course, most contemporary theorists find the notion that epistemological questions can and should be scientifically settled exceedingly odd. If one is inquiring into the nature of knowledge, it will hardly do to limit oneself to the very methods about which one is seeking to theorize. The very fact that psychology is identified as a social science tips its epistemological hand. It suggests that some of the central epistemological issues have been resolved and, having resolved them, psychology is only willing to address second-order epistemological concerns. Like the Epicureans, perhaps, scientists may accept that the metaphysical world exists, but methodologically, it must be treated as if such a world lies in a parallel universe with little capacity to affect changes in our world of everyday experience. Concomitant with this is the idea that scientific method somehow lies beyond the reach of constructive processes that science can discover and explain.

Hammer (1994) provides another instructive example of how one may "safely" speak of epistemology and the predominant way in which it is approached by psychologists. In his study, epistemology is operationalized as a learner's belief about the structure of a domain's knowledge, that domain's content, and how one learns within the domain. Hammer conducts interviews with students in an introductory physics class to determine how their prior knowledge of the domain influences their learning and approaches to material. What is left out of this scheme is the learner's beliefs about knowledge generally (for the existence of the domain as an cogent entity is assumed) as well as his or her beliefs about how knowledge of a given domain relates to one's broader understanding (p. 151). There seem to be at least three alternative senses in which we speak of knowledge and, more to the point, three senses in which the epistemological interests of social scientists differ from their more humanistic colleagues. Figure 4.1 differentiates among these differing meanings of knowledge.

We might say that Hammer is using a somewhat restrictive definition of epistemology—one whose investigation provides valuable information regarding attitudes and beliefs about the domain of physics (C), which is, after all, his objective in this particular study. My point is that, though it serves the purposes of this sort of structured investigation, it carefully avoids implicating overarching

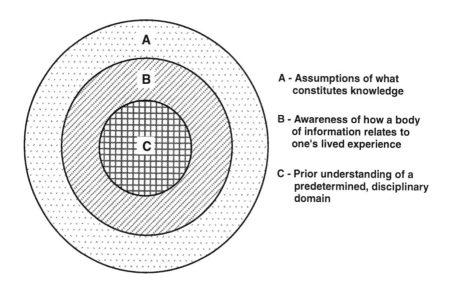

A - Assumptions of what constitutes knowledge

B - Awareness of how a body of information relates to one's lived experience

C - Prior understanding of a predetermined, disciplinary domain

FIG. 4.1.   Usages of the term *epistemology.*

issues of how that domain is embedded in an individual's life outside the class-room (B) or, as in epistemology's more philosophical sense, interrogates what counts as knowledge (A). This is not a criticism of Hammer's construct validity; again, his definition serves his purpose—it only suggests the ways in which an empirical investigation of epistemology can be conducted differ from how knowledge beliefs are viewed from the perspective of less methodologically constrained epistemologists.

Perhaps the restrictions placed on epistemology in education-related fields reflect the fact that psychology's standing as a good scientific citizen has long been under attack from both within and outside the field and thus, it may be especially susceptible to ignoring the issue of foundations if only to defend its status among the sciences. Most social sciences have long suffered from a disciplinary inferiority complex. Evans' (1995) textual analyses of popular press reports suggest that, in the world of journalism, social science has to fight for the respect accorded "real" science (e.g., his analyses reveal that natural scientists' findings are typically labeled *scientific* whereas social scientific research is often written of in terms of *opinion*.) While psychology may not be uniquely insecure, its social scientific credentials are still questioned in and outside the discipline, and it seems reasonable to assume that this insecurity has made many psychologists sensitive to issues of construct operationalization (as we see with epistemology) and methodological rigor (Baars, 1986; Danzinger, 1990; Gergen, 1985).

Of course, as related in Chapter Two, psychology was not always as wedded to empirical methods as it has been for most of this century. Prior to Wundt, psychology was considered by many to be a largely speculative enterprise. As in philosophy, psychology's domain was largely humanistic, little concerned with quantification and the establishment of empirical fact. As such, it was largely practiced by gentleman–philosophers. What made Wundt's psychology new was its turn away from speculative accounts that dominated the field and its reach toward the growing status associated with scientific method and experimentation. Psychology was not alone in this, and as the other social sciences expanded, they encroached. The competition for disciplinary intellectual space at this critical time almost certainly encouraged psychology to forego the methodological messiness and the almost phenomenological accounts of, say, Durkheim's sociology. Like most of his contemporaries, Vygotsky did not seem overly concerned with the epistemological consequences of his theories, but instead, saw himself contributing to a progressive theory firmly rooted in the social scientific tradition, one that better accounted for the data. We have no evidence in his writing that he viewed his project as one that furthered either antifoundationalism or cultural relativism.

The scientification of psychology early in this century ironically created an obsession with method at the expense of theory. The socialness of psychology is widely recognized as a potentially crippling area of contention for psychologists who rightly despair of their discipline's inability to rationally debate the value of theory. Danziger (1990) argues that consideration of the thoroughly constructed nature of the knowledge produced by psychology has been ignored for two opposing reasons: because it is too obvious to merit investigation and it poses clear threats to the scientific status of the field. Unlike the physical sciences, psychology rarely operates on the found world; its practitioners must create its objects of inquiry. Objects such as surveys, tests, test scores and indirect measures of attitude, arousal, and representation are human constructions with a more or less tenuous relationship to the phenomena they claim to mirror. While the physical sciences also heavily rely on the products of human fabrication, the artifactual nature of cognitive psychology and its dependence on linguistic constructs is both one of psychology's distinctive and intellectually challenging elements as well as one that is most threatening to its scientific status. For this reason, Danziger suggests that, relative to the natural sciences, psychology generally prefers to settle its arguments on methodological grounds and that "investigative practice therefore constitutes an area of considerable anxiety within the discipline of psychology. Concern with questions of methodological orthodoxy often takes the place of concern about theoretical orthodoxy when research or its results are discussed and evaluated" (p. 5).

In Dashiell's classic *Fundamentals of Objective Psychology* (1928), it is strenuously argued that the psychological and scientific study of "human beings and their modes of activity should be completely divorced from [philosophical] considerations, not because it is opposed to them, but because it is independent of them and irrelevant" (p. 15). He admits that psychological method is uninterested in "observing concrete persons as wholes in complex social situations" and instead focuses on specific causal sequences "from which to develop formal laws, principles, even formulae, which will serve as statements of general validity, and thus form the subject matter of a pure science" (p. 9). Elsewhere, Dashiell notes that "Man is an animal—a living organism. Nothing else is so important for the reader to keep in mind if he does not wish to lose his bearings in making a survey of the principles of human behavior" (p. 4). Even if our modes of behavior and our lifestyles are markedly superior to those of lower forms of life in their complexity and refinement, these dimensions of human experience "are most adequately viewed, however, as only vast complications of animal traits" (p. 22).

Of course, quoting an early behaviorist does little to represent the educational psychological perspectives of the 1990s. Yet, there is something in the clarity of Dashiell's message and in the directness of his claim that, although we may judge it as reductive by today's standards, continues to speak to the scientific values of contemporary education and psychology. Bazerman (1988) observes that:

> Psychology, by treating the individual as a separate biological behavioral unit can create a disengaged, objectified discourse that seems to separate both the experimental object and the experimenter from the historically evolved forms of culture

in which humans act. Indeed, as we have seen, one of the important themes in the rhetoric of experimental psychology is to represent one's experimental subjects as sufficiently clean *tabulae rasae* and the conditions of one's experiments far enough removed from daily life so as not to be contaminated by the uncontrolled complexities that move our lives. (p. 278)

Thus, to the scientist, we are remarkable animals that may behave and think in very complex ways but who ultimately remain material beings whose actions and thoughts are amenable to being couched in psychological laws, principles, and formulae—Newtonian clockwork of the highest order.

The Individual Versus the Social

Constructivism's "bad" side cannot help but make us uneasy, for if we intend for our pedagogy to be directed in some positive manner, we have to believe that certain, predictable causes and effects are obtained in the classroom. The constructivist argument that students are responsible for their own knowledge construction processes seems to make those assumptions untenable.[9] As Jonassen (1994) puts it, "If each individual is responsible for knowledge construction, how can we as designers determine and insure [sic] a common set of outcomes for learning, as we have been taught to do?" (p. 35). And so there is yet another source of tension between the constructivist account of knowledge and its social constructionist dimension for the educator: the constructivist's ultimate interest in the individual learner and the social constructionist's attention to the social forces that act on individuals. It is at this point that the strain of juggling the concerns of social construction with those of education are most apparent. The constructivist account attempts to understand, and in doing so, support the efforts of the individual learner while a social constructionist understanding, though it has been used to support pedagogical innovations, often seems incapable of addressing issues of individual agency.

Constructivism in psychology, as Gergen (1985) argues, continues to work within the endogenic world view—the world reflected in the traditional Western dualisms separating the mind from the body or the knower from that which is known. Conversely, social constructionism attempts to break away from such dualism by viewing the knower as part and parcel of socially constituted knowledge (i.e., the exogenic stance). He notes that unlike constructivists such as Vygotsky (whose sociohistorical theories were promulgated in support of cultivating individual competencies, cf. Salomon, 1993), social constructionists make scant reference to psychological processes within the individual. Instead, they are interested in matters such as "negotiation, cooperation, conflict, rhetoric, ritual, roles and social scenarios" (Gergen, 1995, p. 25) while sociohistoricists and early constructivists have focused on mental processes such as abstraction, generalization, attention and representation.

---

[9]As Anderson et al. (1996) point out, constructivists such as Lave and Wenger have explicitly refrained from making specific pedagogical recommendations.

Social constructionists who set their sights on the dynamics of social consensus building often lose sight of the individual learner—the focus of traditional constructivist theories. Put another way, the educable unit that educators deal with is the individual student; we do not teach bodies of consensus builders, we can only teach their constituent members. For this reason a social constructionists' preoccupation with social processes is at odds with the focus on individual agency to which practically every model of Western education subscribes. Similarly, constructivists might view cognitive activity as distributed throughout social matrices of which individuals are only a part, but when they adopt the role of educator it is this part with which they must be concerned. Berthoff (1996) quickly sums up the unattractive elements of antifoundationalism for educators when she notes that an "insistence that the map is not the territory becomes the claim that without the map there is no territory": an ontological claim that, if true, makes educational (or any other) efforts useless (p. 18).

It is understandable, then, that most educators prefer to ignore the epistemological implications of constructivism, but this thumbnail sketch, like all such sketches, elides disconfirming evidence that there are, in fact, educators and educational technologists that have adopted what might be called the "strong" version of constructivism and have, indeed, taken a very epistemologically aware stand. Hay (1994) for instance, very clearly lays out the tenets that characterize postmodernism and rightly argues that postmodernist thought has laid three crises at the doorstep of education: crises of representation, authority, and subjectivity. His treatment of these three crises highlights epistemological problems that any discussion of preauthentication entails. Yet, observers such as Hay also manage to avoid the problems by creating a disjuncture between theory and practice that enables them to be both constructionists and "productive" technologists. Although Hay assures educators early on that "these crises are not insurmountable," he does little to surmount them. Basically, he leaves us with a thoughtful problematization of education typically given by reflective constructivists, and we are tacitly reminded that a few constructivists in education have gotten adept at playing two competing roles: postmodern educational critic (in which capacity they can problematize) and curriculum developer (in which capacity they must propose activities, construct learning environments, etc.).

Averting the Threat

One needs not put much credence in "radical" constructivism (the antirealism of a Feyerabend, Baudrillard, or Derrida, for instance) to find the epistemological implications of constructivism unnerving; simple constructivism will do. When sociologists of knowledge Berger and Luckmann (1967) sought to escape what they saw as the debilitating effects of antifoundationalism, they did so abruptly. They simply announced that the "sociology of knowledge . . . cannot solve these [epistemological] problems within its own proper frame of reference" and thus, "firmly bracketed any epistemological or methodological questions about the validity of sociological analysis," even though such questions were begged throughout their book (p. 14). In their bid for theoretical cogency, we might extend one of Gergen's metaphors and suggest that many constructivist technologists have, like Berger and Luckmann, resisted turning into the dreaded epistemological *cul-de-sac* not by successfully negotiating detours, but by shortening their trip to avoid the turn-off altogether.

My understanding of this disjuncture is shared by other educators (e.g., many of the contributors to the Steffe and Gale collection on the subject of constructivism in education), and yet, it is fair to say that constructivism's epistemological challenges are not widely acknowledged or discussed. Such avoidance is accomplished, perhaps, by the constructivism-in-educational technology conversation's ability to focus our attention elsewhere—either on the weakness of foundationalism and the transmission model of learning it spawned, or by highlighting the mediating theories, or most significant in my opinion, by permitting constructivism to slide between its social scientific status and its ethical implications. I will briefly touch on each of these in turn.

Often described as a "recent revolution," the move from objectivism to constructivism in matters of educational psychology seems to be a topic that currently engages the energies of many technologists (e.g., Bednar, Cunningham, Duffy, & Perry, 1991; Cooper, 1993; Duffy & Jonassen, 1992). Accounts of this revolution suggest that antiquated theories of education prevail in many classrooms (and in educational technology's own tradition of instructional design) and then detail why this situation is unsatisfactory by recounting what has become a fairly standard critique of the transmission model of learning and its basis in objectivist epistemology. Instead, the argument goes, careful reconsideration of the work of early theorists such as Vygotsky and, above all, Piaget should lead us to the view that students construct knowledge in accordance with their own prior understanding and available resources and that educational technologies should be developed to accommodate this view.

Drawing inspiration from constructivism's founding fathers rather than from its postmodern and epistemologically contentious proponents, educational technology journals perpetuate an often stark good guy–bad guy distinction that pits constructivism and enlightened educational technology against the worst sort of transmission model excess (e.g., those especially annoying puzzles and word problems that are often held up as the paradigmatic tasks from which constructivism rescues us) and the discredited instructional design paradigm. Noteworthy in educational technology's approach to the topic is that it shifts the debate from only the crudest objectivism to an often tepid constructivism. Constructivism, as we have seen, has been rather common currency in psychology circles for some time now. Of course, the issue of when to date the rise of constructivism depends on whose history book one is reading from, but even a generous compliment to constructivism's youth could not plausibly date contemporary constructivism's "arrival" after the late 1970s. While it has undergone an admittedly gradual process of acceptance in the 1980s and 1990s, it seems remarkable to portray constructivism as up and coming. Fighting the good fight against objectivism has the rhetorical consequence (intended or not) of diverting attention away from the epistemological discomfort posed by constructivism.

As Confrey (1995) notes, the social scientific interest in constructivist principles does not seek the rejection of universalism (as a social constructionist would), but contents itself with the bedrock claim that mental processes are inherently social. In the case of education and educational technology, this permits a more productive tangent, usually centering on a mediating theory that has been extrapolated from constructivist theory. The relative importance of mediating theories to the constructivism that gave rise to them becomes clearer when one considers the authorities most commonly invoked in the technologist literature; they are largely those educational psychologists and technologists who already digested constructivist theory and devoted their efforts to developing functional mediating theories (e.g., Spiro and his colleagues in the area of cognitive flexibility, Collins and his collaborators in discussions of cognitive apprenticeship, etc.). Thus, many educational technologists are working from secondary sources (those theories and theorists that mediate the more primary cognitivist literature). Because these secondary sources have begun the movement toward making practical pedagogical recommendations and have already selected a subset of issues with which they wish to deal, the antifoundationalism latent in constructivism appears less salient and more avoidable. In short, educational practices and technologies that draw more heavily from mediating theories are less likely to call attention to epistemological issues than they would if they were drawing from primary constructivist theory (such as sociohistoricism and Bartlett's early constructivism) that sometimes makes allusion to the problematic status of knowledge.

Finally, it is clear that in educational technology, constructivism is celebrated not only for its adequacy to psychological explanation or even to pedagogical theories, but for the destabilization of an objectivistic epistemology and its valuation of identity and experience that give it an important ethical appeal as well. In her response to Steven Tripp's criticism of an earlier paper on situated knowledge, Damarin (1994) claims that what Tripp "ignores in his discussion of technologies, including the technologies of instruction and situated learning, is the social and economic situatedness of the technology's use, and the power relations and politics which contribute to the establishment, continuation, modification, or demise of the technological arrangements of a particular time and place" (p. 17). What is sometimes called *radical pedagogy* or *liberation pedagogy* is thus another face of the constructivist metatheory that educators can draw on to disarm the threat of antifoundationalism.

The skeleton of a Marxist theoretical framework can be seen in certain strands of situated cognition theory and leading proponents, such as Lave, for instance, offer their analyses from a clearly leftist perspective. For Lave and Wenger (1991), as well as Hay (1993), the theory of legitimate peripheral participation (LPP) slides between the scientist's observation and the practitioner's problem to be solved. Although legitimate peripheral participation is, on one hand, explicitly held up by psychologists (and, as Hay's article illustrates, technologists) as a naturally occurring learning dynamic between novices and experts, it is difficult to speak of it without also suggesting that it is a dynamic to be encouraged and managed, thus shifting between accounts of what is and what ought to be. After acknowledging that the idea of LPP is only intended as an account of learning rather than a proposal for the restructuring of schooling, Hay notes that "there is a similar decentering of learner's authority and knowledge which I find unacceptable," for it is "somewhat like the banking concept Freire criticizes because both aim to create a product—the educated man" (p. 36). When Hay speaks of unacceptability, he is referring to its political unacceptability, not its descriptive or social scientific inadequacy. In the space of a few pages, LPP becomes an ethical stance appealing for its moral import rather than a scientific theory of knowledge acquisition.

It is difficult to overstate the significance of the constructivist metatheory's political, and thus, ethical dimension. Allen (1992) chooses his words well when he asserts that constructivism in educational technology is often advocated with a kind of "zeal and evangelism" (p. 201). At technology-in-education conferences from Syracuse to Singapore, the language of empowerment and marginalization is at least as prominent as that of networking and hypertext and much more in evidence than cognitivistic talk of conceptual change, schema modification, or task environment. Constructivism, it is argued, undermines the sort of hegemonic knowledge that serves the purposes of a dominant elite. And so yet another way in which the antifoundationalist threat is averted is in the identification of constructivism with the politics and ethics of knowledge making and the subsequent focus on power differentials. The political critique is an especially important response to antifoundationalism as it does not depend on a studied ignorance of constructivism-induced vertigo as other methods of finessing do, but pragmatically proposes that a criterion *other* than verifiable correspondence with external reality (the traditional foundationalist ideal) can be the basis for knowledge. Confronted with the antifoundationalism inherent in constructivism, leftist theorists have recommended that the constructions that count (that is, those understandings and world views that are given social sanction) should be constructions that promote political and economical equity while they cheerfully (at least in the case of Richard Rorty) acknowledge that such a position works only if one resists pushing too hard on its logic. In other words, to create a moral order, we should be willing to forego standards of theoretical purity, which would require us to deconstruct a politically satisfying deconstruction.

Before leaving the topic of why and how social constructionism is finessed in the constructivist literature of educational technology, it may be interesting to note the complicity of critics of situated constructivism in ignoring the epistemological ramifications of the theory. It is almost as if all sides have entered on a tacit agreement not to exploit this particular chink in constructivism's armor. As discussed in Chapter Two, critics of the constructivist metatheory largely focused on either the fear that it spells the end of representation and a return to stimulus–response (a criticism I do not find warranted) or the view that second-wave constructivism is old wine in new cognitive bottles (accurate in several respects, but hardly damning). The fact that constructivism undermines a stable conception of knowledge—which one might expect to be especially threatening to educators and social scientists—is rarely alluded to in the technologist literature. What are we to make of this? It suggests the lengths to which those of us who accept constructivism's social scientific nature will go to keep epistemological issues out of sight for this is clearly a battle that few of us wish to fight.

CONCLUSION

Constructivism has, perhaps, become a victim of its own success, for even as it offers a more sensible and theoretically satisfying description of learning, it sets the mark for a satisfactory pedagogical application so high that it may seem unattainable. Preauthentication's major contribution is that it makes this problem less noticeable. Yet, the danger in the constructivist educator's impulse to pre-authenticate is that the precise thing we are seeking—the leverage real-world problems are presumed to offer—is lost. Thick problems solved in collaborative and hypermediated environments become fancier connect-the-dots exercises that might have many merits, but come no closer to making learning more "real" for learners than any other sort of Tower of Hanoi problem. I have argued that this is because constructivism opens the door to philosophical questions usually avoided by social scientists and educators that ground their pedagogical initiatives in social science. There seem to be few secure toeholds on the slippery slope of constructivism. To prevent sliding, technologists present their arguments for constructivist innovations in such a way that they (perhaps, coincidentally) avoid raising epistemological questions. Again, my objective is not to trivialize efforts that have gone into improving instruction, but to call attention to the inadequacy of these efforts as they relate to authenticating learning within a constructivist framework.

To many of the educators and technologists with whom I have spoken over the course of this book's two-year gestation, constructivism is something more than a method but something less than a theory of knowledge. In these formal and informal conversations, two impressions come through over and over again. First, constructivism is presumed to be education-friendly. Constructivism is on our side; it is on the side of student empowerment, social enfranchisement, and teacher creativity and presents enormous opportunities for the application of technology to learning. Equally important, constructivism is presumed to be do-able; facilitating constructivist learning by means of collaborative, multi-mediated, interactive (and thus, authentic) task environments seems to pose few practical obstacles.

But constructivism's epistemological implications must be taken into account if the theory that guides our pedagogical choices is to be cogent; studied ignorance of these implications or mere acknowledgement of their problematic nature do not seem to be satisfying responses. This is not the analytic philosopher's argument for conceptual purity or a niggler's plea that we observe the niceties of theory; the alignment of constructivist theories of learning with social constructionist theories of knowledge is fundamental to educational reform. The practices of preauthentication illustrate how educators have attempted to keep constructivism on a short leash and insofar as preauthentication leads us to think that we have successfully integrated a more commonsensical and empirically satisfying explanation of learning into a paradigm of education with which we are comfortable, we may judge our efforts successful. If no better options were available, pragmatic educators may have no recourse but to find the present cafeteria-style approach to constructivism acceptable. Yet, I believe, we do have better options.

FIVE

Arguing
and Educating

> ...*no one finds it easy to live uncomplainingly and fearlessly with
> the thesis that human reality is constantly being made and unmade,
> and that anything like a stable essence is constantly under threat.
> ...We need some foundation upon which to stand.*
> —EDWARD SAID (1994, p. 333)

THE DILEMMA for educators, as I have presented it, is that the very constructivist theories of learning used to justify their efforts at preauthenticating learning environments seem to foreclose on the possibility of doing exactly that. There seem to be few ropes for educators to grasp as a common reading of constructivism denies the stability of knowledge and thus leaves the door open to education's traditionally objectivist and anticonstructivist inclinations. In educational technology, I argue, we see this in the need to preauthenticate educational tasks and environments. In this chapter, I propose that the rhetorical tradition provides a framework that might be used to resolve the challenge constructivism poses to educators as it is a framework that emphasizes the explicitly dialogic nature of learning and accentuates the role of argument and persuasion. While we may put rhetoric to work in restructuring the challenge of authenticity to education without further ado, allow me first to put forward two prior and related points: first, that a pragmatic understanding of knowledge as the outcome of rational argument salvages sufficient foundations for education, and second, that because of this, rhetoric provides a coherent framework for the process of education that accommodates our constructivist principles.

A WORKABLE FOUNDATION FOR EDUCATION

Most humanistic and social scientific disciplines roughly come to the same conclusion: when called on to make our epistemological assumptions explicit, it makes little sense to speak of a foundation on which reality is firmly based, and as I repeatedly noted, the constructivist metatheory in various guises reflects this widespread skepticism. Antifoundationalist philosopher Tom Rockmore (1992), for instance, speaks of not wanting to drive yet another nail into the "foundationalist coffin." Although he insists that it is "not the case that the debate between foundationalism and antifoundationalism is over, that there is simply nothing further interesting to say, [nor] that proponents of the latter view have definitively vanquished their opponents," such sentiments sound like the gracious comments of a winner (p. 4). Foundationalism, in his view, cannot be resurrected, at least not in academic circles.

Still, many educators resist this antifoundationalist conclusion and wonder what purpose is served by a compass that only tells us we are lost regardless of the direction we turn (Seigfried, 1992). Even if we accept that the world is constructed by individuals drawing on socialized understandings and that the world is thus a product of both active construction and interpretative processes, educators nevertheless would want to improve on earlier interpretations and correct practices we considered unproductive. For this reason, I suggested at the end of the last chapter that a foundation-like basis that constructivists in education have discovered is that of the politics of learning and its ethical implications. Innovations in pedagogy can no longer be promoted solely on scientific grounds — they must be coupled with a demonstrated concern for fairness and equity as well as with the encouragement of greater participation from traditionally underrepresented or underserved groups. Adopting what might be called a kind of *ethical pragmatism*, we may be less bothered by issues of truth than we are by issues of participation and the belief that everyone (or at least every community) be given an equal opportunity to join in the conversation and be alloted a turn in establishing conventions. A quick glance through current education journals or conference programs makes it clear that education is seen as an important vehicle for political, economic, and social betterment — hardly a new view to be sure, but rarely as explicit and as central to the entire enterprise as it is presently. The constructivist's understanding that knowledge is not disinterested and supports certain ideological agendas has been interpreted by many to mean that education should openly embrace its political role and its pedagogies and technologies be put in service of dismantling inequalities. In this view, that which debunks hierarchical power structures is that which our knowledge should be designed to support.

While some educators have found the substitution of ethical foundations for epistemological ones appealing (see Downing, 1995; Rorty, 1979), others have not. Political conservatives have been most vocal in their attacks on the constructivist turn that is infused with a political agenda. Bloom (1987) for instance, is only one of the better known critics of what he sees as a leftist–deconstructivist conspiracy to overthrow the canon and promote a nihilistic relativism in which anything goes (ironically, precisely the situation that ethical pragmatism is designed to forestall). I would argue, however, that the explicit political agenda may not be seen as entirely satisfying for other reasons. First, there is the obvious point that radical pedagogy is not as intellectually cogent as some of its proponents (and critics) assume; we need not rehash the culture wars here to illustrate the point that political foundations within the academy are themselves unstable and not likely to firm up any time soon, if ever. More important, the observation that knowledge is political seems less like a blueprint for socially conscientious action than one that threatens to render the notion of ethical action meaningless. Concepts of justice are, after all, based on rational assessments of fairness—assessments that often avail themselves of not only reason, but of scientific support as well. For instance, Soper (1991) argues:

> It makes no sense to raise questions and problematize if one is unable or unwilling to offer solutions, just as it makes little sense to worry about access to computers in education if one has not rationally (and maybe even scientifically) determined that there is a strong correlation between computer access and educational opportunity. Why argue for networked environments if you are not willing to make a rational case for the positive benefits networking accrues? (p. 122)

But faith in reason, like the foundationalism to which it is so often yoked, has had a hard time of it over the course of the last quarter century. Many radical pedagogists and postmoderns across the academy have attacked rationalism as yet another interested system that creates and maintains hierarchical structures that ill-serve traditionally marginalized groups (Jarratt, 1995; Modleski, 1991). Crosswhite (1996) notes, for instance, that many postmodernists have repeatedly warned that modern rationality has an "imperialistic" tendency, and is an "agent in the annihilation of tribal peoples, local cultures, distinct traditions. . . . In situations of social conflict, it can force minorities out into a public forum dominated by audiences that do not value their differences" (p. 201). Feminist and identitarian (e.g., African American, postcolonial, "queer") theorists draw our attention to the social dominance of these audiences (usually composed of heterosexual White males) whose notion of reasonableness is presumed to count. Rowland (1995), for instance, cites Orr's (1989) view that cultural conceptions of rationality are overwhelmingly masculinist and Gilligan's claims that indirection and narrative, rather than deduction, are more naturally feminist forms of thinking that have been historically suppressed. Gearhart (1979) also argues that "rational discourse . . . turns out to be a subtle form of Might Makes Right" (p. 197). Rowland concludes that, for many postmoderns, "rational argument may be a code-phrase for a patriarchal communication style that devalues the roles played by women" (p. 353). Within the discipline of rhetoric as well, there has been a sense that the current revival of rhetoric not only deals a blow to science as an enterprise, but to rationality as well. In their introduction to *The Rhetorical Tradition*, Bizzell and Herzberg (1990) claim, "Scientific knowledge now appears to progress not by rational observation and the accumulation of facts, but by arguments" (p. 15).

Such statements, however, ignore the simple fact that arguments are rational and that science does rely on the accumulation of facts, even if facts are rhetorically constituted. Although the process of science is an essentially social, argumentative, and textual process, knowledge production also remains essentially rational. Habermas, Toulmin, and Burke, like practically every major contemporary rhetorician, are in essential agreement that both rhetoric and science are rooted in evidence, and, above all, reason. Reason dominated human experience long before the Age of Reason as it dominates in what some would have us believe is our post-Rational Age. Earlier in this century, Durkheim (1915) observed that it is pointless to question humankind's basic rationality; we cannot help but think in terms of causes and effects. We are not only bound to look for patterns in space and time, but also bound to make categories and classification systems that synthesize experience to render it knowable and understandable (cf. Lakoff, 1987). Of course, our pattern perceptions are often inaccurate, and reason also serves to point out the inadequacy of our tacit theories. Similarly, scientific method, the (again, imperfect) codification of rationality, contains within it the mechanisms for its own correction and recorrection. Gellner argues (1992) that unlike mystical traditions or in theocratic societies, "Rationalism is our [Western liberal] destiny. It is not our option, and still less our disease. We are not free of culture, of Custom and Example: but it is the essence of *our* culture that it is rooted in rationalist aspirations" (p. 159).

Although some postmodern critics warn of rationalism's coercive potential, proponents of a *rational pragmatic* approach counter that argument explicitly seeks agreement.[1] The many successes of feminist and other postmodern movements in the academy must be attributed to their success in arguing their case and bringing evidence to bear to support their worldview; in most cases, these successes have not been brought about by means of coercion. In Perelman and Olbrechts-Tyteca's (1969) words, "Recourse to argumentation assumes the establishment of a community of minds, which, while it lasts, excludes the use of violence" (p. 55). Even when physical violence is unlikely, Crosswhite (1996), Myerson (1994), and Scott (1977) remind us that the very idea of persuasion presumes that there is freedom of assent; assent as a result of coercion (which is certainly common) lies outside the realm of rational argument.

As Dewey taught us, experience guards against relativism and solipsism. While knowledge claims are always open to future testing, rational pragmatism

---

[1]Dewey, whom I would label a rational rather than ethical pragmatist, was, of course, politically engaged with the social change and unrest that characterized the growth of labor unions and urbanization, and accordingly, his articulation of pragmatism has a clear ethical dimension. Yet, Dewey remained committed to reason and viewed his own theories as very rational rather than, as Rorty labels them, merely "edifying" (cf. Prawat, 1995).

nonetheless keeps intact the basic constructionist observation that knowledge is ultimately validated socially rather than methodologically (cf. Diggins, 1994, p. 445). Whether it is a single proposition or a series of related statements, the aim of argument is to make an appeal to another's reason and gain that person's assent; a rhetorical appeal is at once affective and cognitive. Aristotle acknowledged that reasonable people could not content themselves with demonstrable fact. For him, rhetoric's chief charm lay in its ability to mediate probabilities in a reasoned fashion. As Perelman (1982) suggests, our concept of audience is dependent on an assumption of rationality—we do not seriously engage in discussions with those incapable or unwilling to be reasonable. Grice (1989) too, of course, has predicated the very definition of communication on a cooperative principle by which individuals agree to engage rationally. Obviously, cultural and physical circumstances have an enormous influence on what counts as rational (e.g., is a herdsman on the Altiplano being unreasonable when he argues for the flatness of the Earth?), and, of course, we may have intuitions and experiential understandings that evade reason's radar. But the essential point is that, unless we are attempting to achieve some aesthetic effect when we engage others in social intercourse, it is almost always on the basis of rational exchange.

To summarize my argument thus far, one common response to the anxiety produced by constructivism's epistemological instability has been to replace essentially epistemological foundations with essentially political and ethical ones. This has the effect of directing our attention away from the antifoundationalist threat and instead provides an ethical forum in which we can justify our constructivist pedagogy. Yet, the problem with such a substitution is that neither politics nor ethics are sufficiently stable from an educational perspective (or even from an ethical perspective for that matter) to be truly pragmatic. We must assume, commentators from Socrates to Said would concur, that our real worlds are sufficiently solid to permit rational exchange. A foundation in reasoned argument, by contrast, preserves the epistemological basis for learning by not rejecting the knowability of the world out of hand. This allows us to argue in the name of good reasons rather than "right thinking" and thus, privileges evidence over mere consensus and mere expedience. The ability to argue is based on our ability to share our worlds with others. We live in a rationalizable world, where we can (and do) engage others in reasonable discourse about practically every subject, including the limits of reason.

CONSTRUCTIVIST LEARNING
AS A RHETORICAL PROCESS

My purpose in restating and defending a rational variety of pragmatism is to make room for a rhetorical perspective on education. If we see knowledge making as the outcome of argumentative processes, we can appreciate education as an essentially rhetorical enterprise, for rhetoric is, in its deepest and most fundamental sense, the advocacy of realities. Accepting knowledge as a product of rational argumentation resolves what seems to be a perennially difficult issue in constructivist education as well as lays the groundwork for an expanded discussion of learning as a rhetorical process. As the study of argument, the discipline of rhetoric directs our gaze toward an issue that lies outside the constructivist dilemma: the ways in which we use sufficiently knowable symbols to impose order on a world that resists indisputable knowability. Rather than enter into the debates that have been ongoing since the birth of philosophy, rhetoric asks questions such as "what do people accept to be real, and why?" In short, rhetoric changes the subject.

The most thoughtful strain of the rhetorical tradition has always been concerned with understanding and conviction based on a knower's representation of the world and the problems that are to be confronted in it—not on eternal verities or powers of objectivity. This concern, accordingly, entails a focus on how the conscious and unconscious manipulation of symbols creates realities capable of commanding the allegiance of individuals and groups. Unlike efforts to ignore epistemological concerns or replace them with political ones, rhetoric suggests a foundation in the dynamics of mental representation and the community-dependent practices of persuasion. In this, Gergen (1985) makes rhetoric's affinities with constructivism clear:

> Constructionism offers no foundational rules of warrant and in this sense is relativistic. However, this does not mean that "anything goes." Because of the inherent dependency of knowledge systems on communities of shared intelligibility, scientific activity will always be governed in are measure by normative rules. . . . There is [therefore] stability of understanding without the stultification of foundationalism. (p. 273)

To this I would add that not only scientific activity, but education as well, can find stability within a rhetoric of *good reasons*—arguments that may vary among communities, but arguments that lend themselves to rational interrogation and falsifiability. Navigating between the Scylla of absolutism and the Charybdis of relativism does not ensure constructivist educators smooth sailing, but matching constructivism to an unflagging commitment to rationality (as good argument does) provides sufficient foundations for education without recourse to raw politics or preauthentication.

Rhetoric Old and New

To accept rhetoric as a framework worthy and capable of restructuring our thinking about education might require our conception of rhetoric to undergo some rehabilitation, especially if that conception is limited to the ways the word is batted about in colloquial as well as in some academic usage. The study of rhetoric, to those outside the discipline, often conjures up images ranging from bombast meant to divert attention from the truth and five-paragraph essays, to baroque excursions into marginalia. This is with good reason; in Chapter One, we saw rhetorical training in one of its most unflattering forms, that of declamation. Considering that pedagogical tradition, a contemporary observer can be forgiven for the impression that the study of rhetoric is rooted in trivialities, depends on a highly mannered aesthetic, and most important, is a variety of *techne* —a practicable and perfectable art—that enables one to be eloquent and persuasive. While declamation's days as the cornerstone of Western education are behind us, the study of rhetoric's entombment in techne continues in our own times, as seen in the composition and speech courses found at most American universities (Goggin, 1995). Though the contemporary composition field is more circumspect in making overt claims, the teaching of writing still presumes that students can be taught to communicate effectively irrespective of the actual situations in which it is used.

Although this technical face of rhetoric is still with us, rhetoric has undergone remarkable growth in scope and influence during this century. Just as the New Psychology gave rise to a significant discipline worthy of academic study, what is often called the New Rhetoric has rescued a potent classical study from centuries of trivialization and obscurity. Whereas early rhetorics and rhetoricians concentrated on lines of argument and their delivery, the New Rhetoric takes a much less localized view of persuasion and considers the broader cultural context in which argument takes place. If one had to identify one sense in which the New Rhetoric has really taken root, it is in a renewed sense of rhetoric's epistemic nature, a nature denied it by techne, but one suggested by the sophists millennia ago.

The exploration of rhetoric's epistemic powers has preoccupied rhetoric-related fields for the last quarter century, and Leff (1978) classifies perspectives on the knowledge-generating potential of rhetoric into four major groupings. The first acknowledges rhetoric's weakest claim to knowledge generation: its ability to create a place in an already accepted paradigm for a new particular. The second argues a stronger case for rhetoric's knowledge making capability in noting its role in establishing consensus to create a social knowledge that complements personal knowledge. The third perspective views rhetoric as establishing the knowledge necessary to mediate the limitations of formal logic, and the last notion of rhetoric being epistemic suggests that knowledge is rhetorical. It is this last view, argued forcefully in Scott's (1967) seminal "On Viewing Rhetoric as Epistemic," that basically parallels what we called social constructionism in the last chapter. In this article, he concludes that "insofar as we can say that there is truth in human affairs, it is in time; it can be the result of a process of interaction at a given moment. Thus rhetoric may be viewed not as a matter of giving effectiveness to truth but of creating truth" (p. 16). Less grand, but equally encompassing, is Crosswhite's (1996) assertion that rhetoric is the means by which all reasonable discourse, including academic discourse, is moderated. He suggests that the utility of rhetoric to education is not simply adjudicating among empirical and theoretical concerns, "Rather, [a pragmatist] conceives of rhetoric as the only viable way to explain the possiblity of reason itself" (p. 15). To call rhetoric the study of argument and persuasion thus delimits an enormous area of study. Modern rhetoricians now comfortably work in content areas that precedent and custom assigned to philosophy, linguistics, literature, and psychology.

Understood along the lines laid out by historian George Kennedy (1992), rhetoric has been transformed from a self-conscious art to a dimension inhering in both thought and language. A sense of rhetoric limited to techne sees its manifestation in utterance, in the sounds or symbols emitted to persuade another, but in Kennedy's words, "rhetoric, as energy, has to exist in the speaker before speech can take place. It is prior in biological evolution and prior psychologically in any specific instance" (p. 4). The phenomenological exigence that prompts discourse is itself an integral part of that discourse. To understand rhetoric in this sense, we may appropriate the *organic soup* metaphor employed by bioevolutionists. Prior to the electric charge that sets off the chemical reactions that result in the creation of life, the stuff of life exists. Similarly, the stuff of rhetoric (e.g., discourse conventions, lines of argument, genres, etc.) lies latent in the soup of consciousness, awaiting its rhetor and its audience. In this way, Kennedy suggests that we can separate the phenomena of rhetoric from the artifactual aspects generally associated with it—a first step toward extrapolating the study of rhetoric away from the study of symbols written on a page or uttered to an audience.

Another of Kennedy's observation is that rhetoric relies on selection and interpretation that is rarely conscious. Of course, this runs afoul of several rhetorical truisms centering on the notion that rhetoric is a practical and strategic art. Indeed, the idea of rhetoric as techne depends entirely on a notion of the rhetor's intended conveyance of meaning. Whereas rhetoric, in one sense, is just such an art, New Rhetoricians (like Vico and Nietzsche before them) suggest that rhetoric is also a dimension of language as intrinsic a part of communication as morphology and syntax. Because language functions symbolically and symbols have an indeterminate relationship to any objective meaning, the very nature of symbols suggests that any message can function persuasively, even if persuasion were not the sender's actual intention. As context imbues symbols with meaning, there is ample opportunity for persuasion to exist independent of persuasive intent. Rhetoric, in its modern avatar, can be seen as a natural extension of human symbolic interaction that may be said to effect changes, but whose effects may not be explicitly intentioned or known to the rhetor or the audience. While the purposefulness of communicative exchange is always present (in the same sense that verbal communication's syntax is always present), it may arise within the transaction between the rhetor and audience rather than in either's prior intention. Should I ask you to come in and have a seat, I may not be meaning any particular effect whereas you may take the invitation as strategic (that is to say, rhetorical) and may respond as such.[2]

For the educator, the value of Kennedy's theses lies in their explication of rhetoric and argumentation's naturalness and thus, rejection of the artifice with which rhetoric is usually associated. Just as we are comfortable with the image of an individual constructing his or her knowledge of the world without any conscious efforts or awareness of doing so (except in formal learning situations), Kennedy invites us to consider that as rhetorical beings we are engaged in the similar process of persuading and being persuaded often (though not always) without intention or motive other than the desire to function normally in our environment. This being said, however, just as education's purpose is to direct learners' metacognition in order that they exert some control over their thinking, many teachers of rhetoric seek to yoke language's natural persuasive potential to the speaker or writer's intentions. Subsequently, the idea of rhetoric in its modern sense signifies both an intrinsic dimension of language as well as the strategic intervention in that dimension.

Rhetoric and/as Constructivism

Although Shotter (1991) enlists rhetoric in a crusade "against cognitivism," I am much more struck by the similarities of the interests of cognitivists and rhetoricians and, with the advent of constructivist and situationist variations on cognitivism, their increasing convergence (p. 69). Whereas psychology approaches its domain from a social scientific framework and rhetoric usually works within a cultural–critical framework, the histories of both disciplines illustrate that each is capable of the other. Just as psychology was long a gentleman–scholar's speculative study, rhetoric has had several periods in which its professionals have sought to make it a science. In establishing our shared object of inquiry, the commonly misunderstood discipline of rhetoric may be demystified for cognitive scientists and educators, just as I would hope that readers coming from rhetoric-related fields may come to appreciate the essentially cognitivistic nature of their own interests.

To contribute yet another definition of rhetoric to the assortment that Plato, Aristotle, Bacon, and Nietzsche have proposed over the millenia, I propose that rhetoric is the symbol-mediated process through which we build and share representations, and representation is the principal site where rhetoric and constructivism are conjoined. Although a detailed cognitivist concept of representation is largely a product of the twentieth century, rhetoricians have always

---

[2]Burke's (1968) distinction between *motion* and *action* is one attempt to tease apart those behaviors that are simply biological from those that are rhetorically intentioned and indicative of greater cognitive complexity, much like Vygotsky's lower order and higher order functions.

been vitally concerned with the ways in which the mind creates an image of reality (cf. Enos, 1976). The sophist Gorgias would have been as comfortable as Newell and Simon (1972) in maintaining that "the behavior of the subject cannot depend on what the problem *really is* [italics added]—neither he nor we know that—but only on what the stimulus is" (p. 64). Thus, rhetoric and cognitivism share an essential focus on representation independent of objective reality. Cognitively speaking, one could say that the goal of every rhetor is one of encouraging a particular problem representation and a particular conception of reality in the mind of his or her audience. If the problem can be made identical for the two sides, theoretically, the solutions to disagreements will be much easier to identify (Cherwitz & Hikins, 1983) and misunderstanding may be remedied (Richards, 1936).

The idea that cognitivism and rhetoric share a common framework has been put forward most explicitly and in most detail by Michael Billig. The title of one of his most cited works, *Arguing and Thinking: A Rhetorical Approach to Social Psychology* (1987), hints at his very generative premise: the very nature of human cognition is rhetorical and argument works both intrapersonally as well as interpersonally. Billig quotes the Eleatic Stranger in Plato's *Sophist* as saying "thought and speech are the same; only the former, which is a silent inner conversation of the soul with itself, has been given the special name of thought" (p. 263E). In response, Billig (1993a) himself states, "Thinking is not merely the silent argument of the soul with itself, but, even more frequently, it is the noisier argument of one individual with another. And rhetoric, as the traditional study of the study and practice of argument, provides an entry to, and understanding of, thinking" (p. 121).

The constructivistic nature of rhetoric is further illustrated in a well-known disagreement between Lloyd Bitzer and Richard Vatz. Bitzer (1968) argues that a "rhetorical situation" is an external reality, or exigence, to which the rhetor responds. The exigence for rhetorical behavior, according to Bitzer, "come into existence because of some specific condition or situation that invites utterance" (p. 4). Conversely, Vatz (1973) argues as a radical constructivist would by insisting that situations are not "out there," that "no situation can have a nature independent of the perception of its interpreter . . ." and that the reality of a rhetorical situation is not objective but rather depends on the rhetor's desire and ability to create it (p. 154). The debate is later joined by Consigny (1974), who successfully puts the issue in perspective by distinguishing between those situational constraints which are pre-existing and those that require the rhetor to construct them for himself or herself before conveying them to the audience, echoing Aristotle's distinction between artistic and inartistic types of proof. Like Kennedy and Billig, Consigny argues that rhetoric is a constructive process, but is not wholly constructed by the individual rhetor; it must draw its material from a reality that exists prior to the rhetor's awareness of it (though at a prior level, of course, all agree that an understanding of this shared reality is also

socially constructed). Returning to the differences between Vygotskian and Piagetian constructivism that we noted in Chapter Two, we may see Consigny's
mediation of the Bitzer–Vatz debate as analogous to the constructivist metatheory's combination of those divergent stains of constructivist thought.

Within both rhetorical and constructivist frameworks, knowledge is produced by systems erected to serve human needs and curiosities in line with the
social and scientific practices that are validated by given communities at given
times. As such, knowledge and information heavily rely on interaction among
knowledge producers, knowledge consumers, knowledge consumers who reproduce that knowledge for others' consumption, and so on. This interaction is
largely discursive and knowledge is brought about through language via activities in which knowers participate. As in Vygotskian theories of activity, language serves as the most important tool we have at our disposal, for it is the
paramount means by which we come to know things and transform knowledge
into actions, objects, and other symbol systems. It is the means by which knowledge is created as well as the process by which knowledge is inculcated in others.
Both constructivism and rhetoric put forward the view that learning entails a deliberate and ongoing reordering of information that comes to us from every cor-
ner of our experience. Rhetoric and constructivism "happen" both in the head
and among them. For the rhetorician, as well as the constructivist, the real world
is always in play. It is always subject to negotiation, and its construction is an end
in itself as well as means to other ends. A rhetorical view of education is, therefore, inextricably bound up in questions of authenticity, and thus, like the constructivist view of education, the rhetorical view posits that *learning* is the name
we give the argumentative processes that transpires among teachers, students,
and their real worlds.

In short, constructive processes cannot be distinguished from rhetorical ones
by suggesting that the latter depend on artifice and intent while the former are
"just what people do." In the same way that I do not set out to construct meaning when witnessing an accident, neither do I intend to be rhetorical when I report that accident, though I have constructed my understanding of the accident,
and my report is, of course, rhetorical (Scott, 1977). In both cases, the underlying representational processes are masked by a belief that we are only seeing,
hearing, experiencing, saying, or writing the world as it really is. In this light,
we can appreciate argument as the quintessential constructive process. Arguments draw on prior experiences, prior reasoning frameworks, knowledge of
social conventions, and the gathering of relevant information to serve as evidence. Cognition is but an internalized variety of public deliberation for, as Billig succinctly suggests, thinking is arguing. The basically dialogic nature of
thinking has been a mainstay in sociohistoricism for a long time (witness Vygotsky's, 1981, observation that even "in their own private [mental] sphere, human
beings retain the functions of social interaction," p. 164). Thus, cognition, from
the educator's standpoint, is essentially the give and take of rhetorical exchange.

The Role of Affect in Cognition and Rhetoric

To the educator already familiar with the spirit as well as the letter of constructivism, it is reasonable to wonder whether a rhetoricized view of cognition offers anything new or if it merely rearticulates some vague constructivist gestalt. I would argue that in one very important way rhetoric extends our understanding of constructivist education: in its attention to affect and motivation. Such attention is sorely needed, for as Gardner (1985) writes, "Though mainstream cognitive scientists do not necessarily bear any animus again the affective realm, against the context that surrounds any action or thought, or against historical or cultural analysis, in practice they attempt to factor out these elements to the maximum extent possible. So even do anthropologists when wearing their cognitive science hats" (p. 41). Zajonc (1980) puts it even more bluntly: "Contemporary cognitive psychology simply ignores affect" (p. 152).

There is some irony in this. Many of the early cognitivist observations strongly implicated affect in every act of cognition, but were set aside and practically ignored as the information-processing tradition proved successful at producing the kinds of insights that cognitivists were primarily interested in, specifically, insights into well-structured problem solving. Zajonc argues that there were a number of forceful and influential emotivists within the cognitivist camp, so to now proclaim that cognitivists have finally discovered affect (as many in the social sciences are now doing) is somewhat misleading. Interest in affect was never lost, only misplaced. Returning to Bartlett's *Remembering* (1932), we see early constructivism's acceptance of the enormous, if shadowy, role that emotion plays in memory:

> A matter of very considerable importance, illustrated in all experiments involving repeated or successive response, is the fact that once a given specific reaction has been set up, it often seems to persist independently of a subject's conscious effort. . . . Both introspective evidence and the most careful observation of behavior agree in indicating that this persistence of a topic is largely due to the tendency of a mood, or attitude, once it is set up, to outlast its own initial determining conditions. Such a function of mood or of attitude may well have a close relation to the mechanism of remembering. (pp. 38–39)

The acknowledgment of affect notwithstanding, Spiro (1982) notes that Bartlett's notion of *attitude* was never clearly defined and remains practically the only aspect of his general theory that has not been resuscitated by contemporary research (p. 553). Spiro suggests four rationales for this neglect: first, affect is personal—it cannot be expressed to others with any precision. Second, even if they were not private, emotions would be poor models from which to extrapolate, as they are part of the broader gestalt of thinking. Third, it is generally assumed that affect is the result of cognition rather than the cause. And finally, affect cannot be analyzed empirically.

Although rhetoric's appreciation for the affective dimension of thinking has a long and complicated history, it too has tried to hold affect at arm's length. This may be due to the fact that rhetoric's oldest manifestation, the sophistic tradition, was chiefly renowned and reviled by philosophers for its ability to rally the hearer's passions in support of its practitioners. Although most rhetorical theorists have rarely been comfortable with the importance of affect in shaping argument, they have never successfully denied the centrality of emotion to the practice of being rhetorical while psychologists have traditionally succeeded in excising affect from cognition. Gorgias, like his sophistic contemporaries, recognized the generative power of symbol manipulation in conjunction with the power of emotions to create the world. With the advent of Aristotle's labeling of pathetic appeals as a variety of artistic proof and continuing through Bacon, Blair, and Whately, theories of argument and persuasion have always acknowledged the importance of emotion to persuasion and understanding. In our own century, one could easily argue that no less than its epistemic powers, renewed appreciation for the pervasive role of affect in social interaction characterizes the New Rhetoric.

Relative to other fields of inquiry, rhetoric's uneven appreciation of affect nonetheless stands out. However satisfying the constructivist turn in psychology might be, the affective dimension of thinking and representation continues to go largely ignored. The attitudes and feelings that most clearly mark what we might call *rhetorical cognition,* are largely absent from the broader movement to observe thinking in context even though, as many social psychologists will attest, "our interactions with the environment are colored by our emotions, because emotions guide attention, they make memory possible, and give an affective color to what is remembered" (Warburton, 1988, p. 196). This may be due, in part, to the fact that constructivists continue to sidestep investigation into cognition that unfolds as part of a communicative transaction. Consider the nature of many of the problems on which many modern constructivists have focused: finding dictionary definitions (Gildea, Miller, & Wurtenberg, 1990), solving math puzzles (Schoenfeld, 1985), and applying mathematical principles to a variety of new problems (CTGV, 1990).[3] What these sorts of tasks have in common is their situated but noncommunicative nature. That is, the individuals under study are observed doing their situated thinking on topics and in contexts that can be characterized as minimally transactive. Although we can accept that most cognitions are, at some level, socially informed, not all cognitions involve the strategic use of discourse. Whereas (to use Lave's, 1988, well-known example) a dieter's informal method of dividing cottage cheese into correct portions is naturally situated within a certain social context, communicating one's method of dividing cottage cheese is socially situated in an entirely different way.

---

[3]I am not claiming that interpersonal transaction is never the subject of research in situated cognition, but it seems clear that the most paradigmatic research in the area has focused on informal problem solving performed individually.

And so while investigators of cheese division and dictionary usage may be able to bracket issues of transactionality, rhetoric extends the situationist framework by re-emphasizing the affective dimension of social thought.[4] In any rhetorical transaction, feelings and thoughts spark and sustain one another, working together to problem solve in the broadest sense of that term. A footnote in Chapter Two noted what I consider to be a striking similarity between the models of activity proposed by Leontiev and refined by Engeström and others, and what rhetorician Kenneth Burke referred to as the dramatistic pentad. Each of these models tacitly guard against essentialization (Burke warns against being "rotten with perfection") and emphasizes that an individual's comprehension is sustained by and sustains ongoing social engagement largely mediated by symbolic action. Yet, what Burke, as well as Vygotsky, left undeveloped in their theory (and both regretted) is the importance of how feelings for others and their arguments contribute to understanding.

To conclude this section, I am reminded of the often-cited adage that rhetoric is "the adaptation of people to ideas and of ideas to people." I propose that constructivism provides us with good reasons for conceiving of education in precisely the same manner. Closely allying rhetorical and constructivist frameworks (and perhaps going so far as to label the rhetorical tradition as a direct precursor of the present constructivist metatheory) offloads much of the necessity for arguing that rhetoric has a natural affinity for education. The rhetorician would approve of Lincoln and Guba's reformulation of inquiry (1985) in which they suggest that we pose the questions, "How can an inquirer persuade his other audiences (including self) that the findings of an inquiry are worth paying attention to, worth taking account of? What arguments can be mounted, what criteria invoked, what questions asked, that would be persuasive on this issue?" (p. 290). Researchers presenting findings to an unknowing audience, as well as teachers offering instruction to novice learners, may count these among the most pertinent questions they can ask.

From a rhetorical perspective, authenticity is a judgment rather than a characteristic inhering in a learning situation, and thus an outcome of a decision-making process. The special contribution rhetoric adds to the basic constructivist position lies first in the metaphor of education as argument (which addresses constructivism's epistemological difficulties) and then in the attention rhetoric pays to the affective dimension of learning. In sum, judging something to be authentic entails an intricate balancing of knowledge and belief. In the case of judgment at the behest of another (as in the classroom interaction of a teacher and student), we can consider this process to be a variety of argument, and thus,

---

[4]Of course, feelings motivate all thinking. The point I wish to make here is that given rhetoric's not only social, but transactive nature, it seems logical that the level of arousal and affective engagement is relatively higher in rhetorical, as opposed to nonrhetorical, cognition. Thus, rhetorical cognition is not uniquely affective, but especially so.

a process that lies in the realm of the rhetorical. Accordingly, we may be persuaded to forsake or modify our present reality in favor of another and thereby
do what may be validated as "learning." A corollary, however, is that under-
going a change in convictions rarely arises as a sole result of being told to
change; like the lightbulb in the joke about the number of psychiatrists it takes to
change one, a learner has to want to change.

CONCLUSION

With the advent of constructivism and situationism in psychology and the
resurgence of what we now call the New Rhetoric, the objects of rhetorical and
cognitive analysis have become less distinguishable. Both have put the emphasis
on thinking and argumentation as the result of experience, actions, prior understandings, and the individual's cultural, economic, and social situation. Both are
premised on the individual's active construction of knowledge and his or her
perceptions of the world.[5] Although rhetoric remains the study of argument and
persuasion, we now appreciate that constructivism is equally rooted in social
interaction and the individual's capacity for drawing on evidence to impose co-
herence on a jumble of perceptions that have no direct relationship to the external world.

For example, in the earlier part of this book the rhetorical task before me was
to create in the reader's mind a sense that authenticity was an objective of education and educational technology deserving serious investigation. While I
thought the evidence available to me was ample, I doubt most readers had taken
talk of authenticity so seriously. Thus, I needed to create a sense of the topic's
significance in the mind of the reader and used a variety of data, theoretical
frameworks, and lines of reasoning to invite the reader to share my understanding. As rhetoricians are fond of saying, the facts do not speak for themselves and
so, I was required to speak for them. This is analogous, I believe, to the position
of educators who have to convince a learner that the educational task he or she is
being asked to perform can be made to meaningfully correspond to that student's real world.

Of course, rhetorical and cognitive processes are not identical—to speak of
them in such a way requires a vantage point so distant and a grain size so large

---

[5]There are many fine works that deal much more extensively with the role of rhetoric and argumentation in education than I have here. James Crosswhite's (1996) book *The Rhetoric of Reason*, which I have already cited, is perhaps the most recent and one of the best such works, although
many regard the Toulmin's *The Uses of Argument* (1958) and Perelman and Olbrecht-Tyteca's
(1969) *The New Rhetoric* as seminal. In the next chapter, I draw on these works and others to emphasize key elements of constructivism that are elided in education's appropriation of that perspective, but I encourage readers interested in a fuller rhetoricization of education to look to these
other sources.

that we risk saying nothing at all. By framing education as argumentation, however, a rhetorical perspective directs our attention toward the gathering of information and evidence, the arrangement of informational inputs in some readily accessible way, the application of reason to the construction of claims, the association and disassociation of different claims, and the exercise of judgment concerning what action to take, always with the needs of a particular audience in mind. Framing a constructivistic view of education as a rhetorical challenge makes constructive processes less abstract and metaphorical and more amenable to useful intervention. More important, perhaps, it squarely acknowledges the epistemological entailments of constructivist educational theory and thus, as I see it, gives constructivism an integrity that our common fall-back position—preauthentication—is incapable of providing.

Unless the teacher can figure out how and why students arrive at the answers or solutions they do, there is little chance that he or she can productively engage or modify their conceptual structures. Within the objectivist–transmission framework, this engagement was simplified by the assumption that a student's unsatisfactory performance is solely due to error or misrepresentation. While behaviorists have shown us that psychological cattle prods can indeed alter behaviors, there is little to suggest that negative reinforcement benefits one's cognitive appraisal in any intended way, leaving us, again, with the rhetorical option: getting the student to understand and appreciate the correspondence of our pedagogy to their prior understanding of the world and to appeal to their future understanding. As long as brain swapping remains within the realm of science fiction, the process of argumentation affords educators the surest means by which to have our student–audience reflect on problems in the manner we think they should and provides students the means by which knowledge is, in Piagetian terms, assimilated and accommodated. Most educators would agree with von Glasersfeld's (1995) conclusion that constructivism means we need to take seriously the truism that "to solve a problem intelligently, one must see it as one's own problem" (p. 14). I would only add that argument is the means of intervention by which others are made to see what one would have them see.

SIX

Negotiating the Real World: Conceptual Obstacles and Opportunities for Education

> *. . . activities of knowledge production (e.g., science) and reproduction (e.g., education) are about convincing, recruiting and enculturating others. In short a constructivist analysis of knowledge foregrounds rhetoric: the powers of persuasion and the difficulties of dispute.*
> —SACK, SOLOWAY, AND WEINGRAD (1992, p. 357)

TVERSKY AND KAHNEMAN'S (1984, 1986) research on *framing effects* calls attention to the everyday phenomenon whereby the same data, expressed differently, leads to a new appreciation of a problem. This chapter's objective is to elaborate on the disciplinary framing effect I introduced in the previous chapter and prompt a new understanding of the problem of authentic learning by shifting between the language of constructivism and that of rhetoric and persuasion. If we revisit constructivism in educational technology armed with an appreciation of the role rhetoric and argumentation play, the challenge of authenticating learning becomes transformed from that of presenting the learner with new and improved "reality kits" to that of persuading learners that the problems with which they are presented correspond in some important way to their own sense of how the real world works. In this light, the constructivist view of education looks very different. But not only different; a rhetorical view can actually make the issue of authenticity "smaller." Applying rhetoric as an Occam's razor, we find that authenticity is more rightfully confined to particular domains, certain topics within domains, and to certain learners.

ISSUES CONSTRAINING CONSTRUCTIVISM

Approaching constructivist learning as a rhetorical, rather than material, challenge invites us to return to the literatures of education and educational technology with an eye toward a number of subtopics and subissues that flow into, or from, the metaproblem of preauthentication. The topics I briefly address below suggest the scope of a rhetorical critique of constructivism as currently embodied in educational practices and technological developments.

The Rockwellian Learner

As we saw in Chapter Two, the limitations of the information-processing tradition in psychology for the purposes of education have been amply documented and commented on. Perhaps foremost among these is the model of the learner that it supposes. Given the epistemological commitments of social science discussed earlier, it is not surprising that Billig (1987) notes that psychology's traditional model "tends to separate the individual from the argumentative or rhetorical context" (p. 119). Information processing's focus on well-structured problems and its under elaborated acknowledgment of the ill structuredness of everyday situations erected and reinforced a model of the learner as a kind of automaton that moved with great efficiency through problem spaces toward clearly identifiable solutions or at least a finite set of possible alternatives. Gergen (1995) refers to a similarly idealized cogitator as the *mechanical self*, while Porter (1994) uses the term *calculating self*. In the field of educational technology, Sack, Soloway, and Weingrad (1992) label this learner model *Cartesian* and they argue that this model was an integral part of the earlier objectivist frameworks for instructional design.

In contrast, a rhetoricized conception of education gives pride of place to a learner or group of learners who may not be quite as efficiency-oriented as we would like. The student as *audience*, a rhetorician would contend, is less a passive sounding board for the educator's lecture, than an active interlocutor who is fully capable of evaluating claims, assessing evidence, and posing rebuttals. Of course, one could easily argue, as many have, that the least contentious tenet of the constructivist metatheory also emphasizes the activeness of the learner, leading one to wonder if a rhetorical framework expands on a constructivism's rejection of the Cartesian learner model in any original way. In theory, one would have to admit that the differences are few. Constructivists drawing inspiration from Vygotsky and Dewey have always argued that learners must be active participants in the learning process for they are the only ones who experience the activities that provide the grist for construction. Acknowledgment of the essentially active nature of learning is also seen in references to empowerment, student centeredness, and participatory education. For instance, Bereiter and Scardamalia's (1989) rationale for promoting their notion of intentional learning is that "to the extent that students take an active role in learning, their own theories of what knowledge consists of and how it is acquired can be expected to matter" (p. 367).

Such claims notwithstanding, just as preauthenticatory practices imply a particular view of the world's knowability, they tacitly recommend a model of the learner that is just as uncomplicated, inexperienced, and complacent as the learner had been in the instructional design paradigm. In contravention of constructivism's theoretical commitments to the contrary, an idealized learner model remains very much with us. Statements such as the following illustrate the subtlety of this:

> Students need to come to view the skills of GBS [Goal-Based Scenarios] as capacities that will empower them to achieve a valued class of goal previously beyond their reach. . . . It is not enough, however, to simply assure students that these skills will enable them the achieve desirable goals. They will need to be given the chance to actually do so. (Schank, Fano, Bell, & Jona, 1994)

Here we see the presumption that students have desired goals in domain X (coincidentally, the domain we are intent on teaching), authorizing us to empower them to do the sort of learning they really want to do. This is important, for in helping them do what they really want, our good intentions are given wide berth. Whereas the transmission model of education simpy ignored the student's wishes, current constructivist practices often co-opt them. If, as Winn (1993a) suggests, the cognitively stable learner lies at the heart of the earlier instructional design paradigm, the model of a learner who is cleansed of inappropriate attitudes and motivations lies at the heart of education generally. To these Cartesian–mechanical–calculating characterizations of the learner, I wish to add another that makes allusion to the American portraitist: the *Rockwellian* learner model. Such a learner is not merely predisposed to efficiency and logic, but is affectively compliant with the educator's desires. Central to the Rockwellian model is the somewhat sentimental presumption that students are fairly bursting with enthusiasm to learn if only we would let them. While constructivists' efforts to deal with the Cartesian learner try to account for variance in domain knowledge, skills, and even personality types (cf. Gegg-Harrison, 1992; Shute, 1993), they rarely address the Rockwellian learner, who may have motivations other than those presumed by the educator.

Constructivism, no less than the information-processing paradigm it has largely replaced, often directs our attention away from issues such as motivation. Csikszentmihalyi (1990) observes that, in hopes of discovering more and more cognitively elegant ways of presenting information, we continue to devote the greater part of our energies developing approaches to learning that emphasize clarity and increased structure, for "the implicit hope is that if we discover more and more rational ways of selecting, organizing, and conveying knowledge, children will learn more effectively" (p. 115). Yet, he counters, it seems increasingly clear that a task's structural difficulty is not the fundamental impediment; "It is not that students cannot learn; it is that they do not wish to" (p. 115). He cites numerous research findings suggesting that students' often dismal performances could not possibly be due to the tasks' cognitive complexity.[1] Unlike most students we meet in our real-world classrooms, the Rockwellian learner learns from educational technologies because he or she has come to the environment eager to learn. Any gaps in this primary motivation are remedied by the interactivity, hypertextuality, and opportunities to collaborate that make problem solving real and shore up any flagging enthusiasm to learn, as enthusiasm is assumed to be the learner's natural state.

From a rhetorical perspective, however, the persistent claim that authenticity is what motivates students to learn requires qualification. A rhetorical perspective asks us to further consider whether, by preauthenticating learner-directed opportunities for students to design their own tasks, we are making learning comfortable rather than authentic. Whereas the expectation that students will participate in their own learning is easy to subscribe to, there is always the fear of having students circumvent, rather than creatively meet, the challenges put before them. We continue in the tradition of the Rockwellian Learner model if we believe that students, left to their own devices, would choose those options and opportunities that made learning most relevant. Not only does this place an enormous burden on the learner's goodwill, but it also presupposes that the learner is sufficiently mature, knowledgeable about the ways and means of education, and has an appreciation of learning's possible outcomes. Clearly, such presumptions are unwarranted and play into either a naive or cynical rhetoric of empowerment. Genuinely student-centered theories of learning distinguish between a pedagogy which responds to a learner's real world, and one that seeks to accommodate the learners' comfort level.

In other words, a rhetorician may observe that technologists often design environments for what Perelman (1982) calls the *universal audience*—that "reasonable and competent" audience to which we direct our ideal arguments. This is rooted in the assumption that rationality is universal and needs no audience. Yet Perelman reminds us that while the universal audience has its uses, it is only a fiction that serves as a heuristic in helping us define our *particular audience*—those living, breathing, alternately reasoning, and alternately competent audiences that we actually encounter in the real world and who would never do as the subject for a *Saturday Evening Post* cover. Rockwellian learners need not be treated as an audience to be persuaded, but as a confused lot that needs to be set right. Constructivism is the theory of learning that has the potential to explode this myth (certainly, the theory has been set out to do exactly that), but in treating authenticity as an educator-given attribute, constructivist educators betray the objectivist assumptions from which we claim to have moved. Preauthentication encourages us to cast a suspicious eye on some educators' claims of student centeredness as well as to consider the quality of that centeredness, for many

---

[1] One example Csikszentmihalyi provides is that 94% of U.S. high-school juniors could not answer questions such as "Christine borrowed $850 for one year from the Friendly Finance Company. If she paid 12% simple interest on the loan, what was the total amount she repaid?"

current technological and pedagogical responses to constructivist theory suggest that students may only be "free" to problem solve as we think they should.

The Issue of Age

In determining whether a situation might rightfully be called "rhetorical," Bitzer (1968) would have us ask, "Who is the audience?" as the appropriateness of the audience is built into its very definition; an inappropriate audience is no audience at all. So, who is an appropriate audience for appeals to authenticity? The question is rarely considered in the literatures of education and educational technology, for the Rockwellian learner model at work in them naturally precludes consideration of the audience's composition. This is seen most clearly, perhaps, in the widespread lack of interest in how or whether age plays any role in authenticating learning, despite the fact that educators from Isocrates to Whitehead have consistently maintained that practically every aspect of education requires modification when applied to students at particular stages in their intellectual development. On those rare occasions when the issue of age is dealt with directly, it is usually to caution the educator that the complexity of preauthenticated pedagogy needs to be adjusted according to the learner's level of expertise (cf. Bednar et al., 1992, p. 26).

In contrast, turning a rhetorical lens to constructivist education suggests that authenticity, like youth, is wasted on the young. In the design of learning environments for young children, the issue of authenticity may be less pressing, as the environment cannot appeal to a cogent sense of the real world because, naturally, young children have a highly malleable sense of, and less of a stake in, what the real world might be. In other words, authenticity's motivational charms may not appeal to people with no immediate intention of getting on in the world. Ironically, the nexus of age or developmental stage and authenticity is one that may be especially difficult for constructivists to tease apart precisely because so much of the sociohistorical and early constructivist research into contextualization used children as the target population. As those theorists had noted, play is vital to early cognitive development, and in such play situations the issue of authenticity per se does not even arise. Thus, even though the youngest learner constructs meaning, children's constructive processes are relatively more amenable to "correction" and less susceptible to arguments for a task's authenticity.

To come at this same point from a very different direction, we might remember that elite-idealist educators since Plato have argued that students are best prepared for a proper education when they are at their least experienced—experience has traditionally been seen as sullying rational thinking for too much context gets in the way of keeping a clear-head. Accordingly, the young and pure of mind are best equipped to engage in the pursuit of truth with the prerequisite freedom from expectations. Perelman and Olbrecht-Tyteca (1969) contend that when the educator "is made responsible for instilling the values of a given society into really young children, the educator must proceed by means of affirmations, without entering into a discussion in which the pros and cons are freely debated. To do so would be contrary to the very spirit of primary education, as all discussion presupposes adherence at the outset to certain theses, failing which no argument is possible" (p. 54). Children do not make particularly skilled interlocutors for even as they are in the process of constructing their real worlds, they are inexperienced in the kind of active dialogism argument presumes. As we mature and acquire a repertoire of messy experience, elite-idealists believe, we become less suited to formal reasoning and more eager to problematize tasks and problem formulations. While, in theory, constructivist educators eagerly acknowledge a learner's prior experience, a rhetorician may caution that at some point children attain sufficient experience to reject educators' arguments for a task's authenticity.

Perkins (1992) also believes the interaction of authenticity with age merits extensive consideration, for buying into a technological environment is critical to its success. To quote him at length:

> Whatever the challenges of cognitive complexity and task management, a rather different kind of challenge concerns learners' attitudes towards the enterprise. When learners are asked to thrash around for themselves to some extent, there are often characteristic reactions such as "Why don't you just tell me what you want me to know?" Such learners are not "buying in" to the constructivist agenda of the instruction, a problem that inevitably stands in the way of a fully engaged learning experience. An ardent constructivist might naturally respond "Well, buying into this sort of thing is part of what they're supposed to learn. They'll come around."
>
> However heartfelt, I am not sure that such a response is entirely reasonable. From the learners' perspective, they are being asked to jump through hoops to discover X for themselves when they could, they think, straightforwardly be told X with some practice to follow to get used to doing things with X. . . . This is a lot to ask. (pp. 163–164)

A lot, indeed. While the educator might find such a Pascalian wager reasonably attractive (i.e., "Trust me when I say that this learning experience will be valuable. If I am correct, you'll be glad you followed my advice, if I am not, no matter, you have not lost anything by playing the belief game"), I think it is only prudent to assume that most students do not give us such benefits of such doubts. Certainly, very young learners may be willing to suspend disbelief in their faith that teacher knows best, but it would be unreasonable to expect such Rockwellian good naturedness among older students. One suspects that most fifteen-year-olds have a keenly developed sense of the bogus—the adult party line against which they recognize and define their own reality. Most things that matter and many things that are "true" come under renegotiation by adolescents who are beginning to understand the interestedness of knowledge claims and beginning to understand that different lessons on the same topic can teach very different, even contradictory, things (cf. Perry, 1970). This critical posture may be especially true of young people in the late twentieth century who are raised on a postmodern diet of savvy and cynicism and such a posture cannot be ignored when we argue for authenticity in education.

Implicating the Educator

If we could conjure up a mental image of a construct like "the education process," we might imagine it as something done to a student, for the ultimate objective of any educational system is to effect change in the novice and this naturally directs our view toward the student. Similarly, a troublesome feature of the preauthenticating practices underlying much constructivist education is the fact that those doing the preauthenticating excuse themselves from the scene, hovering (angel-like) over the learner and learning environment, somehow apart from the cognitive dynamics transpiring below. In a certain sense, constructivism's rhetoric of student-centeredness reinforces this absence by rationalizing the educator's removal from the scene, even while the educator remains in charge.

One is hard pressed to find much analysis in the cognitivist literature in education that actively casts educators and administrators as central actors in learning activities.[2] In this, education reflects its roots in a scientific metatheory, for science also seeks to exempt itself from the forces that operate on the phenomenon under study, and the "view from nowhere" is widely upheld as the scientific ideal. Even in social psychology, Danziger (1990) suggests that conceptualizations of social processes are largely restricted to externally verifiable social psychological phenomenon—that is, the way a social situation influences a given subject's cognitive assessment or response to a stimulus) rather than in the sociological context within which both the experimenter and subject play roles. In this way, the idea that the experimenter is exempted from the constructivist forces that apply to others is consistently maintained.

While the metaphor of *education as argument* points out the importance of genuinely appreciating the learner's attitudes toward the educational environment, it also asks us to consider the other party—the educator. We are less likely to conjure an image of "argument" as narrowly focused on the interlocutor, for the transactive nature of argument forcefully signals that the arguer is at least as much of the process as the person toward whom the argument is directed (especially as the roles of arguer and audience are constantly in flux). If learning is argumentative and thus dialogic, the rhetorical perspective suggests that we

---

[2]An important caveat here is that the more social constructionist tradition within education (e.g., Deweyan and Freirian thought in particular) does, in fact, manifest an interest in collective consciousness and collective agency, though in the view of that tradition's critics, this is often to the detriment of individual learners.

cannot ignore the constructive processes of the teacher. For many of the same reasons that naturalistic research methods have relied on participant observation, a rhetorical perspective on education asks educators and technologists to accept the importance of their own assumptions and meaning-making practices, for as task setters, informational resources, and arbiters of performance, teacher cognition has an enormous impact on student learning (a topic to which we will return).

The Social Construction of the Expert

One of the ways in which the educator is deeply implicated in a learner's cognition is in applying criteria to evaluate student performance, raising another issue that could stand a bit of rhetoricizing—that of expertise. As with the Rockwellian learner model, constructivists who preauthenticate learning share with information processing cognitivists a faith in a static notion of expertise, for the expert provides a touchstone against which educational success can be determined. Rhetorical theory, however, highlights the notion that experts (especially in ill-structured domains) are only contingently bestowed with that title. In recognizing that expert performance is rhetorically constructed at various times for various reasons, educators are reminded that authentic assessment—a critical subject in many education-based literatures—is entirely dependent on the norms of, and consensus among, evaluators. New ripples, trends, tastes, and politics can quickly dethrone experts and replace them with individuals whose performance was previously considered highly inexpert. To use the field of writing as an example, the accomplished student writer of twenty years ago (when what is called the current-traditional paradigm was ascendant) is hardly the exemplary writer of the 1990s. In fact, our current model of expert writing tacitly identifies this earlier expertise as a particularly grievous variety of novice performance.

Thus, while expertise has been operationalized to mean an ability possessed by someone that has done something successfully for a number of years (cf. Hayes, 1985), success at performing a task may tell us at least as much about the social and cultural environment in which success is defined as it does about the cognitive abilities of the putative expert. Gergen (1995) notes that issues of expertise and authority are fairly transparent in transmission models of education and in objectivist epistemological frameworks; experience and experiments are gathered into a body of knowledge, and those who have mastered this information are called authorities. In a constructivist framework, however, "authority does not reside within an individual. . . . Rather, authority is socially accorded, and within most academic spheres it is typically given to those occupying a given discursive position" (p. 30). Naturally, a rhetorician would also point to the important performative dimension of expertise. The status of expert is not necessarily granted to one that knows a content in any objective sense, but is a status granted to the person that possesses the means (and has access to the discursive fora) in which to *perform* knowledge—that is, to write reports, deliver lectures, grant interviews, and so forth.

Although Plato's (1987) character (and sophistic caricature) Gorgias brags that the expert rhetor possesses a power that surpasses that possessed by others ("by virtue of this power, you will have the doctor as your slave, and the trainer as your slave; your money-getter will turn out to be making money not for himself, but for you, who are able to speak and persuade the multitude" [p. 9]), we discern within that boast a germ of truth; expert status is accorded those who can persuade others of his or her expertise. Although one may be an "objectively" expert chess player or mathematical problem solver (i.e., the expert chess player wins a lot and the expert problem solver gets the right answer elegantly and predictably), who is a transcendently expert teacher, manager, psychologist, economist, or writer? For the educator interested in inculcating expertise on the part of our students, the rhetorical view on authenticity would ask that we attend not only our students' ability to demonstrate their understanding of information in traditional ways (e.g., in formal examination), but that we also consider their ability to articulate this understanding and share it with others effectively and convincingly.

Variance in Information Types and Teaching Objectives

Any student of linguistics may recognize my own graduate student experience that, whenever an example was sought to illustrate a "universal" linguistic principle, the professor (after a thoughtful pause) seemed to invariably decide that "let's take . . . oh . . . *English* as an example." Obviously, English is a perfectly good language, but it is hardly paradigmatic, no language is. While English may suit to illustrate the point the professor wishes to make, it is possible, even likely, that the universal principle is, in fact, not universal at all. Similarly, examples of authentic learning proffered by educators and educational technologists are often taken from the domain of, "let's take . . . oh . . . *math*"—or physics, or chemistry. Learning the periodic table, or how to plot the trajectories of objects of a given weight traveling at a given speed or to calculate square roots, are the kinds of learning that educators are fond of authenticating.[3] With few exceptions (the GBS used in *Broadcast News* might be one) the archetypal examples of authentic learning are well-structured problems to which correct answers are possible and empirically verifiable. With even fewer exceptions, discussions of authenticity in educational technology elide the issue of problem type completely.

A rhetorical response to this might be twofold. First, and most obvious, there

---

[3]In Vanlehn and Ohlsson's (1994) lengthy list of AI systems developed to simulate human learning, we can observe that the domains are entirely related to the physical sciences or mathematics. This is interesting, in part, because the conflation of human learning with asocial, well-structured problem solving goes unremarked.

is a sizable chunk of most domains that attenuates much of constructivism's (and rhetoric's) applicability. Greater attention needs to be paid to the question of what sorts of tasks in what kinds of domains are open to arguments for authenticity. The second response is to remind us that educators may have reasons for not wishing to embed their lessons in real-world contexts and that authenticity, in some cases, may conflict with other pedagogical objectives.

Looking more closely at this first point, a rhetorical framework suggests that we should avoid clinging too tenaciously to the trope of authenticity or real-world problem solving with little regard for whether the problem at hand lends itself to authentication. As Anderson et al. (1996) put it, "how tightly learning will be bound to context depends on the kind of knowledge being acquired" (p. 6). For instance, a constructivist math professor may insist that teaching the idea of compounding is best facilitated by embedding it in a word problem using real-world contexts such as paying a mortgage. In this case, the appeal to authenticity is not only mundane but perhaps unnecessary. As with the false cognate of component skill isomorphism discussed in Chapter One, the principles of compounding may benefit from their stipulated contextualization, but this does not require correspondence to the real world in any significant sense.

Rhetoric has a useful tradition of classifying types of problems and content domains. For instance, in *The Uses of Argument*, Toulmin (1958) distinguishes between *analytic* and *substantial* arguments in much the same way that Aristotle introduced his treatise on rhetoric with a distinction between arguments whose topics permit them to progress logically (or dialectically) and those whose topics can only be dealt with probabilistically (that is to say, rhetorically). Similarly, Burke's notion of *recalcitrance* also seeks to distinguish among domain types on the basis of their amenability to rhetorical manipulation. In Burke's view, the harder (more recalcitrant) the domain area, the less amenable that domain will be to explanations that ignore the physical givens. Even if we wish to argue that these givens are rhetorically expressed, as we should, Burke wants us to understand that physics is not as rhetorical (or rhetorical in the same way) as sociology, that there is greater recalcitrance in chemistry than there is in economics, and so forth.

So to return to a point made early in the first chapter of this book, concern for the authenticity of learning applies only to some types of information. In many areas outside the humanities, the real is not as closely tied to the social; most sciences, in fact, only count information as knowledge if it is demonstrably not governed by social convention (Cobb, 1994a). Three quarters of a century ago, for instance, Mannheim insisted that only mathematics and physics could avoid society's creative forces, echoing Aristotle's earlier division of the sciences in which dialectic was considered best suited for formal situations that do not rely on contingencies and probability. What we call hard sciences are defined as such largely because a relatively greater proportion of the knowledge they produce cannot be easily attributed to cultural consensus.

Given the variation among domains, the rhetorician would advise the educator to consider the nature of the knowledge to be taught when proposing to inject authenticity into the classroom. When thinking about what counts as real-world contextualization, we need to consider whether the well structuredness of the problem obviates the need for appeals to authenticity. Most of us would agree that certain physical and formal systems (e.g., those commonly studied in physics or chemistry) lend themselves to social decontextualization much better than do sociology, economics, or history. Salomon and Perkins (1989) allude to this in their reference to *low-road transferability* of information such as tables, formal procedures, and other information and problems that lend themselves to "simple" transfer. The issue of creating authentic learning environments, one suspects, is not as pressing in these more formal knowledge domains as it would be in a domain requiring skills of critique and construction of plausible interpretations. In sum, not all tasks are as dependent on social negotiation as are others and thus, cannot be expected to be influenced by rhetorical claims of authenticity.

This being said, well-structured problem solving can, no doubt, benefit by its embedding in life-like situations as long as we remember that the world of school has a reality that may have little to do with the world outside of school (which, again, is not to say that task such as the mortgage compounding problem cannot benefit from being embedded in a narrative context). For instance, if solving a particular math equation is important to a learner for whatever reason, he or she will presumably be motivated to solve it. The authenticity of the problem would have little role to play in any of this—whether the student saw the problem as having extracurricular transferability or as being embedded in a realistic context is overridden by the student's desire to do well on the quiz or learn enough to move on to the next chapter. By this same token, could we not content ourselves to speak of this problem as an authentic school problem?

Continuing on to my second point, however, it is also worth considering whether authenticity accommodates every sort of pedagogical objective. Although authenticity has become something of a mantra for educators seeking to engage learners, there is much students can learn by engaging in environments and tasks without pretense to genuineness. In fact, there are domains, such as applied ethics, where it has been argued that the idea of what it means to learn may require certain kinds of detachment (cf. Petraglia, 1991, 1994). One reason we may desire this detachment has to do with our interest in introducing students to disciplinary practices that, by their very nature, provide a relatively narrow outlook on their objects of study. A thorough understanding of a disciplinary perspective may be short-circuited in the sort of rich contexts provided by anchored instruction whereby the thickness of the context is privileged over careful and systematic investigation. Another example of how authenticity may be inappropriate can be gleaned from the introductory chapter's Algar scenario in which my colleague's students voiced the opinion that the science-fictive nature of the assignment freed them to be creative in a way that the real world would not permit. The very nature of creativity, it would seem, requires an ability to not only go beyond the information given, but also to transcend the given world as we know it. In other words, a holder of a rhetorical view of education might argue that there are some problems that we may wish to decontextualize for a reason; their occurrence in nature is neither part of their appeal nor part of our pedagogical objective. In fact, some problems' complexity may be precisely what we wish to strip away for purposes uncovering first principles or highlighting similarities among a set of problems.

Finally, we might consider that two pedagogical values tacitly compete in the classroom: first, the idea that reasoning and communicating skills should be applicable to the real world and second, that reasoning and communicating should conform to some standards of objectivity. Although, as educators, we may find it easy to strike a theoretical balance in our own minds, the problems we face in conveying such a balance may be more difficult than we think. We have already dealt extensively with this first value, but the second—that of objectivity—merits a discussion as well. Paul (1982) takes it as self-evident that, "virtually all teachers of critical thinking want their teaching to have a global 'Socratic' effect, making some significant inroads into the everyday reasoning of the student, enhancing to some degree that healthy, practical, and skilled skepticism one naturally and rightly associates with the rational person" (p. 3). Perkins (1987) and others argue that teaching students to objectify knowledge through the deliberate application of artifice will presumably lead them to adopt the kind of clear and structured thinking that most educators appreciate in their students. He suggests that "it is easy enough to develop one's preferred side of a case, but paying careful heed to the other side of the case does not come readily" (p. 45). With practice in artifice, Perkins believes that such objectification will come as second nature to students. Merrill (1992) too believes that "to insist on all instruction occurring only in the context of use, is to deny some of the great advantage of learning from instruction versus learning only from experience" (p. 105).

Both Merrill's and Perkins' observations reflect the situation in the social sciences and humanities, especially, whereby many teachers view having students carefully weigh facts, opinions, and the interests of others as part of their general mission (Berlo, 1960; Young, Becker, & Pike, 1970). This is no doubt informed by the widely perceived need to move young adults away from the egocentrism with which they often arrive at a university (cf. Pascarella & Terenzini, 1991; Perry, 1970). For many teachers of journalism, critical thinking, applied ethics, writing, and speech, objectivity may even be an essential part of the course content and there is a long-standing tradition in education (still very much with us today) that values the objective stance as an exercise in intellectual rigor. One may also admit to a common postmodern impulse among many of us that actually prefers that students do not come to conclusions. In my capacity as a writing instructor, I too have generally valued the student response that acknowledged and analyzed the problematic nature of issues over that which argued strongly in favor of one side or the other as students too readily do in everyday situations.

Somewhat paradoxically, then, constructivism is often accompanied by what Rorty (1991) called a postmodern bourgeois liberal theory of education, which seems to place great moral stock in training students to objectify, to the extent possible, the points of view presented them. This moral impetus is seen in educational technology where one finds the belief that collaborative, multimediated, and hypertextualized technologies leverage our ability to see many sides of a problem and free us up from the narrowness our natural biases encourage. The problem here seems very real indeed. Can we reason through an authentic situation without invoking values and attitudes that encourage personal bias? If so, one must wonder what we mean by authentic, for no real-world problem is approached in a value-neutral way. Many educators may say that the solution is that students must be trained to reflect on their commitments, for commitment need not be antithetical to rationality. I agree; we need not set up a false dichotomy between being reasonably objective and being reasonably committed. Not only are the two not mutually exclusive, but Paul is correct, I think, in suggesting that the two are, in fact, linked: People must cultivate the emotional disposition to be rational (in Siegal, 1989, p. 40). While we might dismiss an objectivity versus authenticity dichotomy as unnecessary and simplistic, however, the issue poses an interesting question for constructivist educators training their students to critically think through real-world problems. The classroom is a difficult place to make subtle distinctions vivid, and when the classrooms are populated by eighteen-year-olds who, as Perry (1970), Paul (1982), and Kohlberg (1986) suggested, are likely to reflect less on their assumptions in any case, the integration of being "objective," on one hand, with being "of this world," on the other, is more difficult still.

To summarize this point, I believe a rhetorical perspective on education requires us to reflect on whether, in a particular instance, claims of authenticity are worth the bother; could we not substantiate our pedagogical innovations' effectiveness without reference to the real world? As the authentication of a problem has been shown to be so difficult to attain, we might take some consolation in the awareness that it may not even be desirable in many cases.

Multiple Realities and Comfortable Contradiction

As many social, clinical, and cognitive psychologists have demonstrated, the flexibility of our real worlds depends on how our reality is structured. If asked to adjust our reality, we have to be able to accommodate the adjustment within our present frames of reference. As a corollary, we generally resist adding information to our repertoire of knowledge that overtly contradicts other information we believe we know. Widespread acceptance of this corollary is revealed in the fact that few phrases from psychology have permeated the educational culture as much as *cognitive dissonance* has. Festinger's phrase is meant to explain why the mind draws attention to certain logical disjunctures and prompts the individual to devote the mental resources necessary to resolve them, much like the Piagetian notion of disequilibrium. Both cognitive dissonance and disequilibrium stem from the seemingly logical assumption that we cannot believe "P" and "not P" simultaneously. This relates to the topic of authenticity not only in the assumption that there is a single real world (the preauthentication error) but further, that this real world is cogent. When this cogency is undermined, psychologists and educators have traditionally assumed, the result can only be confusion and a compulsion to restore what is presumed to be a balance. The rhetorical perspective refutes this.

Brummett (1976) accounts for the fact that contradictory truths exist by noting that each individual belongs to a variety of communities and thereby, possesses multiple frames of mind. He contends that:

> conflicting truths arise when two or more validating contexts have opposed meanings. For example, people may be torn between the desire to further the common welfare and the desire to protect self interests. This conflict is possible because the meanings assigned to either pattern are generated by different validating contexts. Motivations for one context or another are in a rhetorical opposition that presents the individual with a choice. (p. 35)

Whereas the Rockwellian learner model leads us to label a conflicted learner as either confused or underinformed, the rhetorician recognizes him or her as typical. Consider the many maxims that seem contradictory but nonetheless coexist comfortably in our minds: "too many cooks spoil the broth" versus "many hands make light work," "look before you leap" versus "he who hesitates is lost." Billig (1993a) suggests that traditional psychology, with its scientific commitments, holds out the hope that "experimental methodology will settle once and for all the competing truths of the many hands lightening the work or the multiplicity of cooks spoiling the broth" (p. 127). Conversely, he argues, the rhetorical perspective maintains that "such contradictions are not considered to be matters in desperate need of resolution, but are part of the resources which enable common sense thinking" (p. 127). Rhetoric points to the human proclivity to make multiple sense of information presented, and just as important, such sense making's perpetual evolution. Although a conversation might return to the same topic, it never returns in precisely the same terms. When representing the same context at two different times, variables not only shift but are added and deleted, certain variables are bound to be given more or less weight, and the very constitution of the variables may radically vary depending on mood, intention, and other factors that impact memory instantiation.

As Billig (1993) points out repeatedly, cognitivist assumptions have failed to recognize the human capacity—indeed, the propensity—to transcend particu-

lar categorizations. According to him, "there is a tendency within cognitive social psychology to overlook the rhetorical context of categories, and thereby to
underestimate the extent to which the selection of categories can be a matter of
controversy" (p. 136). Whereas computational models of mind have focused on
carefully delineating their terms, both Billig and Burke caution that they have
been largely unsuccessful in operationalizing metaphor and the other linguistic
means by which "P" can be "not P." Cognitive scientists have long accepted
that memory might be encoded in at least three distinct ways: semantically,
episodically, and in terms of actions (Boekaerts, 1985) while social psychologists
have argued that memory also encodes information affectively. Whereas constructivists in education have readily accepted the idea that information may be
represented in multiple ways, we have generally assumed that these encodings
are mutually reinforcing—a version of the blind men and the elephant story. A
rhetorical perspective, on the other hand, accepts that seeming contradictions
may not be signs of irrationality as much as they are opportunities for clarification and rational exchange and that different encodings often lead to seeming
contradictions that may never have to be reconciled. We can, and do, believe
seemingly contradictory things, for experience and language creates many such
opportunities.

Thus, rhetoric highlights the multiplicity of realities—the fact that we are
not tied to a common conception of the real—and thus the authentic, as well as
the idea that in each of us competing realities coexist. Although the notion of
cognitive dissonance is certainly useful in sorting out formally incommensurate
propositions, constructivists should join rhetoricians in acknowledging that the
primacy of symbol usage in thinking and the attendant flexibility of symbols
makes it possible, indeed necessary, that we be comfortable with contradiction
in our everyday lives and in the understandings of our students. For the educator, this poses both challenges and opportunities. First, it undermines any comfortable assumption that once a student learns something, it stays learned. Whitehead's cautions regarding inert knowledge, though still relevant in certain domains, may appear quixotic in others; we may never be able to bring our multiple understandings to bear on any given subject, and while knowledge makes
sense on a certain level, there are no assurances that at another level, such
knowledge will not be resisted, thereby inhibiting transfer. Couched in terms of
cognitive flexibility, the rhetorical perspective argues that not only do we all
take different paths through problem spaces, but that we are also capable of multiple paths, all of which may lead us through different spaces to different conclusions, and we cannot rely on cognitive dissonance to stop us.

Tolerance for Failure

Strommen (1995) begins his review of a constructivism-in-educational technology anthology (edited by Duffy and Jonassen, 1992) with the observation that,
"Instructional technology design is the most self-confident field I can name.

Long after constructivism began to shake the foundations of educational theory and practice, ITD continued to plug away with a quiet certainty about the nature of learning, the nature of instruction, even the nature of knowledge itself " (p. 77). The arrival of constructivism has done little to dampen this determined optimism. Because of this, a final, fundamental, and perhaps the most radical lesson I believe a rhetorical perspective on education can offer suggests that constructivism means learners are free to fail. Education, generally, is an optimistic enterprise in the sense that our theories of knowledge and the Rockwellian learner model felicitously join to create a teaching situation in which—done right—successful learning outcomes are practically guaranteed. As Csikszentmihalyi argues, this situation promotes the belief that education should be wholly invested in alleviating cognitive difficulty: if students do not learn, it is up to educators to make the content more cognitively processable. Not only does this ignore the motivational issues involved in education, but it perpetuates a thoroughly unconstructivistic framework in which the educator exercises control over learning.

Faith in the predictability of educational outcomes leads us to treat educational problems and tasks as if they are sitting ducks, helpless in the face of the pedagogical and/or technological firepower arrayed against them. Yet, if we decide to forego simply telling students that what they are learning is authentic and instead opt to persuade them to adopt the understanding we wish them to, we have to be prepared for the possibility that the most thoughtful pedagogy and advanced technologies may fail in the face of student apathy or counterarguments. A rhetorical perspective reminds us that there is no guarantee of success in making learning authentic: Although we may argue for a given task's authenticity, evidence one audience finds compelling, another audience finds inadequate. What Aristotle identified as rhetoric's natural concern with probable outcomes instills in the rhetorically sensitive educator an explicit awareness of the limits of persuasion and thus success. In Book One of *Rhetoric*, for instance, Aristotle reminds us that the rhetorician who discovers the available means of persuasion does so with no assurances that the means employed will succeed. He advises us to set our sights a bit lower and suggests that a more reasonable objective is to come "as near such success as the circumstances of each particular case allows" (p. 6).

Simons (1993) asks us to consider that "constructive learning can not be expected to result from constructive learning environments automatically. Learners, in their long history of experiences with learning, develop persistent beliefs, habits and styles related to learning activities that will make it difficult for some of them to work and learn in constructive learning environments" (p. 310). In Simons' words we see a sensitivity to the rhetorical task at hand—we are not just asking that students commit to learning additional information, but rather that they overcome a number of ingrained beliefs that may have deep roots in their extracurricular lives. Even within purely academic contexts, however, learners encounter a broad variety of tasks and teachers that may undermine a given teacher's constructivist efforts. Designers of pedagogical innovations, technological and otherwise, must consider that their environment will supplement, coexist with, and compete with other environments created for the student in other courses. Another consideration, of course, is that the evaluative nature of schooling has obvious consequences for our ability to convince students to buy into the authenticity of the tasks we set. Students expect (and largely accept) that their purpose in learning has generally more to do with performing well in school than in genuinely preparing them for tasks they may encounter in everyday life. While students have come to demand that schooling adequately credential them for the world of work, Damarin (1994) suggests, "Traditionally, school is widely regarded as distinct and remote from 'real life'; unless this tradition is abandoned, 'authentic activities' will be de-authenticated in the eyes of students simply by introducing them to schools!" (p. 21). The point is legitimate: school carries with it (or perhaps one should say that many practices imbue schooling with) the aura of inauthenticity. It may, in fact, be a place where a kind of reverse alchemy—transforming the authentic to the inauthentic—must be anticipated and engaged.

The constructivist literatures of education and educational technology tell stories of "getting it right," of figuring out what is going wrong, and then remediating the error rather than revisioning the basic structure of the enterprise and the motivations of learners. Ironically, education's aversion to failure may be one of the reasons why students' reality counts so little in our academic calculations. It might be considered rude or defeatist to acknowledge that students have lives outside school that are more important to them than the lives with which we are willing and able to work. Instead, many educators, constructivist or otherwise, are eager to presume a greater degree of goodwill and dedication on the part of students than my experiences as a teacher (and especially as a former student) suggest is warranted. Far from denigrating students, acknowledgment of their freedom to fail validates them as complex individuals with aspirations that may have very little to do with the Rockwellian desire to learn whatever is put before them—a self-serving myth that perhaps does more to lend cogency to our theories of learning than to truly demonstrate respect for student centeredness. Taking constructivism seriously means facing the discomfort of not knowing ahead of time what students accept as an everyday or real-world problem and instead viewing authentication as an ongoing process that presents the teacher with many rhetorical opportunities but no guarantees.

REINVIGORATING CONSTRUCTIVIST THINKING IN EDUCATIONAL TECHNOLOGY

Every argument has a starting point. According to Perelman and Olbrecht-Tyteca (1969), starting points for arguments can be identified as one of two kinds. For a rhetor, the first and easiest starting point sets out to fit the argument at hand into an already accepted worldview. The second starting point, however, is one in which we cannot presume that a shared worldview is already in place, and requires us to begin by first establishing this worldview. Throughout this book, I have suggested that in the case of creating authentic learning environments, educators have been too quick to presume that we can launch our arguments from the first starting point. That is, our rhetoric of authenticity is predicated on the assumption that we are all "on board" when it comes to identifying the real world and knowing authenticity when we see it. Conversely, I argued that constructivist theory recommends we recognize that arguments for authenticity require us to first establish a common reality before building on it. My own powers of persuasion notwithstanding, I suspect that this rhetorical framework for constructivist education readily makes sense to many educators, for as the epigraph introducing this chapter clearly demonstrates, educators have not been oblivious to the essentially rhetorical nature of the task confronting them (cf. Brown, 1990).

In a short essay that asserts many of the claims I presented in this chapter, Jonassen (1994) notes the critical difference between the dominant technological paradigm of the 1960s and 1970s and our present constructivist paradigm lies in the technologists' assumptions regarding the predeterminability of learning processes and outcomes. In contrast to instructional design, "constructivism believes that learning outcomes are not always predictable and that 'instruction' should foster, not control, the processing of the learner" (p. 35). He further notes that "constructivist instruction" is an oxymoron if, by instruction, we mean a process of getting knowledge into students' heads. The real challenge facing technologists, according to Jonassen, is to consider the goals of instruction in a particular context and then adjust the strategies, models, and tactics necessary to attune the nature of the task to the perspective of the student. Just as educational technology provided a useful backdrop for problematizing our common reactions to constructivism, I believe it also exhibits a great deal of creative and rhetorical thinking in education that has the potential to move us toward a more cogent constructivist pedagogy.

*The Movement Toward
Knowledge Negotiation*

There are many signs that a rhetorical turn is beginning to take hold in educational technology. For instance, growing attention to co-construction in the technologist literature is certainly encouraging. Rhetoricians since Aristotle agreed with his contention that audiences are more easily convinced when they are invited to participate in their own persuasion (Lunsford, 1979). Much of the power of everyday argument is derived from the rhetor and interlocutor's participation in social knowledge that reminds them of their mutual dependence and shared assumptions. Burke has identified this sharing (or *consubstantiality*) as the basis of rhetoric and the motivation for all human action. To the degree that co-construction is taken to draw the educator into the dynamics of knowledge building, it provides a basis for a rhetorical view of education.

Elsewhere in the technologist literature, Baker (1994) draws from Cohen (1992) to make the point that an important distinction for the design of intelligent tutoring systems is that between acceptance and belief. Acceptance, he explains, is a sort of metacognitive judgment (i.e., one decides to accept another's claim), whereas belief is more deeply ingrained in an individual's existing worldview. Although in rhetoric, Perelman argues that if acceptance is not tied to a belief system, we are left with relatively fragile understandings that can be overturned or easily forgotten, Baker notes that we would also do well to acknowledge that just because someone may be compelled to accept an argument, they may not be compelled to believe it. The distinction between acceptance and belief demonstrates an appreciation for the subtlety of argument and the problems we encounter in the classroom and the mere fact that Baker signals this as a critical issue facing AI tells us something about the direction in which AI in education is moving. In the area of shell design, we also see some rhetorical possibilities. Zucchermaglio (1993), Winn (1993b), and others have called for *empty* or *shell* environments to circumvent the issue of excessive teacher intervention in learning. Because empty environments only provide general scaffolding for the learning process and are largely devoid of any prespecified content, their emptiness leads some teachers to find them pedagogically uninteresting. Still, appropriating the minimalist credo of less being more, shell design may be rhetorically appealing in that it supports the learner's constructive processes by not imposing predetermined content and thereby creating a pedagogical space that lends itself to genuine coconstruction.

Yet, even while lauding the advances shell and other minimally intrusive technologies afford constructivism, Vosniadou (1994) acknowledges that "they are not free of problematic elements themselves. Students must still realize the similarities and differences between the simulations to which they have been exposed and in the multi-media environments and the real life tasks" (p. 13). Teachers, she argues, must be able to articulate those differences and lend support for the similarities. In this, she is seconded by Driver, Asoko, Leach, Mortimer, & Scott (1994) who argue that:

> If students are to adopt scientific ways of knowing, then intervention and negotiation with an authority, usually the teacher, is essential. Here, the critical feature is the nature of the dialogic process. The role of the authority figure has two important components. the first is to introduce new ideas or cultural tools where necessary and to provide the support and guidance for student to make sense of these for themselves. The other is to listen and diagnose the ways in which the instructional activities are being interpreted to inform further action. . . . The teacher is

the often hard-pressed tour guide mediating between children's everyday world and the world of science. (p. 11)

I believe Driver and her colleagues are making much the same point I am making here, even if we would perhaps emphasize different parts of their statement. Whereas they may suggest that the teacher is conducting a sort of shuttle diplomacy between the worlds of science and student experience, a rhetorical perspective on learning (as well as key constructivist concepts such as activity) suggests that neither of these worlds are stable enough sites of knowledge to permit shuttling. Instead, the challenge educators face has less to do with giving the right information (or offering students an empty shell within which they can discover their own knowledge) than in engaging the learner in a dialogic process that gives the learner an opportunity to articulate his or her understanding and offers the educator the best hope of intervening in it. In Cunningham's (1992) words, "perhaps the most distinguishing feature of constructivism . . . is its emphasis on argument, discussion and debate" (p. 157).

Within some AI circles, an even more explicitly rhetorical perspective on learning is finding some advocates (cf. Pilkington, Hartley, Hintze, & Moore, 1992). We see this reflected in a recent call for papers to be presented at a conference on argumentation and agent communication in which Zuckerman (1995) notes that:

> With the increased sophistication of tasks performed by computers and the increased use of computers in collaborative settings, argumentation has become an important component of the interaction between computers and users. For example, knowledge-based systems must present arguments to justify their recommendations, intelligent tutoring systems need to explain why a particular proposition is or isn't true, and negotiation systems need to justify what a particular course of action is better than some alternative.

The issue of justification seems to be just one of a number of signs pointing to a growing acknowledgment of deductive logic's inadequacy for creating authentic interaction between learners and environments. Educational technology's growing awareness of the importance of taking a justificatory stance toward engagement with students is encouraging and in technologist conversations elsewhere, we can find even more fully formed rhetorical frameworks.

On the other side of the Atlantic, for example, European (principally British) computer scientists working on tutoring systems have produced a distinctive approach that can potentially bring the full weight of a rhetorical perspective to bear on educational technology. An anthology edited by Moyse and Elsom-Cook (1992) dubbed this approach *knowledge negotiation*. Unlike the more typical AI environments that contain the correct knowledge and are to be used to lead students to the ideal understanding the environment already possesses (again, the full technology approach to educational technology), a knowledge negotiating system does not presume to possess all the answers and instead, seeks to negotiate problem solutions with learners. Although some of its tenets have precursors in other intelligent tutoring systems, Moyse and Elsom-Cook correctly argue that this approach is unique in that earlier learning environments designed to permit students to explore a variety of viewpoints (e.g., Papert's Logo) only permitted this exploration in predetermined ways.

Like cognitive flexibility theory, the knowledge negotiation approach holds that there is a need to represent multiple viewpoints, but unlike most of the systems that have adopted the cognitive flexibility rationale, knowledge negotiation questions whether, in every instance, there is a pre-existing truth to be learned. In their introduction to the anthology, Moyse and Elsom-Cook (1992) claim that their general goal is "to build adaptive systems where the current definitions of the domain to be tutored, and the process of tutoring it, are determined by a repeated process of negotiation between system and student" (p. 13). Baker (1994) summarizes the knowledge negotiation approach to intelligent tutoring by listing eight of its tenets:

1. Some (or all) tutors do not possess complete knowledge for the domains they teach.

2. For some domains there is no single, privileged, or correct viewpoint on knowledge.

3. There exists domains, or parts of them, that contain no knowledge, but only a number of different competing and arguable sets of justifiable beliefs.[4]

4. For some problems in some domains, there are multiple correct or acceptable solutions.

5. For domains that possess some or all of characteristics 1 to 4, teachers should not aim to simply transmit their own knowledge (beliefs, viewpoints, solutions, etc.) to the student.

6. The tutor should not have complete control over the tutor–learner interaction in domains that possess some or all of Characteristics 1 to 4.

7. The representation of the domain to be taught or learned, and the problem solutions themselves, should be jointly constructed by teacher and learner.

8. Negotiation mechanisms and representations to support them are required in teaching and learning interactions with respect to domains that possess some or all of characteristics 1 to 4.

We see that this list encompasses many of the issues I suggested a rhetorical perspective would raise. For instance, it demonstrates a sensitivity to the importance of domain (characteristics 2 and 3) as well as acknowledges the role of the teacher in controlling the knowledge-making process (characteristics 5 and 7).

---

[4]While I subscribe to what I think is the author's intended meaning of this tenet, a rhetorical perspective, to my mind, would question the distinction made here that contrasts knowledge and justified belief.

Yet, Moyse and Elsom-Cook acknowledge that there are important definition-related questions that must be determined before technologists can set out to build such systems (for instance, "what do we mean by *negotiation?*"). As Baker (1994) further notes, work on negotiation in AI has generally relied on idealized utterances, and these are further limited by the narrow range of speech act types investigated (specifically, questions and requests). He concludes that a negotiative technological environment must be capable of distinguishing between those aspects of arguments on which it is appropriate to negotiate with a given learner and those that are not (p. 204). This is clearly a tall order and not one that will be filled in the immediate future by either artificial or human intelligence. Even if a knowledge negotiation approach only provides a theoretical basis on which to build, however, from a rhetorical perspective, it seems like a promising foundation.[5]

A Case in Point: Reality Check

Writing to an audience of educational technologists, Vosniadou (1994) best articulates the nature of the practical challenges facing educators generally:

> The creation of learning environments that allow existing representations to be externalized and examined can facilitate conceptual change and can contribute to the creation of metaconceptual awareness. . . . Such learning environments help students to make their representations public and to examine them objectively. It makes it possible for students to draw the hidden implications of these representations, to discuss them with others, and to change them. (p. 15)

Subtitled "A Rhetorical Approach to Constructivist Learning," *Reality Check* is a prototype of educational software that my colleagues at Georgia Tech and I are currently developing. It embodies many of the lessons knowledge negotiation offers the constructivist educator and educational technologist.[6] Using the metaphor of education as argumentation, *Reality Check* prompts educators and students independently to construct a task profile by identifying relevant

---

[5]One should be careful not to overstate AI's rhetorical awakening, however. Lynette Hunter (1991) notes that AI has the potential to radically transform communication practices, but though it can "contribute a great deal on technique and device, and a growing amount on strategy . . . there is little or nothing on stance, the centre of rhetoric which is concerned with material interaction. . . . [This stems] from its grounding the representational strategies of science that claim adequacy and exactitude. When AI does not find such exactitude, it simply moves on, does not address the difficulty, sees it as a failure rather than the potential location for social context" (p. 281). Like the educational enterprise it occasionally serves, the AI community is also often caught in a rhetoric of success (a preoccupation with getting it right), which may lead it to overlook its real rhetorical potential.

[6]*Reality Check* is part of a NewMedia Center project funded, in part, by the EduTech Institute and the Graphics, Visualization, and Usability Center at Georgia Tech. In addition to myself, the Reality Check design team is principally comprised of Bryce Glass and Greg VanHoosier-Carey.

variables and giving reasons and evidence for their relevance in order to articulate and compare their senses of how elements of the task correspond to the assignment and the "real world." *Reality Check* does not support construction of a neatly rational profile of the task from either the educator's or learner's perspectives. It does not attempt to force closure on points of discrepancy, but instead tries to make explicit and describe as fully and multidimensionally as possible, the gap between the two. In keeping with the guidelines outlined earlier in this chapter, *Reality Check* is only intended for use in those circumstances in which the disciplinary content, the educator's objectives, and the learner's intellectual development are appropriate. This means that it is not intended for use with well-structured problems, tasks where the teacher finds pedagogical value in rigidly stipulating a context within which they must be performed, or elementary (and even many secondary) school children.

The four steps that make up *Reality Check*'s protocol are (a) the entry of the assignment, (b) a teacher profiling activity, (c) a student profiling activity, and finally, (d) a teacher–student joint analysis. In the first step, the teacher simply enters the particulars of an assignment into *Reality Check*. After the assignment narrative has been entered, *Reality Check* prompts the teacher to identify the criteria he or she wishes to use for profiling the assignment and then asks the teacher to apply that criteria to the assignment. Examples of such criteria might be "parts of the task requiring greatest amount of student creativity and initiative," or "parts of the task that will figure most heavily in its evaluation." Once the teacher has marked up the assignment in this way, *Reality Check* prompts him or her to go back and annotate elements of the assignment narrative with justifications for why the various choices were made.

Independent of the teacher's marking and annotation, students mark up the assignment narrative much as the teacher did using the criteria selected by the teacher. Just as their teachers were, students are then returned to the result of each mark up routine and asked to annotate the elements to justify their selection and prioritization of elements along each criterion.

Once both the teacher and the student have profiled their understandings of the assignment, *Reality Check* uses the mark up and annotation routines to constrast the evidence each side finds relevant in performing the task as part of an academic assignment. It highlights the the differences between alternative profiles and suggests areas in which the educator and learner appear to have serious disagreements. For instance, *Reality Check* might flag places where the teacher thinks it is important that students use tools he or she normally associates with the task, whereas students may not realize these tools exist, that they are permitted to use them, or that the employment of these tools really make a difference. Or perhaps *Reality Check* would signal that the student feels the designated evaluator of the task makes little difference to its execution, whereas the teacher thinks this is a critical consideration and will be looking for sensitivity to this issue in his or her assessment of the student's performance.

Thus, the outcome of a teacher–student dyad's use of *Reality Check* is a textual as well as graphical representation of the task that identifies the variables and the evidence each side finds relevant in peforming the task. In the final and most important step, the teacher and student come together to discuss these representions and to negotiate their divergent understandings. In this negotiating phase, teachers and students may discover that they are in more agreement than *Reality Check*'s analysis suggested, for *Reality Check*'s purpose is not so much to produce an accurate picture of the gap between the student and teacher's task representation but rather to provide an opportunity for negotiation of the task that might not happen otherwise. In other words, *Reality Check*'s real function is to prompt sustained reflection of one's task representation in relation to another's and to provide structure for a dialogue between the teacher and student.

Although this is a necessarily sketchy overview of *Reality Check,* it may be sufficient to illustrate several ways in which we are attempting to use technology to support knowledge negotiation objectives. First, a system such as *Reality Check* demonstrates how, instead of presenting learners with preauthenticated materials, environments might challenge the learner to reflect on the contextual disjunctures they encounter in the environment and to speculate on the implications these disjunctures might have for their performance of the task. This does a few things, but perhaps most important (to use Nix's [1990] terminology) it *dignifies* the learner by making explicit the experiential superiority of the human learner to the mechanistic environment. While lending learners dignity might be a worthwhile end in itself, as educators, we might find dignity useful; it makes the learner cognizant of the importance and relevance of his or her own prior knowledge and understanding and in doing so, it makes the learner an active participant in the learning experience. By inviting learner rejoinders to our construction of a problem space, we shift the didactic nature of instruction more toward genuine co-construction. Engaging learners in this sort of dialogue might give them a metacognitive awareness of their own reasoning and invites students to consider the ways in which their task representations differ from their teachers' as well as from their peers.

From a rhetorical perspective, one of the appealing attributes of a system such as *Reality Check* is that it explicitly acknowledges the separation of the context of instruction from the contexts in which knowledge may be used outside of school. As mundane an observation as this is, this separation is one that preauthenticating practices have been erected to mask. Of course, the educator as well may find value in having students explain how their understanding of the assignment differs from his or her own. This provides the educator with a wealth of information about how learners are interpreting the assignment to construct the problem space and may assist the teacher in discovering ways of overcoming cognitive and motivational difficulties students encounter. If patterns of learner reactions seem to point to similar disjunctures between their understanding of the problem and the teacher's representation of the problem, this would provide a valuable check on the appropriateness of the task's contextualization for the group of learners for whom it is meant.

Finally, and most fundamental, perhaps, *Reality Check* highlights the argumentative nature of education and allows the teacher to present his or her case for the importance of the task to the overall assignment and the relevance of the assignment to the learner's real world. By setting up alternative narratives in this way, *Reality Check* explicitly invites the teacher and student to participate in a kind of negotiation in which evidence is exchanged and positions are clarified, whereby each party in this educational activity can better understand the other and, ultimately, make productive use of this understanding. *Reality Check* pulls the educator into the knowledge-construction process in a way that permits students to see the educator as a reasonable, pedagogically motivated individual rather than an arbitrary task setter. While a prototype such as *Reality Check* is hardly paradigmatic of a knowledge negotiating or rhetorical approach, I believe it nonetheless illustrates one way that technologies can be used to advance constructivist pedagogy without running afoul of constructivism's basic theoretical commitments.

CONCLUSION

Learning entails the conscious application of the learner's cognitive abilities within an educational environment in order to make sense of the world. Technological environments and tools might support such sense making, but as Jonassen, Campbell, & Davidson (1994) suggest, they are not responsible for learning—the learner is—and "that will not change regardless of how engaging [educational technologies] become." They further argue that the sooner "we reject our conceptions of media and conveyors of instructional interventions and accept and design them as intellectual partners in the knowledge construction process, the sooner we can support meaningful change in the learning process" (p. 39). Casting authenticity in education not only as a consequence of constructivism, but also as a rhetorical challenge prompts a new appreciation for both constructivism and education. This appreciation, in turn, enables us to look more critically at current theory and practice and suggest where more productive lines of inquiry and pedagogical innovation might lie.

As we have also seen, the idea that education is a rhetorical and argumentative process is not entirely new to either educators or technologists. In fact, just as the evolution toward authenticity may characterize the cognitivist enterprise, evolution toward a rhetorical view of education seems to encapsulate many of the conversations currently underway in educational technology. The knowledge negotiation approach to intelligent tutoring, in particular, opens up exciting possibilities for educators generally—both for the metaphors it employs and for its willingness to grapple with constructivism's epistemological challenge.

SEVEN

Conclusion:
Slowing Down
for the Rhetorical Turn

GERGEN (1995) opens his essay on the "mechanical self" with the observation that "One can scarcely overestimate the power of the concept of objectivity in contemporary affairs" (p. 265). The allure of objectivity is all the more impressive when one considers that even the constructivist account, an account that we may expect to be especially careful in this regard, appears as easily seduced by idea of the real world's objectivity as the information-processing account it has sought to supplant in the field of psychology and the transmission model it rejects in education. Constructivists' failure, revealed in preauthenticatory practices, lies in our often unreflective attempts at squeezing an unsettling theory of knowledge into a comfortable, elite-idealist framework. Such a misappropriation of constructivist theory, I argued, allows the real world to remain compliantly stable, for only alternative pathways, not alternative real worlds, are conceded.

Yet, in setting out these arguments, I tried to show myself to be sympathetic to constructivists in education who find it difficult to create the proper space in education to allow constructivism to really take root. In Chapter Four, I described some of the obstacles education faces in accommodating an unmitigatingly antifoundational theory of learning and, in Chapters Five and Six, I gave my own response to these obstacles: we can avoid the worst excesses of relativism by casting education as an ongoing argumentative process in a broader rhetorical framework. This only begs other questions for some. While it may be easy for the rhetoric enthusiast to rattle off the benefits of adopting a rhetorical perspective on learning, the rhetorical perspective poses challenges of its own.

Although this book focuses on what I think is educators' justified fear of antifoundationalism, there may be reason to fear rhetoric as well. To be a successful rhetor requires that one reject the available means of coercion and put himself or herself into the role of persuader. Educators generally lack this self-perception. Just as Levine suggests that being a scientist means not being a rhetorician, we can easily imagine that being an educator has traditionally meant foregoing what Dewey termed "warranted belief" in favor of truth. We have not constructed our role—we have not been encouraged to construct our role—as one that requires skill at warranting. The rhetorical turn might not be appealing to those who wonder if, by taking on the metaphor of education as argument, we have not exchanged the behaviorist's black box for Pandora's. In other words, a commitment to persuasion might suggest to some educators that the knowledge bazaar is open.

Yet, adopting a rhetorical stance toward education does not mean cajoling students to learn or engaging in a lot of postmodern handwaving about the end of authority. Instead, I am merely rearticulating the point, made more eloquently by various educators and psychologists over the years, that the construction of problems and their solutions by learners is unavoidable. The manner in which a student's problem-solving process unfolds—even when grossly inaccurate, inefficient, or otherwise unacceptable from an educator's perspective—is not random but reflects prior efforts on the student's part to make sense of the task in a way that conforms with his or her knowledge of the world. As Bruner (1990) notes, issues of right and wrong need not be reducible to absolute truths and absolute falsities. Instead, "the best we can hope for is that we be aware of our own perspective and those of others" (p. 25).

For the truly constructivist educator, then, the idea that we argue for knowledge is a statement of fact rather than a recommendation. It is not our prerogative to permit alternative constructions of the way the world works. Instead, we must first acknowledge them as the logical consequence of a constructivist view of learning and then engage these constructions in a manner we find beneficial to the learner. The practical consequence of this has less to do with presenting a different, more "liberating," face to our students than with developing, in the profession, our own understanding of what it is we are doing as educators—more of a private conversation than a public confession. Just as Augustine had to reconcile the certainty of Scripture with the need to employ rhetoric to persuade nonbelievers in the early fifth century, so must educators attempt to reconcile their faith in the value of their knowledge with the frank acknowledgment that others may not readily share that faith.

Yet, a rhetoricized constructivism is not only difficult for traditionalists; a moderate rhetorical turn may be disappointing to some radical pedagogists who find the rhetorical perspective too tame for their liking. For members of educational communities who feel themselves less beholden to scientific method, the tension induced by antifoundationalism is too readily ignored. In their view, relativism goes without saying, or at least, it should (Fuller, 1993). For instance, we may consider McCloskey's (1997) response to Dilip Gaonkar (1993) who, according to McCloskey, joins conservative newspapers in dredging up "the canard about 'relativism' every time they comment on the Culture Wars" (p. 109). McCloskey believes it suffices to quote Bruno Latour's (1988) response to the charge of relativism, a response he characterizes as "sharp and compelling":

Those who accuse relativists of being self-contradictory can save their breath for better occasions. I explicitly put my own account in the same category as those accounts I have studied without asking for any privilege. This approach seems self-defeating only to those who believe that the fate of an interpretation is tied to the existence of a safe metalinguistic level. . . . This belief is precisely what I deny. This reflexive position is the only one that is not self-contradictory. (p. 109)

Likewise, educational theorist Henry Perkinson (1993) forcefully argues for accepting relativism in the guise of an "evolutionary epistemology" in which he claims learning is unintentional. As students are wholly responsible for their own understanding, in his view, it is pointless for a teacher to have any particular objective he or she wishes students to meet and students themselves should not have any particular purpose for learning. Rather, in Perkinson's view, teachers should be content to assist students in adopting a critical stance toward information. Subscribers to such views can also be found in educational technology circles. At a recent National Science Foundation-sponsored conference on technology in education, for instance, there were spokespersons for the view that the most educative environment is one in which students assign themselves their own grades and in which the teacher is assigned that position not by professional accreditation, but through the exercise of classroom democracy (i.e., students vote on what they wish to learn and who is qualified to teach them).

While such suggestions may be accommodated within a constructivist framework (and Perkinson demonstrates how they can be), I suspect that they strike most educators and rhetoricians as unworkable. From the education side, these suggestions appear to deny the essentially formative and evaluative nature of schooling by which I mean that the very idea of education presumes that students are developing, rather than merely exhibiting, already existing knowledge and skills and that the classroom is structured hierarchically with the teacher as the central authority who must be empowered to legitimize and regulate student learning (cf. Petraglia, 1995). Rhetoricians might add that excessively radical recommendations also seem to flout the rational foundations to which most of us subscribe: Perkinson's theories makes little sense in a society and material context that insists on the recalcitrance of certain hierarchies. So we may not be chastened by Latour's suggestion that we save our breath, and instead may use that breath to repeat the question, for rigorously defending a system of thought that dismisses rigor or systematicity (and yet, insists on its academic value) is not without its own logical shortcomings, however quickly its defenders shrug them off.

An illuminating exchange in regards to this is one found in the journal *Educational Psychologist* in which Carl Bereiter (1994), whose long career has made him a mainstay on both the behaviorist and cognitivist scenes, calls for "progressive discourse" in reconciling postmodernism to educational scientism. In his article, Bereiter articulates a very carefully crafted response to what he acknowledges is the epistemological instability to which postmodern and constructivist theory gives rise. He first proposes that science is not committed to objectivity (as its critics traditionally maintain), but to progress. Furthermore, he argues that in appealing to progress, science need not appeal to the real world but to the reasoned arguments made by inquirers. Teachers, he suggests, can thus lead students toward better comprehension of phenomenon in the name of progress rather than in the name of truth, a shift that acknowledges the importance of discursive practices in creating understanding.

In their response, Fenstermacher and Richardson (1994) criticize Bereiter for what they perceive as a latent resistance to the postmodern program. In essence, they complain that he is not sufficiently radical in his repudiation of objectivity. Bereiter's effort at reconciling education to antifoundationalism, in their view, falls short in many ways, but essentially in its insistence on teacherly authority. They argue that:

> When Bereiter moves to the educational implications of his progressive-discourse theory, one can see why equal participation in the discourse is not one of his criteria. The first authority is Bereiter himself, who, as a learning theorist developed prescriptions for teachers. . . . The next authority is the teacher, whose role is to lead students forward by having them examine authoritative texts and other expert sources and come to common interpretation of their meaning. The teacher would also determine whether the discourse is progressive and would intervene if it were not. (p. 51)

Fenstermacher and Richardson go on to take issue with Bereiter's endorsement of scientific progress, which they claim is at odds with real postmodern agenda that, because it rejects the idea of objectivity in science, must also debunk the notion of progress.

Yet, Bereiter's stance is quintessentially rhetorical and keeps with the constructivist spirit: we argue for the superiority of our claims in the name of better (read: rationally satisfying) understanding. Bereiter does not suggest that knowledge is the same as mere consensus (a common take on social constructionism that continues to have some currency in pockets of cultural studies), but that through systems that make sense to a culture we can sustain a rhetoric of good reasons; claims that draw from evidence that hold up within their cultural framework. Fenstermacher and Richardson, perhaps without intending to, are only highlighting what is obvious to most educators: the educational enterprise, at heart, is one that requires foundations. In response to their critique of authority, one might counter that the basic vocabulary of education (which assigns roles with words like *instructor, educator, teacher, student*) contains within it a knowledge differential and the barely tacit assumption that the knowledge constructed by the person standing in front of the classroom lies in a superior relationship to that of the people that sit facing that person. In addition, their claim that a rejection of objectivity is tantamount to a rejection of progress is simply wrong: as Bereiter suggests, we can argue for progress quite independent of objectivity as long as we are willing to be proven wrong and are open to better, more progressive arguments.

To conclude then, adjusting our pedagogical stance to one that persuades learners rather than informs them—in other words, taking the rhetorical turn —poses several significant and very different challenges. Chief among these is that of overcoming our ingrained beliefs about persuasion and education on the one hand, and an uncritical embrace of antifoundationalism on the other. Constructivism without a dialogic and argumentative dimension either sets up a false and unnecessarily antagonistic dichotomy pitting the educator against the learner—a dichotomy that has at stake the question of whose real world is to be acknowledged—or else it prompts a kind of "anything goes" response that serves no one's interests, least of all the student's. Instead, an argumentative framework acknowledges that teachers and educational institutions have objectives, but learners have real worlds that may be an obstacle in achieving them.

On the rear cover of a recent book (Backman, 1991), in an aggressive, eye-catching typeface, a series of short sentences read: "WORDS ARE TOOLS. IMAGES ARE REAL. INFORMATION IS POWER. CHANGE IS INEVITABLE. TRUTH IS RELATIVE." The book, *Sophistication*, is about the ressurection of sophism, but these few sentences could just as easily summarize the challenge constructivism presents educators. More than any new movement in cognitive science or any book on authenticity, teacherly common sense tells us that life is multifaceted and complex and that any attempt to prescribe what counts as real or authentic is doomed to failure. This same common sense suggests that there is little to be gained by upholding education's professional, yet stultifying, conceit that we control the worlds within which our students learn. This being said, however, education is and will remain a largely foundational enterprise that can only be tempered by an awareness of those foundations' constructedness. Metaphors drawn from the study of rhetoric, I propose, demonstrate how we might view the real world within its proper scope, that is, within the realm of argument, persuasion, and ultimately, of negotiation.

Glossary

(*Note:* Italicized words are defined elsewhere in the glossary.)

ACTIVITY THEORY   A theoretical framework that takes much of its shape from the work of Vygotsky and his colleague Leontiev, and attempts to account for the way in which individuals and groups use mediational tools (such as language) to meet everyday objectives.

ANTIFOUNDATIONALISM   The generic *epistemological* view that there are no secure foundations for knowledge, a view that is reflected in movements ranging from classical skepticism to contemporary deconstructionism. Although many contemporary theorists insist that *pragmatism* and *social constructionism* are essentially antifoundational, others argue that they may be "founded" upon utility or consensus, respectively (see also *foundationalism*).

AUTHENTICITY   Although the contested nature of this term is a focus of this book, it may succinctly be defined as the quality of having correpondence to the real world (see *preauthentication*).

COGNITIVISM   The interest in/concern with the ways in which humans discover, store, and retrieve information. Although some modern critics have found it rhetorically effective to conflate "cognitivism" with the *information-processing paradigm*, in this book I take the broader view that *sociohistoricism*, *situated cognition*, and various forms of *constructivism* are also varieties of cognitivism.

COGNITIVE SCIENCE   An interdisciplinary body of interests related to human thinking that typically draws contributors from fields such as psycholinguistics, philosophy, education, psychology, and computer science.

CONSTRUCTIVISM   The *social scientific* (and, especially, psychological) view that individuals actively construct meaning based on their prior experience. Such a perspective is often juxtaposed to earlier correspondence and *information-processing* views of learning. Early constructivist thought is generally attributed to Bartlett and Piaget, while more contemporary constructivism is often linked to Vygotsky and the *sociohistoricists*. Although constructivism can be defined within psychology, after Chapter Two I conflate constructivism with the broader *constructivist metatheory* (see also *situated cognition*).

CONSTRUCTIONISM, See SOCIAL CONSTRUCTIONISM

CONSTRUCTIVIST METATHEORY My term for the widespread approach to learning that combines elements of many strains of educational, philosophical, and psychological thought, especially Deweyan *progressivism*, Vygotskian *sociohistoricism*, Piagetian developmental theory, *social constructionism*, and philosophical *pragmatism*. In this book I argue that most teachers, researchers, and *educational technologists* subscribe to the constructivist metatheory rather than to any one of these constituent strains.

DISTRIBUTED COGNITION The view that thinking is dispersed across human organizations and environments. In computer science, a similar view is reflected in parallel processing.

DUALISM The term for the Cartesian separation of the observer from the phenomena he or she observes. A dualist perspective thus characterizes any enterprise we call "science." *Social constructionist* theories are founded on the refutation of dualism, however, and emphasize the interaction of the observer with the phenomenon observed. For this reason, the *constructivist metatheory* to which many educators subscribe must also reject dualism, though the metatheory's simultaneous status as a *social scientific* account of cognition creates many problems, the most obvious of which, I suggest, is *preauthentication*.

EDUCATIONAL TECHNOLOGISTS A group of specialists, often with disciplinary ties to computer science, that seeks to leverage cognitive theories of learning with electronic technologies. This book's de facto definition are those educators that participate in the conversations carried on in journals devoted to educational technology.

ELITE-IDEALISM I have coined this term to describe a traditional view of education that emphasizes the exalted nature of education and thus the superiority of the educated person to individuals who do not receive formal schooling. Because of its focus on "academic" rather than applied learning it may be counterposed to *vocationalism*. Although it has come under sustained attack by *progressivism* for much of this century, the elite-idealist tradition persists in many subtle ways.

EPISTEMOLOGY Used in two senses; in its most common, philosophical sense, epistemology is the study of knowledge and its sources. In Piaget's *social scientific* sense of "genetic epistemology," however, it is the study of how an organism (specifically, the human child) uses its senses to understand the world. In this social scientific sense, key aspects of philosophical epistemology are elided, most notably the reliability of the senses and the correspondence of sensate feelings to external reality (see *foundationalism* and *antifoundationism*).

FOUNDATIONALISM   The *epistemological* perspective that knowledge is rooted in, and can be built up from, an immutable truth, whether that truth is a supreme being (e.g., God), human capacity (e.g, rationality, sensory perception), or method (e.g., science) (see *antifoundationalism*).

INFORMATION-PROCESSING PARADIGM   The form of *cognitivism* that first displaced behaviorism in the United States, variations of which are sometimes called "symbol-processing" or "stored-schema" paradigms. In its crudest form, the information-processing paradigm presumes that informational inputs are external to the processor's (or learner's) experience and that cognition is therefore the essentially algorithmic processing of stable data. Still dominant in artificial intelligence circles, the information-processing paradigm is often contrasted to *constructivist* views of cognition.

PRAGMATISM   One of the philosophical threads that contribute to the *constructivist metatheory*, pragmatism is a broad perspective, developed at the turn of this century by figures such as Peirce, James, Mead, and, most significantly for education, Dewey. Pragmatism grounds knowledge in viability and utility rather than in the traditional foundations of rationality or scientific method. While neo-pragmatists (Richard Rorty may be the most best known of this group) insist that pragmatism is therefore *antifoundational*, others have argued that it is not so dogmatic as to reject all bases for knowledge.

PREAUTHENTICATION   The educational practice whereby "authentic" learning technologies, environments, or pedagogies are devised prior to, and independent of, a learner and a specific learning context. A central point of this book is that preauthenticatory practices, as seen in the field of *educational technology*, highlight the philosophical tensions latent in *constructivism*.

PROGRESSIVISM   The framework for education, commonly associated with Dewey and contrasted to what I have called *elite-idealism*, that conceives of learning as rooted in experience. Progressivists argue that the best sort of education is one that unites a learner's curricular and extracurriular lives and blurs the lines among different spheres of learning.

RHETORIC   Traditionally limited to the study of argumentation and persuasion, more recently (with the ascendance of the New Rhetoric movement) rhetoric has come to encompass the study of how individuals and/or groups intentionally and unintentionally use symbols such as words, images, and concepts to represent the world to themselves and to others. I argue in this book that *constructivist* theories of learning demand a rhetorical perspective on education.

SITUATED COGNITION (also Situationism) The psychological view that thinking is embedded in context and draws upon social, cultural, and material resources that are never exactly the same for any two individuals or in any two contexts. Drawing on *sociohistoricism*, situated cognition relies heavily on the notions of *distributedness* and *activity* and is a key thread of the *constructivist metatheory*.

SOCIAL CONSTRUCTIONISM The largely philosophical view (although it has important roots in sociology, anthropology, linguistics, and rhetoric) that what we take to be true about the world is a product of our interaction with others, both synchronistically (i.e., interpersonally) and, through culture and ideology, diachronistically. Social constructionism is thus primarily an epistemological stance that feeds into the *constructivist metatheory* (see also *antifoundationalism*).

SOCIAL SCIENTISM The application of scientific method (e.g., operationalization and control of variables, commitment to falsifiability, separability of observer and the observed, etc.) to the realm of human behavior. In this book, I have argued that *constructivism* in psychology is essentially social scientific (and thus *foundational*) whereas *social construction* is essentially *antifoundational*. For this reason, the *constructivist metatheory* that draws from both therefore contains an internal *epistemological* contradiction.

SOCIOHISTORICISM The school of psychology associated with Vygotsky and his collaborators, sociohistoricism asserts that individual cognition is the result of internalizing external (i.e., social) knowledge and practices via *activities* embedded in cultural and material circumstances. Rediscovery of sociohistoricist thought has motivated the movement to *situate cognition* as well as the revival and amendment of earlier *constructivist* thought.

SCHEMA PROCESSING, See INFORMATION-PROCESSING PARADIGM

VOCATIONALISM The view that education should principally serve to prepare students for the world of work. Within the *elite-idealist* framework, vocationalism (in the form of apprenticeship) was considered an alternative to education.

References

Agre, P. E. (1993). The symbolic worldview: Reply to Vera and Simon. *Cognitive Science, 17,* 61–69.

Allen, B. S. (1992). Constructive criticisms. In T. Duffy & D. Jonassen (Eds.) *Constructivism and the technology of instruction* (pp. 183–204). Hillsdale, NJ: Lawrence Erlbaum Associates.

Allen, B. S., & Hoffman, R. P. (1993). Varied levels of support for constructive activity in hypermedia-based learning environments. In T. Duffy, J. Lowyck, & D. Jonassen (Eds.), *Designing environments for constructive learning* (pp. 261–283). Berlin: Springer-Verlag.

America 2000 Commission. (1991). *America 2000: An overview.* ED1.2: AM3/7.

Amsel, A. (1989). *Behaviorism, neobehaviorism, and cognitivism in learning theory: Historical and contemporary perspectives.* Hillsdale, NJ: Lawrence Erlbaum Associates.

Anderson, J. R. (1990). *Cognitive psychology and its implications* (3rd ed.). New York: Freeman.

Anderson, J. R., Reder, L. M., & Simon, H. A. (1995). *Applications and misapplications of cognitive psychology to mathematics education.* [Internet]. Available: World Wide Web, http://sands.psy.cmu.edu/personal/ja/misapplied.html.

Anderson, J. R., Reder, L. M., & Simon, H. A. (1996). Situated learning and education. *Educational Researcher, 25*(4), 5–11.

Aristotle. (1932). *Rhetoric.* L. Cooper (Trans.). New York: Appleton-Century.

Ausubel, D. P. (1968). *Educational psychology: A cognitive view.* New York: Holt, Rinehart & Winston.

Baars, B. (1986). *The cognitive revolution in psychology.* New York: Guilford.

Backman, D. (1991). *Sophistication: Rhetoric and the rise of self-consciousness.* Woodbridge, CT: Ox Bow.

Bagley, C., & Hunter, B. (1992, July). Restructuring constructivism and technology: Forging a new relationship. *Educational Technology,* 22–28.

Baker, M. (1994). A model for negotiation in teaching–learning dialogues. *Journal of Artificial Intelligence in Education, 5*(2), 199–254.

Balsam, P. D. (1985). The functions of context in learning and performance. In P. Balsam & A. Tomie (Eds.), *Context and learning* (pp. 1–21). Hillsdale, NJ: Lawrence Erlbaum Associates.

Bantock, G. H. (1963). *Education in an industrial society.* London: Faber & Faber.

Barclay, W. (1959). *Educational ideals in the ancient world.* London: Collins.

Bartlett, F. (1932). *Remembering: A study in experimental and social psychology.* London: Cambridge University Press.

Bazerman, C. (1988). *Shaping written knowledge: The genre and activity of the experimental article in science.* Madison: University of Wisconsin Press.

Beach, R., & Lundell, D. (1996, October). *Early adolescents' use of computer-mediated communica-*

tion in writing and reading. Paper presented at the NRRC conference on computers and literacy, Decatur, GA.

Becker, H. S. (1972). A school is a lousy place to learn anything in. *American Behavioral Scientist, 16,* 85–105.

Bednar, A. K., Cunningham, D., Duffy, T., & Perry, J. D. (1992). Theory into practice: How do we link? In T. Duffy & D. Jonassen (Eds.), *Constructivism and the technology of instruction* (pp. 17–34). Hillsdale, NJ: Lawrence Erlbaum Associates.

Bell, P., Davis, E. A., & Linn, M. C. (1995). *The knowledge integration environment: Theory and design.* Paper presented at the Computer Support for Collaborative Learning Conference.

Bellamy, R. K. E. (1996). Designing educational technology: Computer mediated change. In B. Nardi (Ed.), *Context and consciousness* (pp. 123–146). Cambridge, MA: MIT Press.

Bereiter, C. (1994). Implications of postmodernism for science, or, science as progressive discourse. *Educational Psychologist, 29*(1), 3–12.

Bereiter, C., & Scardamalia, M. (1989). Intentional learning as a goal of instruction. In L. Resnick (Ed.), *Knowing, learning, and instruction* (pp. 361–392). Hillsdale, NJ: Lawrence Erlbaum Associates.

Berger, P., & Luckmann, T. (1967). *The social construction of reality.* New York: Anchor.

Berlin, J. (1987). *Rhetoric and reality, writing instruction in American colleges, 1900–1985.* Carbondale: Southern Illinois University Press.

Berlin, J., & Inkster, R. (1980). Current-traditional rhetoric: Paradigm and practice. *Freshman English News, 8,* 1–14.

Berlo, D. (1960). *The process of communication.* New York: Holt, Winston & Rinehart.

Berthoff, A. E. (1996). Problem-dissolving by triadic means. *College English, 58*(1), 9–21.

Best, J. H., & Sidwell, R. T. (1967). *The American legacy of learning.* Philadelphia: Lippincott.

Billig, M. (1987). *Arguing and thinking: A rhetorical approach to social psychology.* Cambridge, England: Cambridge University Press.

Billig, M. (1993a). Psychology, rhetoric and cognition. In R. H. Roberts & J. M. M. Good (Eds.), *The recovery of rhetoric: Persuasive discourse and disciplinarity in the human science* (pp. 119–136). Charlottesville, VA: University Press of Virginia.

Billig, M. (1993b). Studying the thinking society: Social representations, rhetoric, and attitudes. In G. Breakwell & D. Canter (Eds.), *Empirical approaches to social representations.* Oxford, England: Clarendon.

Bitzer, L. (1968). The rhetorical situation. *Philosophy and Rhetoric, 1,* 1–14.

Bizzell, P., & Herzberg, B. (Eds.). (1990). *The rhetorical tradition.* New York: St. Martin's Press.

Bloom, A. (1987). *The closing of the American mind.* New York: Simon & Schuster

Boekaerts, M. (1987). Problem solving behavior: New perspectives for ecologically valid research. *Journal of Structural Learning, 8*(3–4), 195–224.

Bolter, J. D. (1991). *Writing space.* Hillsdale, NJ: Lawrence Erlbaum Associates.

Bowen, B. (1994). Telecommunications networks: Expanding the contexts for literacy. In C. Selfe & S. Hilligoss (Eds.), *Literacy and computers* (pp. 113–129). New York: MLA.

Boyd, W. (1947). *The history of Western education.* London: Adam and Charles Black.

Bredo, E. (1993). Reflections on the intelligence of ITSs: A response to Clancey's "Guidon-Manage revisited." *Journal of Artificial Intelligence in Education, 4*(1), 35–40.

Bredo, E. (1994). Reconstructing educational psychology: Situated cognition and Deweyan pragmatism. *Educational Psychologist, 29*(1), 23–35.

Brief, J-C. (1983). *Beyond Piaget: A philosophical psychology.* New York: Teachers College Press.

Brown, A. L., Ash, D., Rutherford, M., Nakagawa, K., Gordon, A., & Campione, J. C. (1993). Distributed expertise in the classroom. In G. Salomon (Ed.), *Distributed cognitions: Psychological and educational considerations* (pp. 188–227). Cambridge, England: Cambridge University Press.

Brown, A. L., & Palincsar, A. S. (1989). Guided cooperative learning and individual knowledge acquisition. In L. Resnick (Ed.), *Knowing, learning, and instruction* (pp. 393–452). Hillsdale, NJ: Lawrence Erlbaum Associates.

Brown, J. S. (1990). Towards a new epistemology of learning. Keynote address to ITS 1988 (Montreal). In C. Frasson & J. Gauthiar (Eds.), *Intelligent tutoring systems at the crossroads of AI* (pp. 266–282). Norwood, NJ: Ablex.

Brown, J. S., Collins, A., & Duguid, P. (1989). Situated cognition and the culture of learning. *Educational Researcher, 18*(1), 32–42.

Brown, J. S., & Duguid, P. (1994, October). Practice at the periphery: A reply to Steven Tripp. *Educational Technology*, pp. 9–11.

Brubacher, J. S. (1950). *Modern philosophies of education*. New York: McGraw-Hill.

Bruffee, K. (1986). Social construction, language and the authority of knowledge. *College English, 48*, 773–787.

Bruffee, K. (1990). Response to *JAC* interview with Richard Rorty. *JAC, 10*, 145–146.

Bruffee, K. (1993). *Collaborative learning: Higher education, independence, and the authority of knowledge*. Baltimore: Johns Hopkins University Press.

Brummett, B. (1976). Some implications of "process" on "intersubjectivity": Postmodern rhetoric. *Philosophy and Rhetoric, 9*(Winter), 21–51.

Bruner, J. (1961). The act of discovery. *Harvard Educational Review, 31*, 21–32.

Bruner, J. (1990). *Acts of meaning*. Cambridge, MA: Harvard University Press.

Buck, G. (1901). Recent tendencies in the teaching of English composition. *Educational Review, 22*, 371–82.

Burgess, T. (1993). Reading Vygotsky. In H. Daniels (Ed.), *Charting the agenda: Educational activity after Vygotsky* (pp. 1–29). New York: Routledge.

Burke, K. (1945). *A grammar of motives*. New York: Prentice-Hall.

Burke, K. (1968). Dramatism. In D. Stills (Ed.), *International encyclopedia of the social sciences* (pp. 445–452). New York: Macmillan.

Button, H. W., & Provenzo, E. F. (1983). *History of education and culture in America*. Englewood Cliffs, NJ: Prentice-Hall.

Ceci, S. J., & Ruiz, A. (1993). Inserting context into our thinking about thinking: Implications for a theory of everyday intelligent behavior. In M. Rabinowitz (Ed.), *Cognitive science foundations for instruction* (pp. 173–188). Hillsdale, NJ: Lawrence Erlbaum Associates.

Chambliss, J. J. (1968). *The origins of American philosophy of education*. Hague, The Netherlands: Nijhoff.

Cherwitz, R. A., & Hikins, J. W. (1983). Rhetorical perspectivism. *The Quarterly Journal of Speech, 69*, 249–266.

Choi, J-I., & Hannafin, M. (1995). Situated cognition and learning environments: Roles, structures, and implications for design. *Educational Technology Research and Development, 43*(2), 53–69.

Chomsky, N. (1964). A review of B. F. Skinner's verbal behavior. In J. A. Fodor & J. J. Katz (Eds.), *The structure of language: Readings in the philosophy of language* (pp. 547–78). Englewood Cliffs, NJ: Prentice-Hall.

Cicero. (1921). *De Oratore* (Book I). (E. W. Sutton & H. Rackham, Trans.). Cambridge, MA: Harvard University Press.

Cizek, G. J. (1995). Crunchy granola and the hegemony of the narrative. *Educational Researcher, 24*, 26–28.

Clancey, W. (1992). Representations of knowing: In defense of cognitive apprenticeship. *Journal of Artificial Intelligence in Education, 3*(2), 149–168.

Clancey, W. (1993). Guidon-manage revisited: A socio-technical systems approach. *Journal of Artificial Intelligence in Education, 4*(1), 5–34.

Clark, J. M. (1995). *Cognitive apprenticeship, motivation, and college writing: Theoretical and peda-

gogical considerations. Unpublished doctoral dissertation. Bowling Green State University, Ohio.

Clarke, M. L. (1971). *Higher education in the ancient world.* London: Routledge & Kegan Paul.

Cobb, P. (1994a). Constructivism in mathematics and science education. *Educational Researcher, 23*(7), 4.

Cobb, P. (1994b). Where is the mind? Constructivist and sociocultural perspectives on mathematical development. *Educational Researcher, 23*(7), 13–20

Cognition and Technology Group at Vanderbilt. (1990). Anchored instruction and its relationship to situated cognition. *Educational Researcher, 19,* 2–10.

Cognition and Technology Group at Vanderbilt (1992a). An anchored instruction approach to cognitive skills acquisition and intelligent tutoring. In J. W. Regian & V. Shute (Eds.), *Cognitive approaches to automated instruction* (pp. 135–170). Hillsdale, NJ: Lawrence Erlbaum Associates.

Cognition and Technology Group at Vanderbilt. (1992b). Technology and the design of generative learning environments. In T. Duffy & D. Jonassen (Eds.), *Constructivism and the technology of instruction* (pp. 77–89). Hillsdale, NJ: Lawrence Erlbaum Associates.

Cognition and Technology Group at Vanderbilt. (1993, March). Anchored instruction and situated cognition revisited. *Educational Technology,* 52–70.

Cohen, L. J. (1992). *An essay on belief and acceptance.* Oxford, England: Clarendon Press.

Cohen, Y. A. (1971). The shaping of men's minds: Adaptations to imperatives of culture. In M. Wax, S. Diamond, & F. Gearing (Eds.), *Anthropological perspectives on education.* New York: Basic.

Cole, M. (1985). The zone of proximal development: Where culture and cognition create each other. In J. Wertsch (Ed.), *Culture, communication, and cognition: Vygotskian perspectives* (pp. 146–161). Cambridge, England: Cambridge University Press.

Cole, M. (1990). Cognitive development and formal schooling: The evidence from cross-cultural research. In L. Moll (Ed.), *Vygotsky and education* (pp. 89–110). Cambridge, England: Cambridge University Press.

Cole, M., & Engeström, Y. (1993). A cultural–historical approach to distributed cognition. In G. Salomon (Ed.), *Distributed cognitions: Psychological and educational considerations* (pp. 1–45). Cambridge, England: Cambridge University Press.

Collins, A. (1991). The role of computer technology in restructuring schools. *Phi Delta Kappan, 73*(1), 28–36.

Collins, A. (1994, November–December). Goal-based scenarios and the problem of situated learning: A commentary on Andersen Consulting's design of goal-based scenarios. *Educational Technology,* 30–32.

Collins, A., Brown, J. S., & Holum, A. (1991). Cognitive apprenticeship: Making thinking visible. *American Educator,* (Winter), 6–11, 38–46.

Collins, A., Brown, J. S., & Newman, S. (1989). Cognitive apprenticeship: Teaching the crafts of reading, writing, and mathematics. In L. Resnick (Ed.), *Knowing, learning, and instruction* (pp. 453–494). Hillsdale, NJ: Lawrence Erlbaum Associates.

Confrey, J. (1990). What constructivism implies for teaching [Monograph]. *Journal for Research in Mathematics Education, 4,* 107–122.

Confrey, J. (1995). How compatible are radical constructivism, sociocultural approaches, and social constructivism? In L. Steffe & J. Gale (Eds.), *Constructivism in education* (pp. 185–225). Mahwah, NJ: Lawrence Erlbaum Associates.

Conklin, J. (1987). *A survey of hypertext* (MCC Tech. Report No. STP-365-86).

Consigny, S. (1974). Rhetoric and its situations. *Philosophy and Rhetoric, 7,* 175–186.

Cooper, P. A. (1993, May). Paradigm shifts in designed education: From behaviorism to cognitivism to constructivism. *Educational Technology,* 12–18.

Cornbleth, C. (1987). The persistence of myth in teacher education and training. In T. Popkewitz (Ed.), *Critical studies in teacher education* (pp. 186–210). London: Falmer.

Costall, A. (1991). Frederic Bartlett and the rise of prehistoric psychology. In A. Still & A. Costall (Eds.), *Against cognitivism: Alternative foundations for cognitive psychology* (pp. 39–54). New York: Harvester-Wheatsheaf.

Costall, A., & Still, A. (1991). Cognitivism as an approach to cognition. In A. Still & A. Costall (Eds.), *Against cognitivism: Alternative foundations for cognitive psychology* (pp. 1–6). New York: Harvester-Wheatsheaf.

Coulter, J. (1983). *Rethinking cognitive theory.* New York: St. Martin's Press.

Covey, P. K. (1990). Integrating emotion in moral reasoning and learning. In R. Kozma & J. Johnston (Eds.), *Educational computing in the humanities.* Hillsdale, NJ: Lawrence Erlbaum Associates.

Crosswhite, J. (1996). *The rhetoric of reason: Writing and the attractions of argument.* Madison: University of Wisconsin Press.

Csikszentmihalyi, M. (1990). Literacy and intrinsic motivation. *Dædalus,* (Spring), 115–140.

Cunningham, D. J. (1992). In defense of extremism. In T. Duffy & D. Jonassen (Eds.), *Constructivism and the technology of instruction* (pp. 157–160). Hillsdale, NJ: Lawrence Erlbaum Associates.

Damarin, S. K. (1994, October). The emancipatory potential of situated learning. *Educational Technology,* 16–22.

Danziger, K. (1990). *Constructing the subject: Historical origins of psychological research.* Cambridge, England: Cambridge University Press.

Dashiell, J. F. (1928). *Fundamentals of objective psychology.* Boston: Houghton Mifflin.

Davydov, V. V. (1995). The influence of L. S. Vygotsky on education theory, research, and practice (S. Kerr, Trans.). *Educational Researcher, 24*(3), 12–21.

Davydov, V. V., & Radzikhovskii, L. (1985). Vygotsky's theory and activity-oriented approach in psychology. In J. Wertsch (Ed.), *Culture, communication, and cognition: Vygotskian perspectives* (pp. 35–65). Cambridge, England: Cambridge University Press.

de Groot, A. D. (1965). *Thought and choice in chess.* Hague, The Netherlands: Mouton.

Dember, W. (1974). Motivation and the cognitive revolution. *American Psychologist, 29,* 161–168.

Dewey, J. (1897). My pedagogic creed. *School Journal, 54,* 77–80.

Dewey, J. (1938). *Experience and education.* New York: Collier.

Dewey, J. (1961), *Democracy and education.* New York: Macmillan.

Diggins, J. P. (1994). *The promise of pragmatism: Modernism and the crisis of knowledge and authority.* Chicago: University of Chicago Press.

Dillenbourg, P., & Schneider, D. (1993). Designers did not wait for situationists: A response to Clancey's viewpoint "Guidon-Manage revisited." *Journal of Artificial Intelligence in Education, 4*(1), 41–48.

Donaldson, M. (1978). *Children's minds.* London: Fontana.

Douglas, P. H. (1921). *American apprenticeship and industrial education.* New York: Longman.

Downing, D. B. (1995). The political consequences of pragmatism; or cultural pragmatics for a cybernetic revolution. In S. Mailloux (Ed.), *Rhetoric, sophistry, pragmatism* (pp. 180–205). Cambridge, England: Cambridge University Press.

Driver, R., Asoko, H., Leach, J., Mortimer, E., & Scott, P. (1994). Constructing scientific knowledge in the classroom. *Educational Researcher, 23*(7), 5–12.

Duffy, T. M., & Jonassen D. H. (1992). Constructivism: New implications for instructional technology. In T. Duffy & D. Jonassen (Eds.), *Constructivism and the technology of instruction* (pp. 1–16). Hillsdale, NJ: Lawrence Erlbaum Associates.

Dunn, T. G. (1994). If we can't contextualize it, should we teach it? *Educational Technology Research and Development, 42*(3), 83–92.

Durkheim, E. (1915). *The elementary forms of the religious life: A study in religious sociology* (J. Swain, Trans.). London: Allen & Unwin.

Ede, L., & Lunsford, A. (1990). *Singular Texts/Plural Authors: Perspectives on Collaborative Writing.* Carbondale: Southern Illinois University Press.

Elkind, D. (1979). Piaget and developmental psychology. In F. Murry (Ed.), *The impact of Piagetian theory on education, philosophy, psychiatry, and psychology* (pp. 3–15). Baltimore: University Park Press.

Ellis, R. (1990). *Instructed second language acquisition.* Oxford, England: Blackwell

Engeström, Y. (1987). *Learning by expanding: An activity-theoretical approach to developmental research.* Helsinki: Orienta-Konsultit.

Engeström, Y. (1990). *Working, learning and imagining: Twelve studies in activity theory.* Helsinki: Orienta-Konsultit.

Engeström, Y. (1993). Developmental studies of work as a testbench of activity theory: The case of primary care medical practice. In S. Chaiklin & J. Lave (Eds.), *Understanding practice: Perspectives on activity and context* (pp. 64–103). Cambridge, England: Cambridge University Press.

Engeström, Y., & Escalante, E. (1996). Mundane tool or object of affection? The rise and fall of the postal buddy. In B. Nardi (Ed.), *Context and consciousness* (pp. 325–374). Cambridge, MA: MIT Press.

Enos, R. L. (1976). The epistemology of Gorgias' rhetoric: A re-examination. *Southern Speech Communication Journal, 42,* 35–51.

Evans, W. (1995). The mundane and the arcane: Prestige media coverage of social and natural science. *Journalism and Mass Communication Quarterly, 72*(1), 168–177.

Feinberg, W. (1975). *Reason and rhetoric: The intellectual foundations of 20th century liberal education policy.* New York: Wiley.

Fenstermacher, G., & Richardson, V. (1994). Promoting confusion in educational psychology: How is it done? *Educational Psychologist, 29*(1), 49–55.

Fiske, S. T., & Linville P. W. (1980). What does the schema theory buy us? *Personality and Social Psychology, 6*(4), 543–557.

Floud, J. E. (1973). *Social class and educational opportunity.* Westport, CT: Greenwood.

Fodor, J. (1972). Some reflections on L. S. Vygotsky's *Thought and Language. Cognition, 1,* 84.

Ford, P. L. (1904). *The works of Thomas Jefferson.* New York: Putnam.

Friedmann, G. (1950). *Ou Va le Travail Humain* [The future of work]. Paris: Gallimard.

Frymier, A. B., & Shulman. G. (1995). "What's in it for me?": Increasing content relevance to enhance student motivation. *Communications Education, 44,* 40–50.

Fuller, S. (1993). *Philosophy, rhetoric, and the end of knowledge.* Madison: Wisconsin University Press.

Gaonkar, D. P. (1993). The idea of rhetoric in the rhetoric of science. *Southern Communication Journal, 58*(4), 258–295.

Gardner, H. (1985). *The mind's new science.* New York: Basic.

Garrison, J. (1995). Deweyan pragmatism and the epistemology of contemporary social constructivism. *American Education Research Journal, 32*(4), 716–740.

Gearhart, S. M. (1979). The womanization of rhetoric. *Women's Studies International Quarterly, 2,* 195–201.

Gegg-Harrison, T. (1992). Adapting instruction to the student's capabilities. *Journal of Artificial Intelligence in Education, 3*(2), 169–181.

Gellner, E. (1992). *Reason and culture.* Oxford, England: Blackwell.

Gergen, K. (1985). The social constructionist movement in modern psychology. *American Psychologist, 40*(3), 266–275.

Gergen, K. (1995). Social construction and the educational process. In L. Steffe & J. Gale (Eds.), *Constructivism in education* (pp. 17–39). Hillsdale, NJ: Lawrence Erlbaum Associates.

Gergen, K. J. (1994). The mechanical self and the rhetoric of objectivity. In A. Megill (Ed.), *Rethinking objectivity* (pp. 265–287). Durham, NC: Duke University Press.

Gibson, J. J. (1966). *The senses considered as perceptual systems.* Boston: Houghton Mifflin.

Gildea, P. M., Miller, G. A., & Wurtenberg, C. L. (1990). Contextual enrichment by videodisc. In D. Nix & R. Spiro (Eds.), *Cognition, education, and multimedia: Exploring ideas in high technology* (pp. 67–81). Hillsdale, NJ: Lawrence Erlbaum Associates.

Goggin, M. D. (1995). The disciplinary instability of composition. In J. Petraglia (Ed.), *Reconceiving writing, rethinking writing instruction* (pp. 27–48). Mahwah, NJ: Lawrence Erlbaum Associates.

Good, H. G. (1947). *A history of Western education.* New York: MacMillan.

Goodman, P. (1962). *Growing up absurd.* New York: Random House.

Goodman, Y. M., & Goodman, K. S. (1990). Vygotsky in a whole-language perspective. In L. Moll (Ed.), *Vygotsky and education* (pp. 223–250). Cambridge, England: Cambridge University Press.

Gray, S. H. (1993). *Hypertext and the technology of conversation: Orderly situational choice.* Westport, CT: Greenwood.

Greeno, J. G. (1989). A perspective on thinking. *American Psychologist, 44*(2), 134–141.

Greeno, J. G., & Moore, J. (1993). Situativity and symbols: Reponse to Vera and Simon. *Cognitive Science, 17,* 49–59.

Greeno, J. G., Moore, J., & Smith, D. R. (1993). Transfer of situated learning. In D. Detterman & R. Sternberg (Eds.), *Transfer on trial: Intelligence, cognition, and instruction* (pp. 99–167). Norwood, NJ: Ablex.

Grice, P. (1989). *Studies in the way of words.* Cambridge, MA: Harvard University Press.

Haan, N. (1975). Hypothetical and actual moral reasoning in a situation of civil disobedience. *Journal of Personality and Social Psychology, 32,* 255–270.

Hacking, I. (1983). *Representing and intervening.* Cambridge, England: Cambridge University Press.

Hamlyn, D. W. (1990). *In and out of the black box: On the philosophy of cognition.* Oxford, England: Basil Blackwell.

Hammer, D. (1994). Epistemological beliefs in introductory physics. *Cognition and Instruction, 12*(2), 151–183.

Hanks, W. F. (1991). Foreword. In J. Lave & E. Wenger (Eds.), *Situated learning: Legitimate peripheral participation* (pp. i–viii). Cambridge, England: Cambridge University Press.

Harré, R. (1986). The step to social constructionism. In M. Richards & P. Light (Eds.), *Children of social worlds* (pp. 287–317). Cambridge, MA: Polity Press.

Harris. J. (1989). The idea of community in the study of writing. *College Composition and Communication, 40,* 11–22.

Hay, K. E. (1993). Legitimate peripheral participation, instructionism, and constructivism: Whose situation is it anyway? *Educational Technology, 33*(3), 33–38.

Hay, K. E. (1994). The three activities of a student: A reply to Tripp. *Educational Technology, 34*(8), 22–27.

Hayes, R. (1985). Three problems in teaching general skills. In S. Chipman, J. Segal, & R. Glaser (Eds.), *Thinking and learning skills* (Vol. 2, pp. 391–406). Hillsdale, NJ: Lawrence Erlbaum Associates.

Hayles, N. K. (1993). Constrained constructivism: Locating scientific inquiry in the theatre of representation. In G. Levine (Ed.), *Realism and representation: Essays on the problem of realism in relation to science, literature, and culture* (pp. 27–43). Madison: University of Wisconsin Press.

Hendley B. P. (1986). *Dewey, Russell, Whitehead: Philosophers as educators.* Carbondale: Southern Illinois University Press.

Hmelo, C. E., & Nararyanan, N. H. (1995). Anchors, cases, problems, and scenarios as contexts for learning. *Proceedings of the 17th Annual Conference of the Cognitive Science Society* (pp. 5–8).

Hoffman, M. L. (1984). Interaction of affect and cognition in empathy. In C. Izard, J. Kagan, & R. Zajonc (Eds.), *Emotion, cognition, and behavior* (pp. 103–131). New York: Cambridge University Press.

Honebein, P. C., Duffy, T., & Fishman, B. (1993). Constructivism and the design of learning environments: Context and authentic activities for learning. In T. Duffy, J. Lowyck, & D. Jonassen (Eds.), *Designing environments for constructive learning* (pp. 87–108). Berlin: Springer-Verlag.

Hooper, S. (1992). Cooperative learning and computer-based instruction. *Educational Technology Research and Development, 40*(3), 21–38.

Hoppe, H. U. (1993). Cognitive apprenticeship—The emperor's new method? A polemical reaction to the debate on situated cognition and cognitive apprenticeship. *Journal of Artificial Intelligence in Education, 4*(1), 49–54.

Hunter, L. (1991). Rhetoric and artificial intelligence. *Rhetorica, IX*(4), 317–340.

Hutchins, E. (1995). *Cognition in the wild*. Cambridge, MA: MIT Press.

Jarratt, S. C. (1995). In excess: Radical extensions of neopragmatism. In S. Mailloux (Ed.), *Rhetoric, sophistry, pragmatism*. Cambridge, England: Cambridge University Press.

Jonassen, D. H. (1992). Cognitive flexibility theory and its implications for designing CBI. In S. Dijkstra, H. P. M. Krammer, & J. J. G. van Merrienboer (Eds.), *Instructional models in computer-based learning environments* (pp. 385–403). Berlin: Springer-Verlag.

Jonassen, D. H. (1994, April). Thinking technology: Towards a constructivist design model. *Educational Technology*, 34–37.

Jonassen, D. H., Campbell, J. P., & Davidson, M. (1994). Learning with media: Restructuring the debate. *Educational Technology Research and Development, 42*(2), 31–39.

Jonassen, D. H., Mayes, T., & McAleese, R. (1993). A manifesto for a constructivist approach to uses of technology in higher education. In T. Duffy, J. Lowyck, & D. Jonassen (Eds.), *Designing environments for constructive learning* (pp. 231–247). Berlin: Springer-Verlag.

Jones, B. F., Knuth, R. A., & Duffy, T. (1993). Components of constructivist learning environments for professional development. In T. Duffy, J. Lowyck, & D. Jonassen (Eds.), *Designing environments for constructive learning* (pp. 125–137). Berlin: Springer-Verlag.

Karier, C. J. (1986). *The individual, society and education: A history of American educational ideas*. Urbana: University of Illinois Press.

Kennedy, G. A. (1992). A hoot in the dark: The evolution of general rhetoric. *Philosophy and Rhetoric, 25*(1), 1–21.

Kohlberg, L. (1986). A current statement on some theoretical issues. In S. Modgil & C. Modgil (Eds.), *Lawrence Kohlberg: Consensus and controversy*. Philadephia: Falmer.

Kozulin, A. (1986). Foreword. In L. S. Vygotsky's *Thought and language*. Cambridge, MA: MIT Press.

Krashen, S. (1982). *Principles and practice in second language aquisition*. Oxford: Pergamon.

Kuutti, K. (1996). Activity theory as a potential framework for human–computer interaction research. In B. Nardi (Ed.), *Context and consciousness* (pp. 17–44). Cambridge, MA: MIT Press.

Lakoff, G. (1987). *Women, fire, and dangerous things: What categories reveal about the mind*. Chicago: University of Chicago Press.

Langley, P., Simon, H. A., Bradshaw, G. L., & Zytkow, J. M. (1987). *Scientific discovery: Computational explorations of the creative process*. Cambridge, MA: MIT Press.

Latour, B. (1988). *Science in action: How to follow scientists and engineers through society*. Cambridge, MA: Harvard University Press.

Lave, J. (1988). *Cognition in practice*. New York: Cambridge University Press.

Lave, J. (1991). Situating learning in communities of practice. In L. Resnick, J. Levine, & S. Teasley (Eds.), *Perspectives on socially shared cognition* (pp. 63–82). Washington, DC: American Psychological Association.

Lave, J., & Wenger, E. (1991). *Situated learning: Legitimate peripheral participation.* Cambridge, England: Cambridge University Press.

Lee, G. C. (1965). *Education and democratic ideals.* New York: Harcourt Brace.

Leff, M. (1978). In search of Ariadne's thread: A review of the recent literature on rhetorical theory. *Central States Speech Journal, 29,* 73–91.

Leontiev, A. N. (1978). *Activity, consciousness, and personality.* Englewood Cliffs, NJ: Prentice-Hall.

Leontiev, A. N. (1981). The problem of activity in psychology. In J. Wertsch (Ed.), *The concept of activity in Soviet psychology.* Armonk, NY: Sharpe.

Lesgold, A., Eggan, G., Katz, S., & Rao, G. (1992). Possibilities for assessment using computer-based apprenticeship environments. In J. W. Regian & V. Shute (Eds.), *Cognitive approaches to automated instruction* (pp. 49–80). Hillsdale, NJ: Lawrence Erlbaum Associates.

Levine, G. (1994). Why science isn't literature: The importance of differences. In A. Megill (Ed.), *Rethinking objectivity* (pp. 65–79). Durham, NC: Duke University Press.

Lincoln, Y., & Guba, E. (1985). *Naturalistic inquiry.* Newbury Park, CA: Sage.

Linn, M. C., Bell, P., & Hsi, S. (in press). Lifelong science learning on the internet: The knowledge integration environment. *Interactive Learning Environments.*

Lunsford, A. (1979). Aristotelian vs. Rogerian argument: A reassessment. *College Composition and Communication, 30*(2), 146–151.

Luria, A. R. (1976). *Cognitive development: Its cultural and social foundations.* Cambridge, MA: Harvard University Press.

Luria, A. R. (1979). *The making of mind.* Cambridge, MA: Harvard University Press.

Mailloux, S. (1995). Sophistry and rhetorical pragmatism. In S. Mailloux (Ed.), *Rhetoric, sophistry, pragmatism.* Cambridge, England: Cambridge University Press.

Marrou, H. (1982). *A history of education in antiquity* (G. Lamb, Trans.). Madison: University of Wisconsin Press.

Mastracci, M. (1991). Confronting real-world ethics on videodisc. *Carnegie Mellon Magazine, 9*(3), 26–29.

Mavrodes, G. I. (1964). Real and more real. *International Philosophical Quarterly, 4*(4), 554–561.

McClellan, J. L., & Rumelhart, D. (1986). *Parallel distributive processing* (Vol. 2). Cambridge, MA: MIT Press.

McCloskey, D. (1997). Big rhetoric, little rhetoric: Gaonkar on the rhetoric of science. In A. Gross & F. W. Keith (Eds.), *Rhetorical hermeneutics* (pp. 101–112). Albany: SUNY Press.

McLelland, H. (1994, October). Situated learning: Continuing the conversation. *Educational Technology,* 7–8.

Mead, M. (1951). *School in the American culture.* Cambridge, MA: Harvard University Press.

Merrill, M. D. (1992). Constructivism and instructional design. In T. Duffy & D. Jonassen (Eds.), *Constructivism and the technology of instruction* (pp. 99–114). Hillsdale, NJ: Lawrence Erlbaum Associates.

Miller, G. (1956). The magical number seven, plus or minus two: Some limits on our capacity for processing information. *Psychological Review, 63,* 81–97.

Minsky, M. (1961). Steps toward artificial intelligence. *Proceedings of the IRE, 49,* 8–29

Modleski, T. (1991). *Feminism without women: Culture and criticism in a "postfeminist" age.* New York: Routledge.

Moll, L. (1990). Introduction. In L. Moll (Ed.), *Vygotsky and education* (pp. 1–27). Cambridge, England: Cambridge University Press.

Moll, L., Tapia, J., & Whitmore, K. (1993). Living knowledge: The social distribution of cultural resources for thinking. In G. Salomon (Ed.), *Distributed cognitions: Psychological and educational considerations* (pp. 139–163). Cambridge, England: Cambridge University Press.

Mooney, M. (1994). *Vico in the tradition of rhetoric.* Davis, CA: Hermagoras.

Moyse, R., & Elsom-Cook, M. (1992). *Knowledge negotiation*. London: Academic Press.

Myers, G. (1986). Reality, concensus, and reform in the rhetoric of composition teaching. *College English, 48*(2), 154–171.

Myerson, G. (1994). *Rhetoric, reason, and society: Rationality as dialogue*. London: Sage.

Nardi, B. (1996a). Some reflections on the application of activity theory. In B. Nardi (Ed.), *Context and consciousness* (pp. 235–246). Cambridge, MA: MIT Press.

Nardi, B. (1996b). Studying context: A comparison of activity theory, situated action models, and distributed cognition. In B. Nardi (Ed.), *Context and consciousness* (pp. 69–102). Cambridge, MA: MIT Press.

Neisser, U. (1967). *Cognitive science*. New York: Appleton-Century-Crofts.

Neisser, U. (1976). *Cognition and reality*. San Francisco: Freeman.

Neuman, W. R. (1995, January). The psychology of the new media. *Educom Review,* 48–54.

Newell, A., & Simon, H. A. (1972). *Human problem solving*. Englewood Cliffs, NJ: Prentice-Hall.

Newman, D., Griffin, P., & Cole, M. (1989). *The construction ʒone working for cognitive change in school*. Cambridge, England: Cambridge University Press.

Nix, D. (1990). Introduction. In D. Nix & R. Spiro (Eds.), *Cognition, education, and multimedia: Exploring ideas in high technology* (pp. i–iv). Hillsdale NJ: Lawrence Erlbaum Associates.

Norman, D. A. (1981). *Perspectives on cognitive science*. Hillsdale, NJ: Lawrence Erlbaum Associates.

Norman, D. A. (1993). Cognition in the head and in the world: An introduction to the special issue on situated action. *Cognitive Science, 17,* 1–6.

Oakeshott, M. (1966). *Experience and its modes*. Cambridge, England: Cambridge University Press.

Orr, C. J. (1978). How shall we say: "Reality is Socially Constructed Through Communication?" *Central States Speech Journal, 29,* 263–274.

Palincsar, A. S. (1989, May). Less charted waters. *Educational Researcher,* 5–7.

Palincsar, A. S., & Brown, A. L. (1984). Reciprocal teaching of comprehension-fostering and monitoring activities. *Cognition and Instruction, 1*(2), 117–175.

Papert, S. (1979). The role of artificial intelligence in psychology. In M. Piattelli-Palmarini (Ed.), *Language and learning: The debate between Jean Piaget and Noam Chomsky*. Cambridge, MA: Harvard University Press.

Papert, S. (1995, October). *Technology in schools: Local fix or global transformation*. Remarks before a House of Representatives Panel on Technology and Education.

Pascarella, E. T., & Terenzini, P. T. (1991). *How college affects students*. San Francisco: Jossey-Bass.

Paul, R. (1982). Teaching critical thinking in the "strong" sense: A focus on self-deception, world views, and a dialectical mode of analysis. *Informal Logic, 4*(2), 2–7.

Pea, R. D. (1993). Practices of distributed intelligence and designs for education. In G. Salomon (Ed.), *Distributed cognitions: Psychological and educational considerations* (pp. 47–87). Cambridge, England: Cambridge University Press.

Pea, R. D., & Brown, J. S. (1993). Series foreword. In G. Salomon (Ed.), *Distributed cognitions: Psychological and educational considerations* (p. ix). Cambridge, England: Cambridge University Press.

Perelman, Ch. (1982). *The realm of rhetoric* (W. Kluback, Trans.). South Bend, IN: Notre Dame University Press.

Perelman, Ch., & Olbrecht-Tyteca, L. (1969). *The new rhetoric: A treatise on argumentation*. South Bend, IN: University of Notre Dame Press.

Perkins, D. N. (1987). Thinking frames: An integrative perspective on teaching cognitive skills. In J. Baron & R. Sternberg (Eds.), *Teaching thinking skills: Theory and practice* (pp. 41–61). New York: Freeman.

Perkins, D. N. (1990, April). Person plus: A distributed view of thinking and learning. Paper presented at the American Educational Research Asssociation, Boston.

Perkins, D. N. (1992). What constructivism demands of the learner. In T. Duffy & D. Jonassen (Eds.), *Constructivism and the technology of instruction* (pp. 161–165). Hillsdale, NJ: Lawrence Erlbaum Associates.

Perkinson, H. J. (1987). *Two hundred years of American educational thought*. New York: University Press of America.

Perkinson, H. J. (1993). *Teachers without goals, students without purposes*. New York: McGraw-Hill.

Perry, W. (1970). *Forms of intellectual and ethical development in the college years*. New York: Holt, Rinehart & Winston.

Petraglia, J. (1991). *Exploring the effects of realism on arousal and rhetorical representation*. Unpublished doctoral dissertation, Carnegie Mellon University, Pittsburgh, PA.

Petraglia, J. (1994). Mediated realism and the representation of a health care controversy. *Journal of Biocommunications, 21*(3), 10–17.

Petraglia, J. (1995). Spinning like a kite: A closer look at the pseudotransactional function of writing. *JAC, 15*(1), 19–33.

Phillips, D. C. (1995). The good the bad and the ugly: The many faces of constructivism. *Educational Researcher, 24*(7), 5–12.

Piaget, J. (1970). *Genetic epistemology* (E. Duckworth, Trans.). New York: Columbia University Press.

Piaget, J. (1979). The psychogenesis of knowledge and its epistemological significance. In M. Piattelli-Palmarini (Ed.), *Language and learning: The debate between Jean Piaget and Noam Chomsky* (pp. 23–34). Cambridge, MA: Harvard University Press.

Pilkington, R. M., Hartley, J. R., Hintze, D., & Moore, D. J. (1992). Learning to argue and arguing to learn: An interface for computer-based dialogue games. *Journal of Artificial Intelligence in Education, 3*(3), 275–295.

Plato. (1926). *Laws*. New York: Viking Penguin.

Plato. (1987). *Gorgias* (D. J. Zeyl, Trans.). Indianapolis: Hackett Publishing.

Popkewitz, T. S. (1987a). Ideology and social formation in teacher education. In T. Popkewitz (Ed.), *Critical studies in teacher education* (pp. 2–33). London: Falmer.

Popkewitz, T. S. (1987b). Knowledge and interest in curriculum studies. In T. Popkewitz (Ed.), *Critical studies in teacher education* (pp. 335–354). London: Falmer.

Porter, T. M. (1994). Objectivity as standardization: The rhetoric of impersonality in measurement, statistics, and cost–benefit analysis. In A. Megill (Ed.), *Rethinking objectivity* (pp. 197–237). Durham, NC: Duke University Press.

Potts, D. L., Elstein, A. S., & Cottrell, J. J. (1991, September). *Expert/novice differences in reasoning about a medical ethical dilemma: The "escape" dilemma*. Paper presented at the annual meeting of the American Educational Research Association, Chicago.

Prawat, R. S. (1995, October). Misreading Dewey: Reform, projects, and the language game. *Educational Researcher*, 13–22.

Prawat, R. S., & Floden, R. E. (1994). Philosophical perspectives on constructivist views of learning. *Educational Psychologist, 29*(1), 37–48.

Prenzel, M., & Mandl, H. (1993). Transfer of learning from a constructivist perspective. In T. Duffy, J. Lowyck, & D. Jonassen (Eds.), *Designing environments for constructive learning* (pp. 315–329). Berlin: Springer-Verlag.

Pylyshyn, Z. W. (1989). Computing in cognitive science. In M. Posner (Ed.), *Foundations of cognitive science* (pp. 49–91). Cambridge, MA: MIT Press.

Reigeluth, C. M. (1992). Reflections of the implications of constructivism for educational technology. In T. Duffy & D. Jonassen (Eds.), *Constructivism and the technology of instruction* (pp. 149–156). Hillsdale, NJ: Lawrence Erlbaum Associates.

Reitman, W. R. (1965). *Cognition and thought: An information processing approach*. New York: Wiley.

Resnick, L. (1990, Spring). Literacy in school and out. *Dædalus*, 169–185.

Resnick, L. (1991). Shared cognition: Thinking as social practice. In L. Resnick, J. Levine, & S. Teasley (Eds.), *Perspectives on socially shared cognition* (pp. 1–20). Washington, DC: American Psychological Association.

Rest, J. R. (1984). The major components of morality. In W. Kurtines & J. Getwirtz (Eds.), *Morality, moral behavior, and moral development* (pp. 24–38). New York: Wiley.

Richards, I. A. (1936). *The philosophy of rhetoric*. New York: Oxford University Press.

Rockmore, T. (1992). Introduction. In T. Rockmore & B. Singer (Eds.), *Antifoundationalism old and new* (pp. 1–12). Philadephia: Temple University Press.

Rorty, R. (1979). *Philosophy and the mirror of nature*. Princeton, NJ: Princeton University Press.

Rorty, R. (1991). *Objectivity, relativism, and truth*. Cambridge, England: Cambridge University Press.

Rowland, R. C. (1995). In defense of rational argument: A pragmatic justification of argumentation theory and response to the postmodern critique. *Philosophy and Rhetoric, 28*(4), 350–364.

Rush, B. (1798). *Essays, literary, moral and philosophical*. Philadelphia: Bradford.

Russell, D. R. (1995). Activity theory and its implications for writing instruction. In J. Petraglia (Ed.), *Reconceiving writing, rethinking writing instruction* (pp. 51–77). Mahwah, NJ: Lawrence Erlbaum Associates.

Sack, W., Soloway, E., & Weingrad, P. (1992). Re-writing cartesian student models. *Journal of Artificial Intelligence in Education, 3*(4), 381–402.

Said, E. (1994). *Orientalism* (2nd ed.). New York: Vintage.

Salomon, G. (1993). No distribution without individuals' cognition: A dynamic interactional view. In G. Salomon (Ed.), *Distributed cognitions: Psychological and educational considerations* (pp. 111–137). Cambridge, England: Cambridge University Press.

Salomon, G., & Perkins, D. N. (1989). Rocky roads to transfer: Rethinking mechanisms of a neglected phenomenon. *Educational Psychologist, 24*(2), 113–142.

Sampson, A. (1973). *The new anatomy of Britain*. Lanham, MD: Madison Books.

Sandberg, J., & Wielinga, B. (1992). Situated cognition: A paradigm shift? *Journal of Artificial Intelligence in Education, 3*(2), 129–138.

Schank, R. (1992). *Goal-based scenarios* (Tech. Rep. No. 36). Evanston, IL: The Institute for the Learning Sciences, Northwestern University.

Schank, R., Fano, A., Bell, B., & Jona, M. (1994). *The design of goal-based scenarios*. Unpublished manuscript, Institute for the Learning Sciences, Northwestern University, Evanston.

Scott, R. (1967). On viewing rhetoric as epistemic. *Central States Speech Journal, 18*, 9–16.

Scott, R. (1977). On viewing rhetoric as epistemic: Ten years later. *Central States Speech Journal, 28*, 258–266.

Scribner, S., & Cole, M. (1973). Cognitive consequences of formal and informal education. *Science, 182*, 553–559.

Scrimshaw, S. (1932). *Apprenticeship: Principles, relationships, procedures*. New York: McGraw-Hill.

Seigfried, C. H. (1992). Like bridges without piers: Beyond the foundationalist metaphor. In T. Rockmore & B. Singer (Eds.), *Antifoundationalism old and new* (pp. 143–164). Philadephia: Temple University Press.

Seneca. (1990). *Oratorum et Rhetorum Sententiae, Divisiones, Colores* (H. J. Muller, Trans.). New York: Georg Olms Publishers.

Shotter, J. (1991). The rhetorical-responsive nature of mind: A social constructionist account. In A. Still & A. Costall (Eds.), *Against cognitivism: Alternative foundations for cognitive psychology* (pp. 55–79). New York: Harvester-Wheatsheaf.

Shute, V. (1993). A macroadaptive approach to tutoring. *Journal of Artificial Intelligence in Education, 4*(1), 61–93.

Siegal, H. (1989). *Educating reason: Rationality, critical thinking, and education*. New York: Routledge.

Simon, H. A., & Simon, P. A. (1962). Trial and error search in solving difficult problems: Evidence from the game of chess. *Behavioral Science, 7,* 425–429.

Simons, P. R-J. (1993). Constructive learning: The role of the learner. In T. Duffy, J. Lowyck, & D. Jonassen (Eds.), *Designing environments for constructive learning* (pp. 291–313). Berlin: Springer-Verlag.

Singer, B. (1992). Metaphysics without mirrors. In T. Rockmore & B. Singer (Eds.), *Antifoundationalism old and new* (pp. 189–208). Philadephia: Temple University Press.

Smith, L. (1993). *Necessary knowledge: Piagetian perspectives on constructivism.* Hillsdale, NJ: Lawrence Erlbaum Associates.

Smith, W. A. (1955). *Ancient education.* New York: Greenwood Press.

Soper, K. (1991). Postmodernism, subjectivity, and the question of value. *New Left Review, 186,* 120–128.

Spencer, K. (1988). *The psychology of educational technology and instructional media.* London: Routledge & Kegan Paul.

Spiro, R. J. (1982). Subjectivité et memoire [Subjectivity and memory]. *Bulletin de Psychologie, 23,* 553–559.

Spiro, R. J., Coulson, R. L., Feltovich, P. J., & Anderson, D. K. (1988). Cognitive flexibility theory: Advanced knowledge acquisition in ill-structured domains. In *Proceedings of the Tenth Annual Conference of the Cognitive Science Society.* Hillsdale, NJ: Lawrence Erlbaum Associates.

Spiro, R. J., Feltovich, P. J., Jacobson, M.J., & Coulson, R. L. (1992a). Cognitive flexibility, constructivism, and hypertext: Random access instruction for advanced knowledge acquisition in ill-structured domains. In T. Duffy & D. Jonassen (Eds.), *Constructivism and the technology of instruction* (pp. 57–76). Hillsdale, NJ: Lawrence Erlbaum Associates.

Spiro, R. J., Feltovich, P. J., Jacobson, M.J., & Coulson, R. L. (1992b). Knowledge representation, content specification, and the development of skill in situation specific knowledge assembly: Some constructivist issues as they relate to cognitive flexibility theory and hypertext. In T. Duffy & D. Jonassen (Eds.), *Constructivism and the technology of instruction* (pp. 121–128). Hillsdale, NJ: Lawrence Erlbaum Associates.

Spiro, R. J., & Jehng, J. C. (1990). Cognitive flexibility and hypertext: Theory and technology. In D. Nix & R. J. Spiro (Eds.), *Cognition, education, and multimedia* (pp. 163–205). Hillsdale, NJ: Lawrence Erlbaum Associates.

Spivey, N. N. (1987). Construing constructivism: Reading research in the United States. *Poetics, 16,* 169–192.

Steffe, L., & Gale, J. (Eds.). (1995). *Constructivism in education.* Hillsdale, NJ: Lawrence Erlbaum Associates.

Steinberg, I. S. (1980). *Behaviorism and schooling.* New York: St. Martin's Press.

Strommen, E. (1995). A review of constructivism and the technology of instruction: A conversation. *Educational Technology Research and Development, 43*(4), 76–78

Suchman, L. (1987). *Plans and situated actions.* Cambridge, England: Cambridge University Press.

Suchman, L. (1993). Response to Vera and Simon's situated action: A symbolic interpretation. *Cognitive Science, 17,* 71–75.

Sullivan, P. A. (1995). Social constructionism and literary studies. *College English, 57*(8), 950–959.

Tansey, P. J. (1971). *Educational aspects of simulation and gaming.* New York: McGraw-Hill.

Thomas, J. W., & Rohwer, W. (1993). Proficient autonomous learning: Problems and prospects. In M. Rabinowitz (Ed.), *Cognitive science foundations for instruction* (pp. 1–32). Hillsdale, NJ: Lawrence Erlbaum Associates.

Tobin, K. (1995, October). *Constructivism list-serve opening statement.*

Toulmin, S. (1958). *The uses of argument.* Cambridge, England: Cambridge University Press.

Tudge, S., & Rogoff, B. (1989). Peer influences on cognitive development: Piagetian and Vygotskian perspectives. In M. Bornstein & J. Bruner (Eds.), *Interaction in human development* (pp. 17–40). Hillsdale, NJ: Lawrence Erlbaum Associates.

Tversky, A., & Kahneman, D. (1984). Choices, values, and frames. *American Psychologist, 39,* 341–350.

Tversky, A., & Kahneman, D. (1986). Rational choices and the framing of decisions. *Journal of Business, 59*(4), 251–278.

Ulich, R. (1965). *Education in Western culture.* New York: Harcourt Brace.

Valencia, S. W., Hiebert, E. H., & Afflerbach, P. P. (1994). *Authentic reading assessment: Practices and possibilities.* Newark, DE: International Reading Association.

Vanlehn, K., & Ohlsson, S. (1994). Applications of simulated students: An exploration. *Journal of Artificial Intelligence in Education, 5*(2), 135–175.

Vatz, R. (1973). The myth of the rhetorical situation. *Philosophy & Rhetoric, 6,* 154–161.

Vera, A., & Simon, H. (1993). Situated action: A symbolic interpretation. *Cognitive Science, 17,* 7–48.

Vico, G. (1965). *On the study methods of our time* (E. Gianturco, Ed. and Trans.). Ithaca, NY: Cornell University Press.

Ville-Cremer, S., & Eckensberger, L. H. (1985). The role of affective processes in moral judgment performance. In M. Berkowitz & F. Oser (Eds.), *Moral education: Theory and application.* Hillsdale, NJ: Lawrence Erlbaum Associates.

Vishwanathan, G. (1989). *Masks of conquest.* New York: Columbia University Press.

von Glasersfeld, E. (1984). An introduction to radical constructivism. In P. Watzlawick (Ed.), *The invented reality* (pp. 17–40). New York: Norton.

von Glasersfeld, E. (1995). A constructivist approach to teaching. In L. Steffe & J. Gale (Eds.), *Constructivism in education* (pp. 3–15). Hillsdale, NJ: Lawrence Erlbaum Associates.

Vosniadou, S. (1994). From cognitive theory to educational technology. In S. Vosniadou, E. De Corte, & H. Mandl (Eds.), *Technology-based learning environments* (pp. 11–17). Berlin: Springer-Verlag.

Vygotsky, L. S. (1962). *Thought and language.* Cambridge, MA: MIT Press.

Vygotsky, L. S. (1978). *Mind in society: The development of higher psychological processes.* Cambridge, MA: Harvard University Press.

Vygotsky, L. S. (1981). The genesis of higher mental functions. In J. Wertsch (Ed.), *The concept of activity in Soviet psychology* (pp. 134–143). Armonk, NY: Sharpe.

Warburton, D, M. (1988). Emotional and motivational determinants of attention and memory. In V. Hamilton, G. Bowers, & N. Frijda (Eds.), *Cognitive perspectives on emotion and motivation* (pp. 195–220). The Hague: Klewer.

Wartofsky, M. W. (1983). From genetic epistemology to historical epistemology: Kant, Marx and Piaget. In L. S. Liben (Ed), *Piaget and the foundations of knowledge* (pp. 1–18). Hillsdale, NJ: Lawrence Erlbaum Associates.

Wertsch, J. (1981). *The concept of activity in Soviet psychology.* Armonk, NY: Sharpe.

Wertsch, J. (1985). *Vygotsky and the social formation of mind.* Cambridge, MA: Harvard University Press.

Wertsch, J., & Toma, C. (1995). Discourse and learning in the classroom: A sociocognitive approach. In L. Steffe & J. Gale (Eds.), *Constructivism in education* (pp. 159–174). Hillsdale, NJ: Lawrence Erlbaum Associates.

Whitehead, A. J. (1929). *The aims of education.* New York: Macmillan.

Wilson, A. L. (1993). The promise of situated cognition. *New Directions for Adult and Continuing Education, 57,* 71–79.

Wineburg, S. (1989, May). Remembrance of theories past. *Educational Researcher,* 7–10.

Winn, W. (1993a). A constructivist critique of the assumptions of instructional design. In T. Duffy, J. Lowyck, & D. Jonassen (Eds.), *Designing environments for constructive learning* (pp. 189–212). Berlin: Springer-Verlag.

Winn, W. (1993b, March). Instructional design and situated learning: Paradox or partnership? *Educational Technology,* 16–21.

Wittgenstein, L. (1961). *Tractatus logico-philosophicus.* London: Routledge & Kegan Paul.

Wolff, P. P. (1969). *The idea of the university.* Boston: Beacon Press.

Yang, C-S, & Moore, D. (1995). Designing hypermedia systems for instruction. *Journal of Educational Technology Systems, 24*(1), 3–15.

Young, J. H. (1994). A brief history of Emory College. *Emory* (pp. 5–12). Atlanta: Emory Office of Publications.

Young, M. F. (1993). Instructional design for situated learning. *Educational Technology Research and Development, 41*(1), 43–58.

Young, R. E., Becker, A., & Pike, K. (1970). *Rhetoric: Discovery and change.* New York: Harcourt Brace.

Zajonc, R. B. (1980). Feeling and thinking: Preferences need no inferences. *American Psychologist, 35*(2), 151–175.

Zucchermaglio, C. (1993). Towards a cognitive ergonomics of eduational technology. In T. Duffy, J. Lowyck, & D. Jonassen (Eds.), *Designing environments for constructive learning* (pp. 249–260). Berlin: Springer-Verlag.

Zuckerman, I. (1995, August). *Preliminary call for papers.* Workshop on Argumentation for Agent Communication, Budapest, Hungary.

Author Index

Subject Index